D1713164

Demographics
and
Criminality

Recent Titles in
Contributions in Criminology and Penology

Crime and Culture in America: A Comparative Perspective
Parvis Saney

Sex and Supervision: Guarding Male and Female Inmates
Joycelyn M. Pollock

Children and Criminality: The Child as Victim and Perpetrator
Ronald Barri Flowers

Intervention Strategies for Chronic Juvenile Offenders: Some New Perspectives
Peter W. Greenwood, editor

Bandidos: The Varieties of Latin American Banditry
Richard W. Slatta, editor

America's Correctional Crisis: Prison Populations and Public Policy
Stephen D. Gottfredson and Sean McConville, editors

The Structure of Criminal Procedure: Laws and Practice of France, the
Soviet Union, China, and the United States
Barton L. Ingraham

Women and Criminality: The Woman as Victim, Offender, and Practitioner
Ronald Barri Flowers

Police Administration and Progressive Reform: Theodore Roosevelt as
Police Commissioner of New York
Jay Stuart Berman

Policing Multi-Ethnic Neighborhoods: The Miami Study and Findings
for Law Enforcement in the United States
Geoffrey P. Alpert and Roger G. Dunham

Minorities and Criminality
Ronald Barri Flowers

Marijuana: Costs of Abuse, Costs of Control
Mark Kleiman

Doing Time in American Prisons: A Study of Modern Novels
Dennis Massey

DEMOGRAPHICS
AND
CRIMINALITY

THE CHARACTERISTICS OF CRIME IN AMERICA

Ronald Barri Flowers

CONTRIBUTIONS IN CRIMINOLOGY AND PENOLOGY
NUMBER 23

Greenwood Press
NEW YORK • WESTPORT, CONNECTICUT • LONDON

Library of Congress Cataloging-in-Publication Data

Flowers, Ronald B.
    Demographics and criminality : the characteristics of crime in
America / Ronald Barri Flowers.
        p.   cm. — (Contributions in criminology and penology, ISSN
0732-4464 ; no. 23)
    Bibliography: p.
    Includes index.
    ISBN 0-313-25367-6 (lib. bdg. : alk. paper)
    1. Criminal statistics—United States.   I. Title.   II. Series.
HV6783.F58   1989
364'.042'0973—dc19   89-1897

British Library Cataloguing in Publication Data is available.

Library of Congress Catalog Card Number: 89-1897
ISBN: 0-313-25367-6
ISSN: 0732-4464

First published in 1989

Greenwood Press, Inc.
88 Post Road West, Westport, Connecticut 06881

Printed in the United States of America

The paper used in this book complies with the
Permanent Paper Standard issued by the National
Information Standards Organization (Z39.48-1984).

10 9 8 7 6 5 4 3 2 1

To Sleeping Beauty, Cinderella, and Snow White all wrapped in one lovely package of warmth, spirit, support, inspiration, devotion, and endearment—I dedicate this volume and bestow upon you the spirit and affection that says I would marry you all over again—my undying love.

Contents

Figure and Tables

Preface

This book, the fourth in a four-volume set, explores demographic trends in criminality and victimization. To my knowledge, *Demographics and Criminality* is the first book entirely devoted to studying the demographic characteristics of criminality in America. My purpose in writing this volume is to address crime's demographic dimensions so that we might better understand its nature, the population groups most affected by it, and the implications for future responses to this problem.

There is a continual need for greater, more substantive knowledge of the dynamics that embody crime, criminals, victims, criminal justice, and injustice. It is to this end that I devote my examination to topics that have been understudied in past criminological research: namely crime as it relates to children, women, minorities, and demographics. In choosing these important areas to explore, my aim is to fill gaps in the existing literature and influence the direction of future study.

The four-volume set has been designed for professional audiences, scholars and academicians, and students in criminology, criminal justice, law, sociology, psychology, racial and ethnic studies, victimology, and related disciplines. The volumes were written also with a general readership of intelligent, concerned citizens in mind who, in a world fraught with crime and violence, seek to become more informed on the issues that affect us all.

Volume 1, *Children and Criminality*, examines the correlation between children and crime. It stands apart from other studies of this relationship by exploring comprehensively the criminality and victimization of children. This treatise examines the dual phenomenon in historical and contemporary terms, the literature, and various approaches to the dimensions, nature, and explanations of the child as a victim and perpetrator of crime.

Volume 2, *Women and Criminality*, is an in-depth analysis of the tripartite role of women as victims, offenders, and criminal justice professionals.

This unique and thorough examination addresses these roles individually and as they relate to one another, as well as the larger picture of the male role in these areas of study. Explored within this text is the significance of the historical treatment of women, the women's liberation movement, the "new" female criminal controversy, and prominent theoretical and etiological avenues responding to the facets of women and criminality.

Volume 3, *Minorities and Criminality*, studies the relationship between being a member of a racial or ethnic minority in America and being a victim or offender of crime. The examination focuses specifically on blacks, Hispanics, Native Americans, and Asians—minority groups that in one way or another have been most affected by criminality and victimization. This important volume explores the historical and present mistreatment of minorities, patterns in arrest and imprisonment data, explanatory approaches to minority crime, differential enforcement in the law, and future implications.

Volume 4, *Demographics and Criminality*, looks at the relationship of demographic correlates and characteristics to crime in America. The volume probes how various demographic variables such as geography, age, gender, class, race/ethnicity, employment, education, and substance abuse affect crime and victimization patterns. Analysis is given also to the demographic features of career and chronic offenders, family violence, and prisoner groups.

ACKNOWLEDGMENTS

Many thanks must be given to Greenwood Press for the publication of this and the prior volumes, and for its recognition of the need for such criminological literature. Additional gratitude is directed to the editorial staff and their various roles in bringing this work to print.

Finally, I acknowledge the guiding force behind my work as a criminologist, social scientist, and author: my best friend, fellow researcher, and wife—H. Loraine Flowers—without whose excellent secretarial skills and unfailing support, this book would never have been created, let alone published.

Introduction

As we move into the 1990s, it is clear that we are fighting an uphill battle against crime in America. The fronts are more diversified, and the combatants and victims more numerous than ever. The criminal justice system is overwhelmed by the problems it now faces—too much crime, underreporting of crime, prison overcrowding, discriminatory practices, budgetary cutbacks. As a result it is often ineffective in combating and controlling crime, and lacking a clear picture of the incidence and nature of crime.

Criminological study also must share the blame for this inability to solve the problem of crime, for it has placed far too much emphasis on explaining crime and too little on recognizing the demographic trends in crime and victimization, what these tell us about crime, and how best to deal with it. Who is committing crime these days? Who are its victims? Where are these crimes occurring? What demographic factors are present in our criminals and victims? Who is going to prison? How do we better use demographic data on criminality in the future to control crime?

It is these questions that will be explored in this book. By presenting the demographic characteristics of crime, criminals, and victims in greater detail than in other criminological books, it is hoped that the information can be used to address more effectively the complex demographics of crime and seek solutions to crime.

Demographics and Criminality is divided into four parts. Part I explores aggregate demographic features of crime. Chapter 1 looks at the primary ways in which crime is measured. Chapter 2 presents an overall examination of the scope and nature of crime and victimization in America. In Chapter 3, crime is explored through geographical and temporal trends.

Part II examines demographic correlates of criminality. Chapter 4 addresses the correlation between age and crime. In Chapter 5, gender and crime are explored. Chapter 6 looks at the issue of race/ethnicity in criminal involvement. Chapter 7 discusses the link between social class and criminality. Chapter 8 examines the variables of employment, income, education, and marital status in relation to crime. In Chapter 9, the association between substance use/abuse and crime is discussed.

Part III devotes its attention to the demographic characteristics of particular deviant groups. Chapter 10 explores the demographic makeup of habitual and career criminals. The dynamics of familial violence are analyzed in Chapter 11. Chapter 12 profiles the prison population.

Part IV addresses the future of crime in America. Chapter 13 examines the implications of demographics, crime, and victims in the years ahead.

I

DEMOGRAPHIC AGGREGATES
OF CRIME

1

The Measurement of Crime in America

In examining demographics and crime, our first task must be to assess the primary ways in which crime is measured. There are two key sources that tell us the incidence, scope, participants, and trends of crime, criminals, and victims: The Uniform Crime Reports and the National Crime Surveys. Other sources of crime measurement include self-report studies; private, public, and professional studies; and prison statistics. Despite their shortcomings, each form of measurement is important to our overall knowledge of crime in this country.

UNIFORM CRIME REPORTS

The Federal Bureau of Investigation's annual volume, *Crime in the United States: Uniform Crime Reports* (UCR), is generally regarded as the most important source of crime statistics. Established in 1930 as a means to collect data on crime and criminals as voluntarily reported by law enforcement agencies, the UCR now includes statistics from more than 16,000 cooperating city, county, and state law enforcement agencies—representing 96 percent of the country's population.

Offenses are separated into two classifications: Part I and Part II offenses. Part I, or the Crime Index, is the central measure used for gauging fluctuations in the total volume and rate of crime, and consists of eight offenses believed to represent the most serious, frequent, and reported crimes. The eight offenses are subdivided into violent crimes (murder/nonnegligent manslaughter, forcible rape, robbery, and aggravated assault) and property crimes (burglary, larceny-theft, motor vehicle theft, and arson).

Part II offenses consist of 21 other crimes believed to be less serious, including forgery and counterfeiting, vandalism, fraud, prostitution, drunkenness, and runaways (each of these offenses will be presented in the following chapter).

Reporting Crime to the UCR

Law enforcement agencies tabulate Crime Index offenses based on reports of crime received from victims or others as well as crimes discovered by the police themselves. While unfounded or false claims (as determined by police) are subtracted from an agency's total, "actual offenses known" to the police are reported to the UCR program irrespective of whether an arrest is made, property is recovered, or prosecution is undertaken.

Also forwarded to the FBI is the total number of actual Crime Index offenses "cleared" or solved. A crime is considered cleared when (1) at least one individual is arrested, charged, and handed over to the court for prosecution; or (2) when circumstances are beyond police control to make an arrest (for example, suicide). Several crimes can be cleared by a single arrest; conversely, several arrests may clear only one crime. Clearances also are reported when a crime involves juveniles (usually under age 18) only (rather than arrest, the clearance is based on a citation to appear in juvenile court).

Law enforcement agencies further report arrestee characteristics including age, sex, race, and ethnic origin for Part I and Part II offenses.

Crime Rates

An important means by which the UCR measures crime is the crime rate. The FBI computes national crime rates for index offenses per 100,000 people (with the exception of arson, where population coverage is inconsistent). The calculation is determined by dividing the number of reported crimes by the total U.S. population and multiplying this total by 100,000. An example can be seen in the following crime rate for murder per 100,000 population in 1986:

$$\frac{19{,}257 \text{ reported murders}}{233{,}000{,}000 \text{ total U.S. population}} \times 100{,}000 = 8.3 \text{ murders per 100,000 population}$$

Crime rates are more accurate indicators of criminality than absolute crime figures because they take into consideration changes or differences in the total population from one region or time to another. For instance, to simply report the total number of murders annually without regard to population differences from year to year would give a false indication of the relative risk of being a murder victim because the population total could vary by millions from one year to the next.

THE LIMITATIONS OF UNIFORM CRIME REPORTS

Despite the obvious usefulness to criminology of Uniform Crime Reports, there are serious deficiencies in their methodology and data. One of the most critical is the inconsistency of crime reporting from one police department to the next. Although the FBI provides to its contributors such sources as the *Uniform Crime Reporting Handbook* and the *Manual of Law Enforcement Records* in an attempt to ensure uniformity in the recording methodology and reporting of crime, the truth is that law enforcement agencies do not always regard or record crimes the same way. For example, one agency might officially record an assault once it is made known to them, whereas another, after assessing the situation, may decide (using basketball terminology) "no harm, no foul," and disregard it as an offense to be reported. Additionally, police agency recording practices often are dictated by administrative and budgetary directives, political maneuvers, and differential enforcement of laws. The FBI acknowledges this and therefore cautions against comparing statistical data of local agencies. This being the case, it makes the UCR *national* data on crime more suspect.

Another shortcoming is the voluntary nature of supplying information to the UCR program. For one, this means that not every police department participates in the program, leaving some crime unaccounted for. Second, even the participants are not obligated to report everything or anything. Because of the implications of this, it is virtually impossible to know or accurately compare the actual amount of crime nationally or from jurisdiction to jurisdiction.

Furthermore, the FBI limits its collection of crime data to that reported by local police departments, ignoring data reported to other institutions and agencies that might help give a more accurate picture of crime in America.

Perhaps the greatest shortcoming of what the UCR tells us is the vast amount of crime believed to be unreported by or unknown to law enforcement. There are several reasons why crimes fail to come to the attention of the police and therefore cannot be recorded. The most general can be summed up as follows:

- Victims would rather not go through the "hassle" of reporting crimes.
- Victims are too ashamed or embarrassed to want to make the crime known (e.g., in the case of rape).
- Witnesses to a crime do not want to get involved.
- Victims or witnesses fear reprisal.
- Victims regard the offense as a private matter.
- A belief that the offense was too "insignificant" to be reported.
- Lack of faith that the police can be, or even care to be, helpful.
- Fear of self-incrimination.
- The victim is unaware of their victimization (e.g., in a confidence scam).

NATIONAL CRIME SURVEYS

The many failings of official statistics as an accurate measure of crime led to the development of an alternate methodology: surveying the victims of crime. The most comprehensive victimization survey is the National Crime Survey (NCS) program undertaken by the U.S. Bureau of the Census for the Department of Justice's Bureau of Justice Statistics. Begun in 1972, this annual report, entitled *Crime Victimization in the United States*, measures the personal offenses of rape, robbery, assault, and larceny, and the household crimes of burglary, larceny, and motor vehicle theft. The NCS is based on the results of a continuous national sample of households, with individual respondents aged 12 and over. In the most recent survey some 49,000 households, comprising approximately 101,000 respondents, made up the sample.

The NCS gives more-detailed measurements of information than does the UCR. The surveys provide not only the incidence and type of victimization but characteristics of personal and household crime victims (sex, age, race, marital status, income, education, employment, and place of residence); victim-offender relationships; offender characteristics (as perceived by the victim); and crime characteristics (time and place of the victimization, the number of offenders, use of weaponry, victim self-protection, physical injury incurred by victims, economic loss, and work loss). Information is also provided on reasons for reporting or not reporting victimization to the police.

Victimization Rates

Similar to crime rates, NCS measures crime occurrence through victimization rates, which is a much more effective way of assessing victimization, as it relates to changes in the population from year to year, than focusing on the absolute incidence of victimization. Victimization rates are expressed in terms of per 1,000 population aged 12 and over and are computed as follows:

$$\frac{\text{Number of victimizations}}{\substack{\text{Total number of persons} \\ \text{under consideration}}} \times 1,000 = \substack{\text{Rate of victimization per 1,000 individuals} \\ \text{aged 12 and over}}$$

The Dark Figure of Crime

The most important finding of victimization surveys is the existence of a considerable *dark figure* of criminality—that is, hidden or unknown crime—at least insofar as officially recorded statistics are concerned. The omission of this dark figure in official data can be attributed primarily to the following reasons:

- The crimes are known only to the perpetrators (such as forgery).
- The failure of victims or others to report known crimes.
- The crimes are unrecorded even though the police are aware of them.

- The crimes involve consenting persons (such as prostitution).
- Reported, yet officially unrecorded crimes.

Recent NCS data has shown that less than half of all violent crimes are reported to the police (this figure does not reflect official murder statistics, which cannot be measured through victimization surveys); whereas only about one-fourth of the crimes find their way into official statistics.

By implication, the existence of a large amount of unreported, unrecorded crime means that official statistics are not representative of the true crime picture. Furthermore, unknown crime does not make its way into the criminal justice system. The correlation between law-enforcement effectiveness, personnel, and resources is often dependent upon recorded crime; a misrepresentation could affect all areas.

A COMPARISON OF NCS AND UCR DATA

The reality is that because these two forms of crime measurement use different methodologies and target different groups in assessing crime, their data are not very compatible or comparable. Nevertheless, because they are the two most important sources of demographic data on criminality in this country, it is important that we recognize their basic differences and similarities. These can be seen in Table 1.1.

For our purposes, the most conspicuous differences lie in the crimes reported and the type of crimes counted. UCR data is derived strictly from law enforcement agencies and is based primarily on crime reported to them. NCS findings consist of both reported and unreported crimes (as is indicated by the dark figure). The other major difference is that while the UCR basically counts crimes committed against all people, establishments, and so on, the NCS data is limited to only crimes against individuals aged 12 or over and their households.

Both sources count most of the major crimes, though the scope of their data differs (for example, UCR measures commercial and household burglary, whereas NCS measures only household burglary). The NCS does not measure murder and kidnapping.

In sum, NCS data provides a measure of victimization in this country, while UCR statistics are geared toward providing information on crime and arrests of individuals. Although the purpose of each is similar—telling us about the nature of crime in America—the results and methods used are anything but similar.

THE SHORTCOMINGS OF NATIONAL CRIME SURVEYS

Although victimization surveys are a useful complement to official data, they too have methodological and validity problems. One is the age limitation on respondents. Because statistics are not recorded for victims under

Table 1.1

A Comparison of Uniform Crime Reports and National Crime Surveys

Uniform Crime Reports (UCR)	National Crime Survey (NCS)
Offenses Measured:	Offenses Measured:
Homicide Rape Robbery (personal & commercial) Assault (aggravated) Burglary (commercial & household) Larceny (commercial & household) Motor vehicle theft Arson	Rape Robbery (personal) Assault (aggravated & simple) Household burglary Larceny (personal & household) Motor vehicle theft
Scope:	Scope:
Crimes reported to the police in most jurisdictions; considerable flexibility in developing small-area data.	Crimes both reported and not reported to police; all data for the nation as a whole; some data are available for a few large geographic areas.
Collection Method:	Collection Method:
Police department reports to FBI.	Survey interviews; periodically measures the total number of crimes committed by asking a national sample of 60,000 households representing 135,000 persons over the age of 12 about their experiences as victims of crime during a specified period.
Kinds of Information:	Kinds of Information:
In addition to offense counts, provides information on crime clearances, persons arrested, persons charged, law enforcement officers killed and assaulted, and character-istics of homicide victims.	Provides details about victims (such as age, race, sex, education, income, and whether the victim and offender were related to each other) and about crimes (such as time and place of occurrence, whether or not reported to police; use of weapons, occurrence of injury, and economic consequences).
Sponsor:	Sponsor:
Department of Justice Federal Bureau of Investigation	Department of Justice Bureau of Justice Statistics

Source: U.S. Department of Justice, Bureau of Justice Statistics, *Report to the Nation on Crime and Justice: The Data* (Washington, D.C.: Government Printing Office, 1983), p. 6.

the age of 12, we can neither use this information for comparison purposes with other crime data nor be given the opportunity to gain knowledge on the incidence and range of the victimization of younger people.

Underreporting is also likely with victimization surveys, as memory failure, communication barriers, dishonesty, and other reasons influence the accuracy of their figures. The same could be said for overreporting, which may occur for similar reasons and in some instances may actually be encouraged by interviewers who refuse to take no for an answer.

Other problems of the NCS program include the absence in surveys of so-called "victimless" crimes—such as substance abuse and prostitution; improper interviewer techniques; and limited applicability for criminological theory.

SELF-REPORT STUDIES

An alternative to UCR and NCS data is the self-report (SR) method of measuring crime. As opposed to using police reports or victim surveys, self-report studies focus on asking law violators about their participation in criminal activity. These studies generally limit themselves to surveying adolescents and college students, who are asked confidentially whether they have "ever" or during a specific time frame violated juvenile or criminal laws. Another difference between SR surveys and the UCR and NCS programs is that the former are not restricted to measuring only certain crimes or using a standard methodology, since researchers develop their own questions and sample populations in relation to their particular objectives.

What SR measures of crime generally have in common with each other is the finding that youths have committed far more violations of the law than are officially recorded. The first such SR study to use survey methodology was conducted in 1946 by Austin Porterfield.[1] Comparing college students with delinquents who had come before the juvenile court, Porterfield found that the incidence and nature of delinquency of both groups were similar, and that the college students had actually committed far more acts of delinquency during their adolescence than the delinquent group had been charged with.

Hence, both SR research and victimization surveys contend that the dark side of criminality, or hidden violations of the law, is substantial. In fact, self-report studies generally conclude that virtually everyone in the entire population has at one time or another in his or her life committed some form of delinquency or criminality.

The Deficiencies of Self-report Measures

Self-report studies are methodologically unsound, and thus their results must be viewed with skepticism. There is, for one, the question of validity. Because there is no way to know if the respondents were always truthful, the findings of self-report studies are subject to a lack of validity. Over-estimation can result from fabricated offenses; underestimating may be even more likely considering the reluctance of many to incriminate themselves, despite the anonymity of SR surveys, for fear of possible involvement with the authorities.

Another weakness of SR data is the lack of comparability, since methodology, sample groups, and objectives can vary greatly from one study to the next. Other problems relate to the narrow range of subjects, usually young, and unethical researchers' practices such as seeking to verify self-reported data through juvenile court records.

PRISONER STATISTICS

The prevalence of crime in the United States is sometimes also measured by the prisoner population. Several different sources provide us with demographic information and population figures on prisoners. The most prominent are the Bureau of Justice Statistics annuals *Prisoners in State and Federal Institutions, Probation and Parole,* and *Jail Inmates.* There are also periodic official censuses and surveys of prisoners in jails and penitentiaries.

Statistics are available as well for juveniles in juvenile detention facilities through such sources as the Department of Justice Reports, *Children in Custody,* the Youth Development and Delinquency Prevention Administration's *Juvenile Court Statistics,* and the National Center for Juvenile Justice's *National Juvenile Court Processing Estimates.*

The Limitations of Prisoner Data

Although prisoner statistics are reasonably useful as a barometer of the demographics of the inmate population, they are a poor measure of the incidence and nature of crime in America. Since most violators of the law never go to prison, prisoners cannot be truly representative of all criminals. Furthermore, the prison population may indicate more about the differential enforcement of the law, race, social class, and other biases than crime itself. Also, as in other sources of crime data, prisoner statistics and self-reports are subject to methodological problems—honesty, voluntary cooperation, nonvalidation, and incompatibility with other statistical sources—all of which further limit their accuracy as measurements of crime and criminals.

Further limitations exist in data on juveniles in custody. Most juvenile prisoner statistics, such as those listed in *Children in Custody,* measure juvenile confinement by those held in juvenile public or private detention facilities, and therefore do not provide information on the persons under age 18 who are confined in adult jails and prisons. Also, some children in juvenile facilities are detained as nonoffenders (such as dependency, abuse, and neglect cases), yet may be included in statistics with delinquent detainees.

SUPPLEMENTARY SOURCES OF DATA ON CRIME, CRIMINALS, AND VICTIMS

Bureau of Justice Statistics Reports

A number of other Bureau of Justice Statistics (BJS) reports and bulletins are produced that present data on various aspects of crime, such as economic costs, crime and victimization trends, recidivism, career criminals, and capital punishment. These data are derived from prisoner and victim samples, government expenditure and other reports, and additional sources. BJS publications provide useful supplementary data to UCR and NCS research by filling gaps in criminological data, however, such sources also are guilty of weaknesses in their conclusions.

Collectively, Bureau of Justice Statistics research is suspect because its studies often compete with one another in presenting findings on various aspects of crime, criminals, and victims, thereby creating the possibility of a conflict of interest. Further sources are needed both within and outside of the government to challenge or corroborate BJS conclusions. Other drawbacks in BJS reports include their reliance on secondhand information with built-in weaknesses, outdated research findings paired with more recent study, and methodological weaknesses.

Retrospective Studies

Longitudinal research represents an important tool in the study of criminals. Retrospective studies are one such longitudinal approach. These studies rely on officially recognized offenders (usually arrested or imprisoned persons), whose past criminal histories are researched. Official source materials as well as self-report data may be used in retrospective research. The obvious limitations of such an approach lie in its concentration on only known offenders and only previous criminals—to the exclusion of persons who have never entered the justice system or who may be crime-prone.

Prospective Studies

A prospective study of officially recognized offenders is a longitudinal approach that both explores the careers of criminals in its sample group and follows the offenders forward in time, usually for several years. These studies also utilize primarily official data, but they may supplement this data with self-report surveys. Some prospective studies examine the general public, such as a birth cohort study that tracks the criminal and noncriminal careers of a selected group from adolescence to adulthood.

Prospective studies provide a better overall picture than retrospective studies. Nevertheless, they may be limited by methodological weaknesses, the subjects used (such as inner-city rather than rural youths), and the length of time the subjects are tracked. In general, longitudinal research, while useful, may tell us only about the criminal activities and backgrounds of those sampled, rather than of offenders unknown or not studied.

Theoretical Research

Theoretical studies into the causes of crime (which may take sociological, psychological, and radical approaches) are critical for comparison-study purposes and also as learning tools for understanding demographic trends in criminality. Most of these studies, however, are hampered by lack of empirical validity, smallness of sample groups, biases, and subjectivity.

OTHER MEASURES OF CRIMINALITY

The amount and range of crime is also measured through a variety of other studies conducted by criminologists, sociologists, private and public organizations, newspapers, and so on. The nature and success of such research varies widely. When used in combination with more methodologically sound research, these studies have some usefulness in helping us to gain more insight into the characteristics of criminality.

However, in and of themselves, most such studies purporting to tell us about crime are replete with weaknesses. Some rely heavily on official or other data. Others contain too small or unrepresentative sample groups. Still others are subject to exaggerated claims that cannot be substantiated. Obviously, any of these problems can affect the reliability and substantive value of the findings.

Crime statistics are gathered through a number of means. The two most authoritative to date are the Uniform Crime Reports and the National Crime Survey program. Each gives facts and figures on crime from different sources. UCR data is derived from police reports and concentrates mostly on reported crime, crime rates, and arrest statistics; NCS research, on the other hand, is aimed at measuring crime from the victims' point of view. Secondary sources of crime measurement include self-report studies and prisoner statistics. There are methodological problems with each source of data that undermines their findings. Yet all remain important as counterbalancing tools in the study of crime, and together they provide us with our best measurement of criminality and victimization in the United States.

NOTE

1. Austin L. Porterfield, *Youth in Trouble: Studies in Delinquency and Despair, with Plans for Prevention* (Fort Worth, Tex.: Leo Potishman Foundation, 1946).

2

A Dimensional Composite
of Criminality

We know that a substantial amount of crime is committed in the United States each year. But how much and what types of crime are being committed? Who are the criminals? Who is being victimized? What are the economic implications? In this chapter we will address these issues as a prelude to a more detailed breakdown of the demographic characteristics of crime in subsequent chapters.

OFFICIAL CRIME AND CRIMINALS

The Frequency, Distribution, and Circumstances
of Index Crimes

How often does serious crime occur in our society? According to the UCR it is quite often (Figure 2.1). In 1987 a Crime Index offense occurred every two seconds in the United States. One property crime took place every three seconds, whereas a violent crime was perpetrated every 21 seconds. The Index crime that occurred most often during 1987 was robbery—at one victimization every minute of the year.

The distribution and circumstances of Crime Index offenses in 1986 are shown in Table 2.1. Among violent crimes, murder was most often related to arguments. For felony murders, robbery was the primary circumstance. Robbery during 1986 was attributed predominantly to street/highway offenses, followed by commercial house and residence robberies. The majority of aggravated assaults involved such weapons as clubs and blunt objects or personal weapons.

Two-thirds of all burglaries in 1986 involved residences, while the remainder were business property burglaries. Structures were the primary targets of arsonists during the year, accounting for 55 percent of the reported arson; 28 percent involved mobile property.

Figure 2.1
Crime Clock, 1987

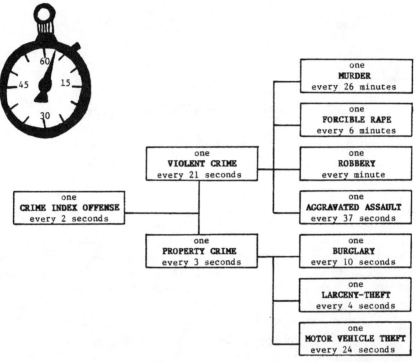

The crime clock should be regarded with caution. It is based upon the most aggregate representation of UCR information and is intended to convey annually reported serious criminality by displaying the relative frequency of occurrence of the Crime Index offenses. This method of presentation is not meant to imply a regularity in the perpetration of Part I offenses; rather it is representative of the annual ratio of crime to fixed time intervals.

Source: U.S. Federal Bureau of Investigation, *Crime in the United States: Uniform Crime Reports 1987* (Washington, D.C.: Government Printing Office, 1988), p.6.

Larceny-theft was the most frequently committed Crime Index offense in 1986, accounting for 55 percent of all crimes and 62 percent of property crimes. As Table 2.1 indicates, the majority of these offenses involved the theft of items and accessories from motor vehicles followed by miscellaneous thefts, theft from buildings, and shoplifting.

Table 2.2 presents an Index offense analysis for 1987 and the percentage change in the number of offenses from 1986. The relative distribution of the offenses changed little from 1986 to 1987. Similarly, the aggregate percentage change in the number of offenses during the period was negligible. Motor vehicle theft, burglary, and robbery had the highest average value of all offenses in 1987.

Table 2.1

Percentage Distribution of Circumstances for Index Crimes, 1986[a]

MURDER

```
Total.................100.0
Felony total............ 19.4
  Robbery................  9.5
  Narcotics..............  3.9
  Sex offenses...........  1.5
  Arson..................  1.0
  Other felony...........  3.4
Suspected felony........  2.0
Argument total.......... 37.5
  Romantic triangle......  2.1
  Property or money......  2.4
  Other arguments........ 32.9
Miscellaneous
Non-felony types[b]...... 18.6
Unknown................. 22.5
```

LARCENY

```
Total....................100.0
Purse-snatching...........  1.2
Pocket-picking............  1.3
Coin machines.............  0.9
Shoplifting...............  14.8
Bicycles..................  7.2
From motor vehicles
  (except accessories)..... 20.7
From buildings............ 15.2
Motor vehicle
  accessories.............. 16.6
All others................ 22.2
```

ROBBERY

```
Total.................100.0
Street/highway.......... 55.6
Commercial house........ 12.3
Gas or service station..  3.1
Convenience store.......  5.3
Residence............... 10.4
Bank....................  1.3
Miscellaneous........... 12.0
```

MOTOR VEHICLE THEFT

```
Total....................100.0
Autos..................... 77.3
Trucks and buses.......... 13.6
Other vehicles............  9.1
```

AGGRAVATED ASSAULT

```
Total.................100.0
Firearms................ 21.3
Knife or cutting
  instruments........... 22.0
Other weapons[c]......... 31.9
Personal weapons........ 24.8
```

ARSON

```
Total....................100.0
Total structure........... 54.6
  Single occupancy
    residential............ 23.4
  Other residential........  9.2
  Storage.................  5.7
  Industrial/manufacturing.  0.9
  Other commercial.........  6.7
  Community/public.........  5.4
  Other structure..........  3.3
Total mobile.............. 28.0
  Motor vehicle............ 25.8
  Other mobile............  2.2
Other..................... 17.4
```

BURGLARY

```
Total.................100.0
Residential............. 66.0
Non-residential......... 34.0
```

[a]Because of rounding, percentages may not add to totals.

[b]Include murders perpetrated while the offender was under the influence of alcohol or drugs.

[c]This distribution is according to the type of weapons used. Other weapons include bats and blunt objects.

Source: U.S. Federal Bureau of Investigation, Crime in the United States: Uniform Crime Reports 1986 (Washington, D.C.: Government Printing Office, 1987), pp. 12, 18, 31, 37.

Clearance of Crime Index Offenses

Law enforcement agencies had only limited success in solving, or clearing, the major crimes that came to their attention in 1987. The clearance rate for Crime Index offenses was only 21 percent. However,

Table 2.2
Offense Analysis, 1987, and Percentage Change from 1986 (13,149 Agencies; 1987 Estimated Population, 225,052,000)

Classification	Number of offenses 1987	Percent change over 1986	Percent distribution[a]	Average value
MURDER..................	17,886	-2.8	.....	$ 107
FORCIBLE RAPE..........	83,885	+0.5	.....	30
ROBBERY:				
Total...............	479,348	-4.5	100.0	631
Street/highway.......	260,957	-6.5	54.4	492
Commercial house.....	60,725	-1.9	12.7	1,017
Gas or service station..	14,535	-5.0	3.0	321
Convenience store.....	27,013	+1.5	5.6	292
Residence...........	49,942	-5.5	10.4	796
Bank...............	6,779	+6.5	1.4	3,013
Miscellaneous........	59,397	-0.4	12.4	668
BURGLARY:				
Total...............	2,945,073	-0.5	100.0	975
Residence (dwelling):..	1,993,689	-0.1	67.7	1,004
Night..............	623,658	-2.5	21.2	808
Day...............	837,645	+0.3	28.4	1,085
Unknown...........	532,386	+2.1	18.1	1,107
Nonresidence (store, office, etc.):..	951,384	-1.3	32.3	914
Night..............	470,533	-3.6	16.0	838
Day...............	189,034	+2.7	6.4	848
Unknown...........	291,817	....	9.9	1,079

16

LARCENY-THEFT (EXCEPT MOTOR VEHICLE THEFT):		+3.4	100.0	404
Total.....................................	6,851,548	+3.4	100.0	404
By type:				
Pocket-picking.........................	74,144	-4.1	1.1	286
Purse-snatching........................	82,319	-5.2	1.2	238
Shoplifting............................	1,046,207	+6.7	15.3	96
From motor vehicles (except accessories)..	1,444,300	+5.2	21.1	434
Motor vehicle accessories..............	1,155,452	+4.8	16.9	288
Bicycles...............................	439,848	-6.8	6.4	172
From buildings.........................	1,001,520	-0.5	14.6	665
From coin-operated machines............	60,843	+2.9	0.9	128
All others.............................	1,546,915	+5.3	22.6	591
By value:				
Over $200..............................	2,340,296	+2.9	34.2	1,074
$50 to $200............................	1,784,405	-0.1	26.0	115
Under $50..............................	2,726,847	+6.3	39.8	18
MOTOR VEHICLE THEFT.......................	1,176,273	+5.1	.....	4,964

aBecause of rounding, percentages may not add to totals.

Source: U.S. Federal Bureau of Investigation, *Crime in the United States: Uniform Crime Reports 1987* (Washington, D.C.: Government Printing Office, 1988), p. 152.

Table 2.3
Index of Crime, United States, 1978-1987

Population [a]	Crime Index Total [b]	Violent Crime [c]	Property Crime [c]	Murder and non-negligent manslaughter	Forcible Rape	Robbery	Aggravated Assault	Burglary	Larceny-Theft	Motor Vehicle Theft
Number of offenses:										
1978 - 218,059,000	11,209,000	1,085,550	10,123,400	19,560	67,610	426,930	571,460	3,128,300	5,991,000	1,004,100
1979 - 220,099,000	12,249,500	1,208,030	11,041,500	21,460	76,390	480,700	629,480	3,327,700	6,601,000	1,112,800
1980 - 225,349,264	13,408,300	1,344,520	12,063,700	23,040	82,990	565,840	672,650	3,795,200	7,136,900	1,131,700
1981 - 229,146,000	13,423,800	1,361,820	12,061,900	22,520	82,500	592,910	663,900	3,779,700	7,194,400	1,087,800
1982 - 231,534,000	12,974,400	1,322,390	11,652,000	21,010	78,770	553,130	669,480	3,447,100	7,142,500	1,062,400
1983 - 233,981,000	12,108,600	1,258,090	10,850,500	19,310	78,920	506,570	653,290	3,129,900	6,712,800	1,007,900
1984 - 236,158,000	11,881,800	1,273,280	10,608,500	18,690	84,230	485,010	685,350	2,984,400	6,591,900	1,032,200
1985 - 238,740,000	12,431,400	1,328,800	11,102,600	18,980	88,670	497,870	723,250	3,073,300	6,926,400	1,102,900
1986 - 241,077,000	13,211,900	1,489,170	11,722,700	20,610	91,460	542,780	834,320	3,241,400	7,257,200	1,224,100
1987 - 243,400,000	13,508,700	1,484,000	12,024,700	20,100	91,110	517,700	855,090	3,236,200	7,499,900	1,288,700
Percent change; number of offenses:										
1987/1986	+2.2	-0.3	+2.6	-2.5	-0.4	-4.6	+2.5	-0.2	+3.3	+5.3
1987/1983	+11.6	+18.0	+10.8	+4.1	+15.4	+2.2	+30.9	+3.4	+11.7	+27.9
1987/1978	+20.5	+36.7	+18.8	+2.8	+34.8	+21.3	+49.6	+3.4	+25.2	+28.3

18

Rate per 100,000 inhabitants:[d]										
1978.............	5,140.3	497.8	4,642.5	9.0	31.0	195.8	262.1	1,434.6	2,747.4	460.5
1979.............	5,565.5	548.9	5,016.6	9.7	34.7	218.4	286.0	1,511.9	2,999.1	505.6
1980.............	5,950.0	596.6	5,353.3	10.2	36.8	251.1	298.5	1,684.1	3,167.0	502.2
1981.............	5,858.2	594.3	5,263.9	9.8	36.0	258.7	289.7	1,649.5	3,139.7	474.7
1982.............	5,603.6	571.1	5,032.5	9.1	34.0	238.9	289.2	1,488.8	3,084.8	458.8
1983.............	5,175.0	537.7	4,637.4	8.3	33.7	216.5	279.2	1,337.7	2,868.9	430.8
1984.............	5,031.3	539.2	4,492.1	7.9	35.7	205.4	290.2	1,263.7	2,791.3	437.1
1985.............	5,207.1	556.6	4,650.5	7.9	37.1	208.5	302.9	1,287.3	2,901.2	462.0
1986.............	5,480.4	617.7	4,862.6	8.6	37.9	225.1	346.1	1,344.6	3,010.3	507.8
1987.............	5,550.0	609.7	4,940.3	8.3	37.4	212.7	351.3	1,329.6	3,081.3	529.4
Percent change; rate per 100,000 inhabitants:										
1987/1986........	+1.4	-1.3	+1.6	-3.5	-1.3	-5.5	+1.5	-1.1	+2.4	+4.3
1987/1983........	+7.3	+13.4	+6.5	....	+11.0	-1.8	+25.8	-0.6	+7.4	+22.9
1987/1978........	+8.1	+22.5	+6.4	-7.8	+20.6	+8.6	+34.0	-7.3	+12.2	+15.0

[a]Populations are Bureau of the Census provisional estimates as of July 1, except April 1, 1980, preliminary census counts, and are subject to change.

[b]Because of rounding, the offenses may not add to totals.

[c]Violent crimes are offenses of murder, forcible rape, robbery, and aggravated assault. Property crimes are offenses of burglary, larceny-theft, and motor vehicle theft. Data are not included for the property crime of arson because of insufficiency.

[d]All rates were calculated in the offenses before rounding.

Source: U.S. Federal Bureau of Investigation, *Crime in the United States: Uniform Crime Reports 1987* (Washington, D.C.: Government Printing Office, 1988). p. 41.

19

violent crimes were cleared 47 percent of the time (70 percent of the time for murder, 53 percent for forcible rape, 27 percent for robbery, and 59 percent for aggravated assault). Property crimes had a lower clearance rate of 18 percent. For individual property offenses, the clearance rates were as follows: burglary, 14 percent; larceny theft, 20 percent; motor vehicle theft, 15 percent; and arson, 16 percent.[1]

Eighteen percent of the Index crime offenses cleared by police during 1987 concerned people under the age of 18. Juveniles were responsible in 21 percent of the property crime clearances and 8 percent of those for violent crime. The rate of juvenile involvement in cleared Crime Index offenses was highest for arson, at 36 percent, and lowest for murder, at 5 percent.[2]

Crime Index Trends

The total number of Crime Index offenses for 1987 was 13.5 million. This represents an increase over the totals in previous years. Table 2.3 outlines Crime Index trends for the periods 1986-1987, 1983-1987 and 1978-1987. The 1987 Crime Index indicates that the number of offenses in the country increased by 2 percent from 1986, 12 percent from 1983, and 21 percent from 1978.

Total violent crime remained virtually the same from 1986 to 1987, while property crime rose by only 3 percent. The 5- and 10-year time frames, however, indicate a significant rise in violent and property crime. The number of violent crime offenses in 1987 was 18 percent higher than it was in 1983, compared to an 11 percent increase in property crime during the period. From 1978 to 1987 violent crime rose 37 percent and property crime climbed 19 percent higher.

Table 2.3 also provides useful comparisons of the rate of Crime Index offenses per 100,000 inhabitants. The crime rate increased 8 percent in the 10-year time frame 1978 to 1987.

Arrests

In 1987, an estimated 12.7 million people were arrested in the United States for all criminal offenses other than traffic violations (see Table 2.4). By this count, the rate of arrests comes to 5,330 per 100,000 people. The vast majority of arrests for Crime Index offenses was for property crimes, specifically larceny-theft, which accounted for nearly 1.5 million arrests in 1987. Nonindex Crime arrests were highest for all other offenses and driving under the influence.

Forty-eight percent of all arrests in 1987 were of persons under the age of 25; 30 percent of the arrestees were under 21; 16 percent were younger than 18; and 5 percent were under the age of 15. For Crime Index offenses, 59 percent of those arrested were under age 25; 44 percent were younger than 21; and 29 percent were under 18. Persons under the age of 25 accounted for

Table 2.4
Total Estimated Arrests, 1987[a]

TOTAL [b]	12,711,600
Murder and nonnegligent manslaughter	19,200
Forcible rape	36,310
Robbery	138,290
Aggravated assault	352,450
Burglary	443,400
Larceny-theft	1,469,200
Motor vehicle theft	169,300
Arson	18,000
Violent crime [c]	546,300
Property crime [d]	2,099,900
Crime Index total [e]	2,646,200
Other assaults	787,200
Forgery and counterfeiting	93,900
Fraud	341,900
Embezzlement	12,700
Stolen property; buying, receiving, possessing	139,300
Vandalism	273,500
Weapons; carrying, possessing, etc.	191,700
Prostitution and commercialized vice	110,100
Sex offenses (except forcible rape and prostitution)	100,100
Drug abuse violations	937,400
Gambling	25,400
Offenses against family and children	58,700
Driving under the influence	1,727,200
Liquor laws	616,700
Drunkenness	828,300
Disorderly conduct	698,700
Vagrancy	36,100
All other offenses (except traffic)	2,836,700
Suspicion (not included in totals)	13,500
Curfew and loitering law violations	89,500
Runaways	160,400

[a]Arrest totals based on all reporting agencies and estimates for unreported areas.

[b]Because of rounding, items may not add to totals.

[c]Violent crimes are offenses of murder, forcible rape, robbery, and aggravated assault.

[d]Property crimes are offenses of burglary, larceny-theft, motor vehicle theft, and arson.

[e]Includes arson.

Source: U.S. Federal Bureau of Investigation, *Crime in the United States: Uniform Crime Reports 1987* (Washington, D.C.: Government Printing Office, 1988), p. 164.

62 percent of the property crime arrests and 47 percent of those arrested for crimes of violence in 1987.[3]

Table 2.5 reflects the percentage distribution of arrests in 1986 by sex, race, and ethnicity. Four out of every five persons arrested nationwide were males. They also represent 89 percent of those arrested for violent crime and

Table 2.5
Total Arrests, Percentage Distribution, by Sex, Race, and Ethnicity, 1986[a]

Offense Charged	SEX[b]		RACE[c]				ETHNIC ORIGIN[d]	
	Male	Female	White	Black	American Indian or Alaskan Native	Asian or Pacific Islander	Hispanic	Non-Hispanic
TOTAL	82.6	17.4	71.3	27.0	1.0	0.7	12.7	87.3
Murder & nonnegligent manslaughter	87.7	12.3	50.3	48.0	0.9	0.8	15.7	84.3
Forcible rape	98.9	1.1	52.0	46.6	0.8	0.5	11.5	88.5
Robbery	92.2	7.8	37.0	62.0	0.5	0.5	13.9	86.1
Aggravated assault	86.8	13.2	58.8	39.8	0.9	0.6	15.3	84.7
Burglary	92.1	7.9	69.1	29.5	0.8	0.6	14.7	85.3
Larceny-theft	69.3	30.7	67.8	30.1	1.1	1.0	12.0	88.0
Motor vehicle theft	90.5	9.5	63.6	34.7	0.9	0.9	16.3	83.7
Arson	86.3	13.7	75.5	23.6	0.5	0.5	7.8	92.2
Violent crime	89.1	10.9	52.2	46.5	0.7	0.6	14.7	85.3
Property crime	76.1	23.9	67.8	30.2	1.0	0.9	12.9	87.1
Crime Index total[e]	78.9	21.1	64.5	33.7	1.0	0.8	13.3	86.7
Other assaults	84.8	15.2	65.7	32.7	1.0	0.7	9.4	90.6
Forgery & counterfeiting	66.1	33.9	66.4	32.6	0.5	0.5	6.7	93.3
Fraud	56.7	43.3	66.2	33.0	0.4	0.4	4.0	96.0
Embezzlement	63.6	36.4	70.1	28.8	0.4	0.7	5.2	94.8
Stolen property; buying, receiving, possessing	88.6	11.4	61.6	37.4	0.6	0.5	14.4	85.6
Vandalism	89.5	10.5	78.5	19.9	0.9	0.7	8.5	91.5
Weapons; carrying, possessing, etc.	92.6	7.4	64.5	34.4	0.5	0.7	15.2	84.8

Prostitution & commercialized vice.	34.6	65.4	59.9	38.8	0.5	0.9	10.1	89.9
Sex offenses (except forcible rape & prostitution)	92.1	7.9	78.1	20.4	1.0	0.6	11.5	88.5
Drug abuse violations	85.5	14.5	67.3	31.8	0.4	0.5	19.9	80.1
Gambling	82.8	17.2	50.7	46.1	0.1	3.1	24.8	75.2
Offenses against family & children	85.0	15.0	66.1	32.3	1.1	0.5	5.1	94.9
Driving under the influence	88.5	11.5	88.7	9.7	1.1	0.6	14.2	85.8
Liquor laws	83.2	16.8	87.6	9.8	2.0	0.6	8.8	91.2
Drunkenness	91.1	8.9	79.7	17.7	2.3	0.2	20.0	80.0
Disorderly conduct	81.8	18.2	67.9	30.7	1.1	0.3	9.5	90.5
Vagrancy	88.1	11.9	66.9	29.4	3.1	0.6	14.9	85.1
All other offenses (except traffic)	84.6	15.4	64.7	33.6	0.8	0.9	11.1	88.9
Suspicion	83.4	16.6	76.1	22.9	0.6	0.4	10.2	89.8
Curfew & loitering law violations	74.5	25.5	75.9	21.9	0.7	1.5	8.6	91.4
Runaways	42.3	57.7	84.3	13.4	1.0	1.4	8.7	91.3

[a]The percentages round out to 100 percent for each category of arrest.

[b]Based on 10,743 agencies; 1986 estimated population 199 million.

[c]Based on 10,699 agencies; 1986 estimated population 198 million.

[d]Based on 9,597 agencies; 1986 estimated population 177 million.

[e]See Chapter 1 for a breakdown of Crime Index offenses.

Source: U.S. Federal Bureau of Investigation, Crime in the United States: Uniform Crime Reports 1986 (Washington, D.C.: Government Printing Office, 1987), pp. 181, 182, 185.

76 percent of the property crime arrests. For all Crime Index offenses, males accounted for 79 percent of the arrests. A scan of Part II offenses by sex shows that more than 90 percent of those arrested for weapons possession, sex offenses, and drunkenness were male.

The distribution by race in Table 2.5 shows that 71 percent of all arrestees in the nation were white, 27 percent were black, and 2 percent were of other races. Blacks were arrested nearly as often as whites for violent crime and gambling, and further exceeded the aggregate percentage of black arrests in a number of other offenses such as property crime, fraud, and prostitution and commercialized vice.

The classification of arrests by ethnic origin shows that non-Hispanics accounted for 87 percent of the total arrests in 1986 and more than 90 percent of the arrests for such offenses as arson, other assaults, forgery and counterfeiting, and gambling. Hispanics were arrested most often for gambling and drunkenness.

The demographic makeup of 1987 arrestees is shown in Table 2.6. The data for 1987 indicates that the characteristics of arrestees were generally the same as they were in 1986.

Table 2.6
Demographic Characteristics of 1987 Arrestees

	TOTAL	PERCENT DISTRIBUTION
AGE		
Under 15	557,278	5.2
Under 18	1,781,240	16.5
18 and over	9,014,629	83.5
Total all ages[a]	10,795,869	100.0
SEX		
Male	8,881,528	82.3
Female	1,914,341	17.7
Total[a]	10,795,869	100.0
RACE[b]		
White	7,386,639	68.7
Black	3,168,129	29.5
Native American	116,916	1.1
Asian	78,625	0.7
Total[c]	10,750,309	100.0

[a]Based on 10,616 agencies and an estimated 1987 population of 202,337,000.

[b]Native Americans include American Indians and Alaskan Natives. Asians include Pacific Islanders.

[c]Based on 10,545 reporting agencies, with an estimated 1987 population of 201,675,000.

Source: U.S. Federal Bureau of Investigation, Crime in the United States: Uniform Crime Reports 1987 (Washington, D.C.: Government Printing Office, 1988), p. 174, 181, 182.

Arrest Trends

Trends reflect increases in arrests in both the short and the long term.[4] In 1987, the number of arrests rose 2 percent above the 1986 total. Adult arrests increased by 3 percent during the two-year period, whereas juvenile arrests decreased by 1 percent. Overall, Crime Index arrests went up 2 percent between 1985 and 1986, including a 1 percent increase for violent crime arrests and a 2 percent jump in property crime arrests.

The five-year trend, 1983 to 1987, shows total arrests and arrests for property crime increasing by 9 percent, with violent crime arrests up 12 percent. The number of arrestees over age 18 grew by 10 percent compared to a 7 percent rise in arrests of juveniles.

Ten-year arrest trends reveal that total arrests from 1978 to 1987 grew by 25 percent. During the period, Index crime arrests were up 18 percent, violent crime arrests increased by 25 percent, and those for property crimes rose by 16 percent. Arrests of persons over age 18 increased 34 percent from 1978 to 1987 for total offenses and Crime Index offenses. Conversely, among persons under age 18, aggregate arrests decreased by 8 percent, and the number of Crime Index offenses dropped by 13 percent.

Over the 5-year and 10-year periods, male arrests rose by 8 percent and 23 percent respectively, compared to 17 percent and 33 percent increases in female arrests during these time frames.

CRIMINAL VICTIMIZATION

The Extent of Victimization

More than 34 million persons aged 12 and over were victims of crime in the United States in 1986, according to the NCS. About one-fourth of all households were touched by crime. As shown in Table 2.7, personal crime victimization was highest for crimes of theft, particularly larceny without contact. Larceny also accounted for the greatest number of household crimes and occurred at the highest rate of all victimizations, 94 per 1000.

NCS data reveals that only 37 percent of all personal and household crime was reported to law enforcement agencies in 1986 (Table 2.8). Half of all violent crime was reported, but only one-fourth of the crimes of theft was. Motor vehicle theft showed the highest percentage of household victimizations that were brought to the attention of the police. In sum, victimization studies indicate that there is a wide discrepancy between official crime data and the actual incidence of criminal victimization.

Violent Crime Victimization

Each year, about 3.2 percent of all Americans, or some 6 million individuals, are violent crime victims.[5] About 1 in 12 persons annually are

Table 2.7
Total Victimization, 1986

	Number of Victimizations	Rate Per 1,000 Population
Total	34,118,000	*
Personal Crimes		
Crimes of violence	5,515,000	28.1
Rape	130,000	0.7
Robbery	1,009,000	5.1
Assault	4,376,000	22.3
Aggravated	1,543,000	7.9
Simple	2,833,000	14.4
Crimes of theft	13,235,000	67.5
Personal larceny with contact	536,000	2.7
Personal larceny without contact	12,699,000	64.7
Household Crimes		
Burglary	5,557,000	61.5
Larceny	8,455,000	93.5
Motor vehicle theft	1,356,000	15.0

Source: U.S. Department of Justice, Bureau of Justice Statistics Bulletin, *Criminal Victimization 1986* (Washington, D.C.: Government Printing Office, 1987), p. 4.

Table 2.8
Percentage of Victimizations Reported to the Police, 1986

All Crimes	37
Personal Crimes	
Crimes of violence	50
Rape	48
Robbery	58
Assault	48
Aggravated	59
Simple	41
Crimes of theft	28
Personal larceny with contact	38
Personal larceny without contact	28
Household Crimes	41
Household burglary	52
Household larceny	28
Motor vehicle theft	73

Source: U.S. Department of Justice, *Bureau of Justice Statistics Bulletin: Criminal Victimization 1986* (Washington, D.C.: Government Printing Office, 1987), p. 4.

victims of crimes of violence. Males aged 16 to 24 tend to have the highest risk of violent crime victimization. Blacks are victimized at a higher rate than any other racial or ethnic group. Black males have a 1 in 30 chance of being murdered in their lifetime, compared to the 1 chance in 178 for white males.[6] Victimization data also show that violent crime rates are higher for unemployed persons than employed, and nearly 80 percent greater for males than females.

Victims of Crime

Tables 2.9 and 2.10 contain selected data on crime victims in 1985. In Table 2.9 we see that teenage victimization rates for both personal crimes of violence and theft are considerably higher than those for victims aged 25 and older. The female rate of victimization is closest to the male victimiza-

Table 2.9
Victims of Crime, 1985 (Rate per 1,000 Population Aged 12 and Over and Rate per 1,000 Households)

| | Personal Crimes | | Household Crimes |
	Violence	Theft	
SEX			
Male	38.8	74.7	
Female	21.9	64.6	
AGE			
12-15	54.1	108.3	
16-19	67.2	122.1)	455.1
20-24	60.2	107.6)	241.4
25-34	37.4	82.7	
35-49	19.9	62.9	194.5
50-64	9.9	40.0	136.6
65 and over	4.5	18.6	78.1
RACE			
White	29.1	70.1	168.5
Black	38.2	63.4	225.8
Other	25.0	72.5	150.1
ORIGIN			
Hispanic	30.1	60.5	235.7
Non-Hispanic	30.1	70.0	171.0

Source: U.S. Department of Justice, Criminal Victimization in the United States 1985: A National Crime Survey Report (Washington, D.C.: Government Printing Office, 1987).

Table 2.10
Selected Characteristics of Crime Victims, 1985 (Rate per 1,000 Population
Aged 12 and Over)

	Personal Crimes	
	Violence	Theft
MARITAL STATUS		
Never married	56.0	107.5
Married	15.0	51.2
Widowed	7.4	90.7
Divorced or separated	53.4	22.5
INCOME		
Less than $7,500	52.1	67.5
$7,500 - $9,999	33.8	62.6
$10,000 - $14,999	31.7	64.5
$15,000 - $24,999	28.0	67.8
$25,000 - $29,999	29.0	68.7
$30,000 - $49,999	22.3	76.1
$50,000 or more	24.6	89.7
EDUCATION		
Elementary school	31.6	53.6
High school	30.9	63.2
College	27.9	88.0

Source: U.S. Department of Justice, Criminal Victimization in the United States 1985: A
    National Crime Survey Report (Washington, D.C.: Government Printing Office,
    1987), pp. 20, 24, 26.

tion rate for crimes of theft. By race, blacks show the highest rate of violent
crime victimization and the lowest rate for theft; by ethnic origin, non-
Hispanics have a higher victimization rate of theft than do Hispanics.
Household victimization rates are highest among households headed by
blacks and Hispanics, as well as among younger heads of household.

As shown in Table 2.10, violent crime rates are highest for persons who
have never married, or who are divorced or separated. The highest victimization rate for crimes of theft belong to persons never married or widowed.
Violent crime victimization rates tend to rise the lower the income.
Conversely, theft victimization is highest among those with incomes over
$30,000, although the rate of victimization is fairly evenly distributed
among other income levels. Educational attainment data on crime victims
reflect a slightly greater rate of violent crime victimization the lower the

education and a higher rate of theft victimization as education rises. Preliminary NCS data for 1986 indicate comparable sociodemographic characteristics for victims of crime.[7]

Victim-Offender Relationship

Most crime is committed by persons who are strangers to their victims. Recent victimization data reveals that strangers account for

- more than 60 percent of all violent crime
- three-fourths of all robberies
- over half of the assaults and rapes
- nearly 70 percent of the crimes of violence against males
- around half of the violent crimes against female victims
- a higher proportion of personal crimes against whites than blacks[8]

Crime is largely an intraracial phenomenon. According to 1986 NCS findings:

- 80 percent of the violent crimes against whites were perpetrated by whites
- 84 percent of the violent crimes against blacks were perpetrated by blacks
- 98 percent of the violent crimes committed by whites were against whites[9]

These trends are consistent for other racial groups as well.

Black offenders, conversely, have been shown to commit over half of their violent offenses against white victims. This inconsistency with the generally intraracial nature of crime is most prevalent for robberies.[10]

Trends in Criminal Victimization

Criminal victimization in the United States has seen a decline in recent years, according to the latest victimization figures. Victimization levels for violent crimes, crimes of theft, and household crimes from 1973 to 1986 are displayed in Table 2.11. The number of total victimizations in 1986 was 746,000 less than in 1985. This represents a 2 percent decline, which is consistent with a trend that has reduced victimization to its lowest level since the NCS program began.

The rate of victimization for personal crimes (violent crimes and theft) experienced approximately a 3 percent reduction in 1986 (about half a million fewer victims than in 1985). The household crimes of burglary, larceny, and motor vehicle theft were down by 200,000 in 1986 from the previous year, however they actually have increased since 1973.

In 1986, around 37 percent of NCS crimes were reported to the police—a

Table 2.11
Victimization Levels for Selected Crimes, 1973-1986

	Number of Victimizations (in 1,000's)			
	Total	Violent Crimes	Personal Theft	Household Crimes
1973	35,661	5,350	14,970	15,340
1974	38,411	5,510	15,889	17,012
1975	39,266	5,573	16,294	17,400
1976	39,318	5,599	16,519	17,199
1977	40,314	5,902	16,933	17,480
1978	40,412	5,941	17,050	17,421
1979	41,249	6,159	16,382	18,708
1980	40,252	6,130	15,300	18,821
1981	41,454	6,582	15,863	19,009
1982	39,756	6,459	15,553	17,744
1983	37,001	5,903	14,657	16,440
1984	35,544	6,021	13,789	15,733
1985	34,864	5,823	13,474	15,568
1986	34,118	5,515	13,235	15,368
Percent change, 1981-86[a]	-17.7%[b]	-16.2%[b]	-16.6%[b]	-19.2%[b]

[a]Total victimizations peaked in 1981.

[b]The difference is statistically significant at the 95% confidence level.

Source: U.S. Department of Justice, Bureau of Justice Statistics Bulletin: Criminal Victimization 1986 (Washington, D.C.: Government Printing Office, 1987), p. 1.

4 percent rise over 1985 figures. The rate of reporting for 1986 represented the highest total ever recorded in the 14-year history of the NCS and was 15 percent greater than the reporting rate for 1973.[11]

Trends in Murder Victimization

NCS research does not measure the crime of murder in its victimization surveys. Instead, murder victimization is tracked through official statistics. In 1986, the UCR estimated that there were 20,613 murder victims in the United States, representing 1 percent of the crimes of violence that were committed. The rate of murder was 9 victims per 100,000 population. Murder has been shown largely to be an acquaintance-related or domestic problem, with three out of every five murder victims being related to or acquainted with their assailant. Unlike the decline shown for criminal victimization, as a whole murder has experienced a short-term increase, up 9 percent in 1986 from 1985, although it has dropped since 1982.[12]

THE COSTS OF CRIME

The costs of crime extend well beyond the physical and emotional trauma of victims. Also at stake are considerable economic costs to both victims and the criminal justice system.

Economic Cost of Victimization

Table 2.12 shows the costs of selected crimes as estimated by recent official and victimization data. The Uniform Crime Reports' figures for 1986 estimate the total national loss owing to conventional crime at $13.5 billion. Motor vehicle theft was responsible for the highest losses at $6 billion. The average value per stolen vehicle at the time of the theft was $4,888. Burglary and larceny losses totaled $6 billion, with the average loss per incident being $960 and $400 respectively. Robberies accounted for $323 million in losses, while arson cost victims $1.2 billion.

Comparative estimates of crime loss can be seen in National Crime

Table 2.12

Estimates of Total Economic Loss to Crime Victims

UNIFORM CRIME REPORTS, 1986		NATIONAL CRIME SURVEY, 1984[a]	
Total Losses	$13.5 billion	Total Losses	$12.5 billion
Robbery Avg. property value per incident: $596	$323 million	Personal crimes	$ 3.4 billion
		Crimes of violence	$ 883 million
		Rape	$ 20 million
Burglary	$ 3.1 billion	Robbery	$ 539 million
Avg. loss per burglary: $960		Assault	$ 324 million
		Crimes of theft	$ 2.5 billion
Larceny-theft	$ 2.9 billion	Personal larceny:	
Avg. property value per theft: $400		with contact without contact	$ 64 million $ 2.5 billion
Motor vehicle		Household crimes	$ 9.1 billion
theft	$ 6 billion	Burglary	$ 3.5 billion
Avg. vehicle value: $4,888		Household larceny Motor vehicle	$ 1.4 billion
		theft	$ 4.2 billion
Arson	$1.2 billion		
Avg. loss per incident: $13,198			

[a]The figures include losses from property damage or theft, cash losses, medical expenses, and loss of pay as a result of victimization.

Source: U.S. Federal Bureau of Investigation, *Crime in the United States: Uniform Crime Reports 1986* (Washington, D.C.: Government Printing Office, 1987); U.S. Department of Justice, Bureau of Justice Statistics, *BJS Data Report, 1986* (Washington, D.C.: Government Printing Office, 1987), p. 22.

Survey data. The Bureau of Justice Statistics estimates that the total economic loss to victims of personal and household crime in 1984 was $12.5 billion. More than $9 billion in losses was attributed to household crimes, with motor vehicle theft and burglary accounting for the greatest proportion of losses. According to these figures, personal crimes cost victims $3.4 billion, with losses of over $800 million coming from violent crimes and $2.5 billion from crimes of theft. The greatest economic losses due to personal crimes resulted from larceny without contact and robbery.

A recent study of NCS data profiled the economic cost of criminal victimization as follows:

- Almost 75 percent of all losses stem from the household crimes of burglary, larceny, and motor vehicle theft.
- Among violent crimes (rape, robbery, assault), the greatest loss is due to robbery.
- The median loss for a victim of violent crime is twice that of a personal theft victim.
- The highest median loss is from motor vehicle theft.
- Most losses are from theft of property or cash (92 percent), property damage (6 percent), and medical expenses (2 percent).
- Two-thirds of medical costs result from assault.
- One-third of all losses are recovered or reimbursed within six months of the crime.
- Median losses from personal and household crimes are higher for black than for white victims. [13]

To get an even better perspective on the tremendous economic costs of criminal personal victimization, consider that in 1986, 96 percent of the crimes of theft resulted in financial losses either in theft or damage terms; 90 percent of the household crimes involved economic losses; and more than one-fourth of all household crimes resulted in financial losses of $250 or more. [14]

Most of the economic losses caused by theft are never fully recovered. Official tabulations of property stolen and recovered in 1987 reveal that only 37 percent of the $11.7 million worth of property stolen nationwide was recovered (Table 2.13). Money and jewelry tend to be among the least recoverable items stolen (less than 6 percent recovered), whereas motor vehicles have the highest recovery rate (65 percent).

Victimization survey findings for 1986 indicate a similar loss-recovery rate for theft losses (Table 2.14). In 7 out of 10 personal and household crimes, there was no recovery of property. As in official indicators, victims of motor vehicle theft were the most likely to recover at least a portion of their losses. Seventy-one percent of all motor vehicle thefts in 1986 resulted in some degree of recovery, according to the NCS.

The impact of the enormous losses attributable to economic crimes such

Table 2.13
Type and Value of Property Stolen and Recovered, 1987 (13,149 Agencies;
1987 Estimated Population, 225,052,000)

Type of Property	Value of Property		Percent Recovered
	Stolen	Recovered	
TOTAL [a]	$11,784,214,000	$4,313,538,000	36.6
Currency, notes, etc............	719,659,000	41,962,000	5.8
Jewelry and precious metals.....	1,143,415,000	61,146,000	5.3
Clothing and furs..............	268,144,000	39,448,000	14.7
Locally stolen motor vehicles...	5,907,293,000	3,854,165,000	65.2
Office equipment...............	177,884,000	15,758,000	8.9
Televisions, radios, stereos, etc..........................	1,056,844,000	52,850,000	5.0
Firearms......................	115,139,000	11,867,000	10.3
Household goods................	209,044,000	14,137,000	6.8
Consumable goods...............	79,492,000	11,975,000	15.1
Livestock.....................	19,533,000	3,105,000	15.9
Miscellaneous.................	2,087,748,000	207,129,000	9.9

[a]All totals and percentages calculated before rounding.

Source: U.S. Federal Bureau of Investigation, Crime in the United States: Uniform Crime Reports 1987 (Washington, D.C.: Government Printing Office, 1988), p. 152.

as burglary and larceny may be more significant than any other aspect of criminal victimization, for this may be the area where the least expertise and fewest recovery systems are available. Law enforcement administrators must employ more policies and personnel to contain economic crimes and recover stolen property.

White-Collar Crime. Neither official nor victimization data concentrates on white-collar offenses and the losses attributable to them. White-collar crime—or illegitimate acts committed within the framework of legitimate enterprise or by otherwise law-abiding individuals of high social standing—includes such offenses as stock fraud, embezzlement, kickbacks, bribery, price fixing, and computer crime. The costs of white-collar crime are not as easily identifiable as those of conventional property crime because of the difficulties in assessing the direct and indirect costs to victims (an example of the latter is the cost of business losses passed on to the consumer). In addition, white-collar crime is much less visible to both the public and law enforcement than street or domestic crime, and therefore its incidence and cost, are more difficult to track.

Several sources, however, indicate that white-collar crime is considerably more costly from a financial standpoint than any other type of criminal activity. The Joint Committee of Congress recently estimated that one-third of the total economic costs of crime—or $44 billion—was the result of white-collar offenses.[15] A comparable estimate was made by the U.S. Chamber of Commerce.[16] Roughly half of all losses from white-collar crime

Table 2.14
Percentage of Victimizations Resulting in Theft Loss and Proportion of Loss Recovered, 1986

Type of Crime	Total	None recovered [b]	Some Recovered				All recovered	Not available
			Total	Less than half	Half or more	Proportion unknown [c]		
All personal crimes [a] (13,037,820)	**100.0**	**71.3**	**7.1**	**1.5**	**1.7**	**3.8**	**3.6**	**18.1**
Robbery (621,730)	100.0	55.3	13.3	2.6	3.2	7.5	7.1	24.4
Crimes of theft (12,401,860)	100.0	72.1	6.8	1.5	1.6	3.7	3.4	17.7
Personal larceny with contact (506,940)	100.0	56.4	20.7	5.0	1.2[d]	14.5	3.7	19.2
Personal larceny without contact (11,894,920)	100.0	72.8	6.2	1.3	1.7	3.2	3.4	17.7
All household crimes (12,307,480)	**100.0**	**68.0**	**8.7**	**1.4**	**2.3**	**4.9**	**5.4**	**17.9**
Burglary (3,552,280)	100.0	63.3	7.1	1.6	2.4	3.2	4.1	25.5
Household larceny (7,869,350)	100.0	76.2	4.6	1.0	1.6	2.0	4.4	14.8
Motor vehicle theft (885,860)	100.0	14.9	50.9	4.6	8.7	37.6	20.0	14.2

Note: detail may not add to total because of rounding.

aIncludes data on rape, not shown separately, but excludes data on assault, which by definition does not involve theft.

bIncludes items that were taken that had no value.

cIncludes items that were recovered that had no value.

dEstimate is based on about 10 or fewer sample cases.

Source: U.S. Department of Justice, *Criminal Victimization in the United States, 1986: A National Crime Survey Report* (Washington, D.C.: Government Printing Office, 1988), p. 74.

are attributable to consumer fraud, deceitful sales practices, and illegal competition.

Tax, Insurance, and Credit Card Fraud. Although tax, insurance, and credit fraud qualify as white-collar offenses, they are as common as non-white-collar offenses (committed outside the realm of legitimate occupation). Estimates suggest that billions of dollars are lost annually from these fraudulent practices:

- Tax fraud — $87 billion
- Insurance fraud — $11 billion
- Credit card fraud — $40-$50 million[17]

The cost of fraud is believed to be about ten times that of property crimes.

Cost to the Justice System

The cost of crime to the American taxpayer is also reflected in the operation of the criminal justice system.[18] Federal, state, and local expenditures for civil and criminal justice operations in 1983 totaled $39.7 billion and were divided as such:

- Local — $23.2 billion
- State — $12.8 billion
- Federal — $4.9 billion

For each dollar spent by the justice system:

- 52¢ went to police protection
- 22¢ went to the courts and other legal services
- 26¢ went to the correctional system

Total civil and criminal justice government spending in 1983 averaged $170 per person.

The magnitude and cost of crime in America are staggering. In 1986, there were 13.2 million serious crimes known to the police, 12.5 million arrests, and 34.1 million victimizations—all at a cost to the victim and the indirect victims (the public) of billions of dollars. These figures likely undercount the magnitude and cost of crime in this country, which for reasons ranging from nonreporting to inconsistent official and victimization data to ineffective law enforcement to unknown financial costs, figure to be much greater.

What has emerged in this chapter are conflicting signals on the direction of crime. On the one hand official data tells us that the crime rate as well as the number of arrests are on the rise. Yet victimization surveys point toward a decline in the rate of victimization. Obviously because these two views represent different sources and methodologies, their conclusions are hard to compare analytically. However, they manage to succeed in adding to the confusion over the greater picture of crime.

While generalizations about crime, its patterns, and its victims and offenders tend to be misleading, some light has been shed on certain trends, namely:

- More crime occurs than is known or admitted to.
- Crime and victimization are primarily a phenomenon of the young.
- Males are victims and offenders much more often than females.
- Whites make up the vast majority of offenders and victims.
- Blacks and other minorities are disproportionately involved in crime.
- Crime is largely intraracial.
- Law enforcement has a low success rate in solving crimes.
- The direct and indirect losses due to crime are exorbitant.

NOTES

1. U.S. Federal Bureau of Investigation, *Crime in the United States: Uniform Crime Reports 1987* (Washington, D.C.: Government Printing Office, 1988), p. 153.

2. Ibid.

3. Ibid., p. 163.

4. Ibid.

5. U.S. Department of Justice, *BJS Data Report, 1986* (Washington, D.C.: Government Printing Office, 1987), p. 8.

6. Ibid.

7. U.S. Department of Justice, *Criminal Victimization in the United States, 1986: A National Crime Survey Report* (Washington, D.C.: Government Printing Office, 1988).

8. Ibid., p. 6; U.S. Department of Justice, *Criminal Victimization in the United States, 1985: A National Crime Survey Report, 1985* (Washington, D.C.: Government Printing Office, 1987), pp. 5, 35.

9. *Criminal Victimization, 1986*, p. 7.

10. Ibid.

11. U.S. Department of Justice, *Bureau of Justice Statistics Bulletin: Criminal Victimization 1986* (Washington, D.C.: Government Printing Office, 1987), pp. 2-3.

12. U.S. Federal Bureau of Investigation, *Crime in the United States: Uniform Crime Reports 1986* (Washington, D.C.: Government Printing Office, 1987), p. 12.

13. U.S. Department of Justice, *Bureau of Justice Statistics Special Report: The Economic Cost of Crime to Victims* (Washington, D.C.: Government Printing Office, 1984).

14. *Criminal Victimization, 1986*, p. 9.

15. As cited in "That Costly White-Collar Mob," *New York Times* (January 2, 1977): sec. 3, p. 15.

16. Chamber of Commerce of the United States. *A Handbook on White Collar Crime: Everyone's Problem, Everyone's Loss* (Washington, D.C.: Chamber of Commerce of the United States, 1974), p. 6.

17. See Elizabeth J. Block, "Bandits Wielding Plastic," *New York Times* (May 22, 1983): F12, F13; Edward Cowan, "Your Honest Taxpayer Bears Watching," *New York Times* (April 11, 1982): E4; Dylan Landis, "Insurance Fraud: Billions in Losses," *New York Times* (July 6, 1982): D1, D2.

18. *BJS Data Report, 1986*, pp. 22-23.

3

Ecological Variations in Crime

Although crime knows few boundaries in our society, it is unevenly distributed among places and according to time. That is, crime has been shown to be more prevalent in some geographical areas, and under certain temporal conditions, than in others. An ecological approach to criminality focuses on the various spatial dimensions of crime and criminals. In this chapter we will explore the demographic ecology of crime.

HISTORICAL TRENDS IN CRIMINAL ECOLOGICAL RESEARCH

Ecological studies of crime date back to the early nineteenth century and the scientific and systematic work of scholars and sociologists who focused on the relationship between criminality and the physical environment. As a biological science, ecology is concerned with how organisms relate to their environment. Human ecology concentrates on the environmental associations between human beings and their physical and social space.

Early scholars in ecological criminology recognized the significance of explaining and exploring the spatial and temporal variations in crime; before one could formulate theories and causes of crime, offer preventive approaches, or deal with criminals, some insight into the spatial distribution of crime and criminals had to be gained. Early writings in criminal ecology described the ecological differences between urban and rural crime. Urban crime was considered to be far more serious and of greater incidence than crime in the rural countryside. Louis Mirth theorized that city life created anomie societally and alienation individually.[1] Others regarded urban living as amoral and normless.[2]

Among the first systematic ecological studies of crime were those carried out in the nineteenth century by André Michel Guerry and by Henry

Mayhew and John Binney. Guerry's "catagraphic method" associated crime and morality in France with man's physical environment.[3] In a study of crime in England and Wales, Mayhew and Binney found that the crime rate was higher than average in industrial centers and below average in the outlying areas of the county.[4] Other prominent early contributors to the study of the spatial ecology of crime include Adolphe Quetelet[5] and Enrico Ferri.[6]

In the United States, the development of an ecological approach in the field of criminology was largely the result of the Chicago school of urban ecology in the 1920s. Concentrating primarily on intraurban crime, these theorists were most concerned with juvenile delinquency in urban America. The most detailed study was undertaken in Chicago (later, other cities were studied as well) by Clifford Shaw and Henry McKay.[7] In describing urban areas as a series of recognizable concentric rings, they found that (1) intraurban crime could be differentiated geographically, and (2) the highest rate of crime and delinquency occurred in the center of cities and decreased with the distance from the center. Calvin Schmid's ecological study of Seattle supported the existence of an inverse association between the rate of crime and the distance from the center of the city.[8]

Other early ecological approaches to crime examined the relationship between criminality and climate, the rhythms of the seasons, and cosmic influences on crime.[9] Although many of the theories linking crime to ecological variables are no longer considered credible or are insufficient as single explanations of criminal behavior, ecology continues to be influential to the understanding of crime and its spatial distribution.

GEOGRAPHICAL DISTRIBUTION OF CRIME

The spatial dimensions of crime are best examined through various geographical subcategories having to do with the relationships between crime and region, community, and population size.

Regional Variations in Crime

One way to examine spatial patterns of crime in the United States is through its regional variations. For official statistical purposes, the nation is divided into four regions: West, South, Northeast, and Midwest. Purely in numerical terms, the South is the most crime-prone region, followed by the West, the Midwest, and the Northeast. As can be seen in Table 3.1, among Index crimes in 1986, the South's percentage was twice that of the Northeast. The South accounted for nearly one-third of the country's total violent and property crimes; the number of murders in the South was nearly twice that of the next closest region, the West. The West and Midwest show relatively equal amounts of Index crime. Although the Northeast had the least

Table 3.1
Percentage Distribution of Crime Index Offenses, by Region, 1986[a]

CRIME	WEST	SOUTH	NORTHEAST	MIDWEST
Murder	22	42	17	19
Forcible rape	24	37	16	23
Robbery	23	31	27	19
Aggravated assault	25	37	17	21
Burglary	25	39	16	20
Larceny-theft	25	36	17	23
Motor vehicle theft	23	31	24	22
Violent crime	24	35	21	20
Property crime	25	36	17	22
Crime Index total	24	36	18	22

[a]Sufficient data on arson are not available for regional estimates.

Source: U.S. Federal Bureau of Investigation, Crime in the United States: Uniform Crime Reports 1986 (Washington, D.C.: Government Printing Office, 1987).

crime overall, it was second only to the South in its percentage of robberies and motor vehicle thefts, while being responsible for around one-quarter of those offenses nationally.

As noted earlier, crime rates are a more effective gauge for measuring crime. Table 3.2 gives the regional rates of Crime Index offenses per 100,000 people in 1986. From this point of view, we see that the rate of crime for Index offenses is highest in the West, followed by the South, the Midwest, and the Northeast. In fact, the West's Crime Index rate is well above the national rate. The differential between the West and other regions is greatest for property crime.

Some researchers have attributed the higher rate of crime in western states to their larger concentrations of ethnic immigrants; others have suggested that the regional differences may be due to a greater representation in the West of young people, who are most likely to be involved in crime. Another explanation given for the higher rates of property crime in the West and South is that warmer weather is more conducive to such crimes.

Despite the fact that the West has the highest rate of overall Index crimes, there is greater variation among individual crimes. For instance, the Northeast, with the lowest Index crime rate among the regions, had the highest rate per 100,000 population for the crime of robbery. The South had the highest murder rate in 1986 and has consistently topped the other regions in this category, though recently the disparity has shrunk, particularly with the West.

Some have blamed the South's higher murder rate on the high incidence

Table 3.2
Rates of Crime Index Offenses per 100,000 Population, by Region, 1986

CRIME	WEST	SOUTH	NORTHEAST	MIDWEST	TOTAL U.S.
Murder	9.2	10.6	6.8	6.6	8.6
Forcible rape[a]	86.0	79.0	55.0	69.0	73.0
Robbery	250.6	199.5	298.2	178.6	225.1
Aggravated assault	422.7	371.2	296.0	290.2	346.1
Burglary	1670.9	1522.5	1042.7	1081.8	1344.6
Larceny-theft	3662.4	3107.4	2472.7	2791.8	3010.3
Motor vehicle theft	584.0	457.8	587.2	448.1	507.8
Arson[b]	64.0	46.0	58.0	48.0	53.0
Violent crime	726.8	64.8	629.3	510.8	617.3
Property crime	5917.4	5087.7	4102.6	4321.7	4862.6
Crime Index total	6644.2	5709.5	4731.9	4832.5	5479.9

[a]The forcible rape rates shown are calculated for female victims only as opposed to the population as a whole.

[b]The rates for arson are tabulated independently owing to lower population coverage for arson data.

Source: U.S. Federal Bureau of Investigation, Crime in the United States: Uniform Crime Reports 1986 (Washington, D.C.: Government Printing Office, 1987), pp. 14, 37, 44-51.

of poverty and minorities in that region. Regional differences in the murder rate also have been attributed to a "subculture of violence," or norms that consider violent behavior to be an acceptable response to particular situations.[10] Some criminologists believe that these norms are more prevalent in the South than in any other region. Regional data on crime is further expressed in arrest statistics. As illustrated in Table 3.3, in 1987 the highest total of arrests in the United States belonged to the southern states, followed by the western, northeastern, and midwestern states. The rate of total arrests, however, was highest in the West and lowest in the Midwest, with the Northeast ranking second highest and the South third. The Crime Index aggregate arrest patterns indicate the following geographical order: South, West, Midwest, and Northeast. But in relative terms per 100,000 inhabitants, the rate of arrests is highest in the western states, followed by the southern, northeastern, and midwestern states. The regional inconsistency of the crime and arrest rates may reflect differences in the participating agencies and estimated populations.

Table 3.3
Regional Arrests, by Number and Rate, 1987 (Rate = Number of Arrests per 100,000 Inhabitants)

Offense Charged	United States Total (10,616 agencies: pop. 202,337,000)	Northeastern States (2,256 agencies: pop. 40,033,000)	Midwestern States (2,703 agencies: pop. 47,688,000)	Southern States (4,201 agencies: pop. 68,394,000)	Western States (1,636 agencies: pop. 46,222,000)
TOTAL	10,784,199	2,209,155	2,156,910	3,602,934	2,815,200
Rate	5,329.8	5,518.4	4,523.0	5,267.9	6,090.6
Murder & nonnegligent manslaughter	16,714	2,591	4,322	5,833	3,968
Rate	8.3	6.5	9.1	8.5	8.6
Forcible rape	31,276	6,024	7,813	10,408	7,031
Rate	15.5	15.0	16.4	15.2	15.2
Robbery	123,306	41,270	20,132	32,489	29,415
Rate	60.9	103.1	42.2	47.5	63.6
Aggravated assault	301,734	64,512	45,129	96,317	95,776
Rate	149.1	161.1	94.6	140.8	207.2
Burglary	374,963	60,725	65,091	140,173	108,974
Rate	185.3	151.7	136.5	204.9	235.8
Larceny-theft	1,256,552	206,120	296,936	411,805	341,691
Rate	621.0	514.9	622.7	602.1	739.2
Motor vehicle theft	146,753	26,939	23,975	45,353	50,486
Rate	72.5	67.3	50.3	66.3	109.2
Arson	15,169	3,134	3,679	4,377	3,979
Rate	7.5	7.8	7.7	6.4	8.6
Violent crime [a]	473,030	114,397	77,396	145,047	136,190
Rate	233.8	285.8	162.3	212.1	294.6
Property crime [b]	1,793,437	296,918	389,681	601,708	505,130
Rate	886.4	741.7	817.2	879.8	1,092.8
Crime Index total [c]	2,266,467	411,315	467,077	746,755	641,320
Rate	1,120.1	1,027.4	979.5	1,091.8	1,387.5

[a] Violent crimes are offenses of murder, forcible rape, robbery, and aggravated assault.

[b] Property crimes are offenses of burglary, larceny-theft, motor vehicle theft, and arson.

[c] Includes arson. Population figures were rounded to the nearest thousand. All rates were calculated before rounding.

Source: U.S. Federal Bureau of Investigation, Crime in the United States: Uniform Crime Reports 1987 (Washington, D.C.: Government Printing Office, 1988), p. 165.

Community Size Variations in Crime

The spatial distribution of crime can also be measured through officially designated community-type aggregations. The most common of these population groupings are Metropolitan Statistical Areas (MSAs), other cities, and rural counties. An MSA consists of a central city or urbanized area at least 50,000 in population and includes suburban areas of less than 50,000 inhabitants. MSAs represented approximately 76 percent of the nation's population in 1986. "Other cities" and rural counties lie outside MSAs and in 1986 comprised 10 and 14 percent of the U.S. population respectively.

Table 3.4 presents Crime Index data by community size for the three aggregate groups in 1986. As would be expected, the amount of crime in MSAs far exceeded that in other cities and rural areas. The rate of crime per 100,000 population in MSAs was higher than the national rate for every Index crime, and with the exception of murder and larceny-theft, was well above the crime rate in the other two community types. Other cities showed the second highest rate of crime and was nearly equal to MSAs in larceny-theft rates. Rural areas had a much lower crime rate than the other population groupings, except in the case of murder, where the rate was higher than in other cities.

Crime distribution by community type also can be expressed in terms of crime rates for offenses known to the police by population group. Table 3.5 distributes the crime rates for cities, suburban cities, and nonsuburban cities in 1986. The rates of Crime Index offenses were highest in cities. However, the overall crime rate for nonsuburban cities was slightly higher than the suburban cities' rate; suburban cities showed a higher rate only for robbery and motor vehicle theft. Because nonsuburban cities include other cities and rural counties outside MSAs, it is unclear how these figures relate to the data presented in Table 3.4, other than that the methodological differences in population groupings lead to somewhat uncomparable results.

Victimization and Geographical Variations

In addition to official data, victimization surveys also track the geographical location of crime, but with an emphasis on victimization rather than "crime" rates per se. Because of this important distinction and differences in methodological procedures and community parameters, the results are not entirely compatible with those in Uniform Crime Reports. National Crime Survey (NCS) data uses three basic geographic areas: central cities, suburban areas, and nonmetropolitan areas.

Findings of a 1985 NCS special report on the geographical distribution of victimization are displayed in Table 3.6. The data shows that central city residents were nearly twice as likely to be victims of violent crime as non-

Table 3.4
Index of Crime, by Community-type Aggregation, 1986

Area	Population[a]	Crime Index[b] Total	Violent Crime	Property Crime	Murder and Non-negligent Manslaughter	Forcible Rape	Robbery	Aggravated Assault	Burglary	Larceny-Theft	Motor Vehicle Theft
United States Total.........	241,077,000	13,210,844	1,488,144	11,722,700	20,613	90,434	542,775	834,322	3,241,410	7,257,153	1,224,137
Rate per 100,000 inhabitants........		5,479.9	617.3	4,862.6	8.6	37.5	225.1	346.1	1,334.6	3,010.3	507.8
Metropolitan Statistical Area.........[c]	184,130,425										
Area actually reporting...	98.1%	11,354,016	1,338,831	10,015,185	17,528	78,614	524,355	718,334	2,750,912	6,135,190	1,129,083
Estimated totals........	100.0%	11,482,370	1,348,327	10,134,043	17,644	79,322	526,550	724,811	2,780,950	6,212,875	1,140,218
Rate per 100,000 inhabitants........		6,236.0	732.3	5,503.7	9.6	43.1	286.0	393.6	1,510.3	3,374.2	619.2
Other Cities............[c]	22,891,469										
Area actually reporting...	94.0%	1,031,496	75,047	956,449	1,077	4,735	10,395	58,840	224,716	687,229	44,504
Estimated totals........	100.0%	1,097,216	80,209	1,017,107	1,154	5,037	11,160	62,758	239,368	730,503	47,236
Rate per 100,000 inhabitants........		4,793.1	350.0	4,443.2	5.0	22.0	48.8	274.2	1,045.7	3,191.2	206.3
Rural Area............[c]	34,056,106										
Area actually reporting...	89.4%	579,263	53,966	525,297	1,588	5,566	4,581	42,231	202,985	288,783	33,529
Estimated totals........	100.0%	631,258	59,708	571,550	1,815	6,075	5,065	46,753	221,092	313,775	36,683
Rate per 100,000 inhabitants........		1,853.6	175.3	1,678.3	5.3	17.8	14.9	137.3	649.2	921.3	107.7

[a]Populations are Bureau of the Census provisional estimates as of July 1, 1986, and are subject to change.

[b]Although arson data are included in the trend and clearance tables, sufficient data are not available to estimate totals for this offense.

[c]The percentage representing area actually reporting will not coincide with the ratio between reported and estimated crime totals, since these data represent the sum of the calculations for individual states, which have varying populations, portions reporting, and crime rates.

Source: U.S. Federal Bureau of Investigation, Crime in the United States: Uniform Crime Reports 1986 (Washington, D.C.: Government Printing Office, 1987), p. 42.

Table 3.5
Crime Rates, Offenses Known to the Police, by Population Group, 1986[a]
(1986 Estimated Population; Rate = Number of Crimes per 100,000 Inhabitants)

Population Group	Crime Index Total[b]	Violent Crime	Property Crime	Murder and non-negligent man-slaughter	Forcible Rape	Robbery	Aggra-vated Assault	Burglary	Larceny-Theft	Motor Vehicle Theft
TOTAL CITIES 8,298 cities; population 148,773,000:										
Number of offenses known........	10,284,922	1,206,162	9,078,760	15,593	64,211	485,453	640,905	2,385,310	5,690,058	1,003,392
Rate.........	7,363.2	863.5	6,102.4	10.5	46.0	326.3	430.8	1,603.3	3,824.7	671.1
TOTAL SUBURBAN CITIES: 1,481 cities; population 41,300,000:										
Number of offenses known........	2,160,142	157,006	2,003,136	1,609	9,370	42,598	103,429	470,956	1,369,331	162,819
Rate.........	5,289.2	384.4	4,521.8	3.6	22.9	96.2	233.5	1,063.1	3,091.1	367.6
TOTAL NON-SUBURBAN CITIES: 3,310 cities; population 22,398,000:										
Number of offenses known........	1,147,475	86,617	1,060,858	1,178	5,378	14,549	65,512	252,255	757,828	50,775
Rate.........	5,406.2	408.1	4,736.4	5.3	25.3	65.0	292.5	1,126.3	3,383.5	226.7

[a]Suburban places are within Metropolitan Statistical Areas (MSAs) and include suburban city and county law enforcement agencies within the metropolitan area. Central cities are excluded. Nonsuburban places are outside MSAs.

[b]Arson rates are not presented in this table because fewer agencies furnished complete reports for arson than for the other seven Crime Index offenses.

Source: U.S. Federal Bureau of Investigation, Crime in the United States: Uniform Crime Reports 1986 (Washington, D.C.: Government Printing Office, 1987), pp. 147-49.

Table 3.6
Victimization Rates for Persons Aged 12 and Over, 1983

Place of Residence and Population	Crimes of Violence	Crimes of Theft
TOTAL ALL AREAS	31.0	76.9
All Central Cities	43.3	92.0
50,000 - 249,999	38.1	89.5
250,000 - 499,999	39.4	85.4
500,000 - 999,999	48.1	104.5
1,000,000 or more	48.2	90.4
All Suburban Areas	29.4	82.0
50,000 - 249,999	25.2	71.5
250,000 - 499,999	30.3	78.6
500,000 - 999,999	30.2	87.8
1,000,000 or more	32.8	92.7
Nonmetropolitan Areas	22.4	57.7

Note: Rates are per 1,000 population aged 12 and over. The population range categories
    shown under the All Central Cities and All Suburban Areas headings are based only on
    the size of the central city and do not reflect the population of the entire metropolitan area.

Source: U.S. Department of Justice, *Bureau of Justice Statistics Special Report: Locating City,
    Suburban, and Rural Crime* (Washington, D.C.: Government Printing Office, 1985).

metropolitan or rural residents during 1983. Central city residents had the
highest victimization rates for crimes of violence and theft, followed by
suburban inhabitants, with nonmetropolitan residents showing the lowest
rates.

Victimization patterns tend to be more varied when examining the central
cities categories. For example, the rates for crimes of theft peaked in the city
size-category of 500,000-999,999, but dropped for cities with a population
of 1,000,000 or more. This city size also had a lower theft victimization rate
than suburban areas with a population of 1,000,000 or more. Violent crime
victimization rates were highest in the larger cities. All central cities' crime
rates were higher than the total crime rates. Suburban victimization rates
for theft and violent crime generally exhibited a rise as community size
increased.

The NCS report found further that while most crimes occurred in the
general vicinity of where the victim lived, suburban dwellers were more
likely to be victimized by violent crime within the city limits of their metropolitan areas than were city residents in the suburbs surrounding their
cities. In 1983, nearly 95 percent of the crimes of violence perpetrated
against residents of cities with a population of 1 million or more took place
within the city itself; in contrast, about two-thirds of the violent crimes
against suburban residents of such cities occurred in the suburbs.[11]

These findings were corroborated by a 1986 National Crime Survey, which revealed that for all personal crimes, the victimization rate was greatest for residents of central cities, followed by suburban area and non-metropolitan area residents. The NCS further reported the following:

- The rate of violent crime victimization was highest for residents of urban areas
- Robbery and assault victimization rates were highest for central city residents
- The rate of robbery victimization was lowest for rural area residents
- The rate of assault victimization was lowest for suburban area residents
- Central city residents had higher victimization rates than suburban residents, except in cities with a population of 1,000,000 or more
- The rate of assault victimization for residents in the central cities categories was lowest for residents in cities of 1,000,000 or more in population[12]

It should be noted that the findings with regard to victimization rates for U.S. cities with 1,000,000 or more residents do not seem to hold true for most other nations.[13] However, in the Soviet Union, the highest crime rates have been shown to be in medium-sized cities rather than in the largest cities.[14]

Population Density and Crime

There has been much debate over the relationship between population density and the crime rate. Some research has shown the relationship to be negligible when the variables of income and ethnicity are considered.[15] However, other studies have concluded that there is a direct correlation between population density and the rates of crime and delinquency.[16] One recent study advanced the notion that the association between density or overcrowding and crime was positive even when the influences of income, education, and racial/ethnic composition were set apart from the effects of population density.[17]

In general, there does appear to be a solid relationship between population density and high crime rates, particularly for more aggressive, violent crimes. Urban counties tend to have the highest per capita crime rates, whereas rural counties tend to have the lowest rates of crime. The exceptions to the latter finding are resort areas that often have high transient and seasonal inhabitants, such as Atlantic City, New Jersey, and Summit County, Colorado.

Metropolitan Crime

Much ecological study of crime has focused on its metropolitan distribution, particularly with respect to central city areas of metropolitan centers.

The general assumption has been that crime rates are highest in central cities and decrease the further the distance away. This inverse linear relationship between crime rates and distance from the center of the city was first proposed by R. E. Park and Ernest Burgess, whose zonal model of urban ecology postulated that central cities have the highest crime rates due to their high concentration of physical and social conditions commonly related to crime.[18] As noted earlier, Shaw and McKay were the first to apply this approach systematically. Since then, a number of other studies conducted in the United States and such countries as Canada and Great Britain have reached similar conclusions.[19]

Official data also essentially support the spatial dimensions of crime. In 1986, MSAs had a crime rate more than three times that of rural areas, and the Crime Index rate for cities was better than three times the rural counties' rate and one and a half times higher than suburban area rates. The differential was even greater for violent crime; the cities' rate was more than four times that of rural counties and over two times the rate for suburban areas.[20]

Researchers have suggested in recent years that the inverse linear relationship between crime rates and the distance from the center of the city may now be outdated, citing among other reasons that "transitional" areas, once a portion of the central city, have since diffused into suburbia.[21] Furthermore, such metropolitan models as Shaw and McKay's, where the central business district lies at the core of the metropolis, is certainly not descriptive of all or even most U.S. cities today. Many cities have multiple business districts; others have developed industry on their suburban fringes.

There are also indications that the spatial distribution of crime is changing. While the rate of urban crime has risen in recent decades, in some areas the growth has been slower than in suburban and rural areas. Neighborhood change and greater criminal mobility may be partly responsible for this.

Several types of theories seek to explain the spatial distribution of crime. Such social theories as anomie, drift, and differential association regard criminality as a pathological reaction to environmental stimuli, among them poverty, disorganization, depression, and exploitation.[22] These theories tend to concentrate on areas within the city where offenders are likely to amass, and so generally imply that they live close to the scene of the crime. The main problem with such an approach is that it fails to account adequately for increased offender mobility and shifts in crime distribution.

Opportunity theories are more concerned with the targets of crime than with criminals.[23] These theories focus on the availability of and the chance to profit from potential victims of criminals. The spatial variable that appears to connect social and opportunity theories is access to victims. The distance between criminals and possible victims can affect the probability of a crime being committed. Opportunity theories allow for the increased mobility of offenders, which means that increased opportunities may well be opportunities further from traditional areas where many criminals live.

Traditional criminological theory posits that property criminals are less likely to commit crimes in their own neighborhood owing to the possibility that they might be recognized.[24] However, as familiarity with an area and easy access are thought to be prime considerations in the commission of most crimes, it is believed that few offenders journey very far from home, and rarely into areas where they might be too conspicuous. Recent trends suggest that traditional theory is less applicable to many urban criminals today whose motivation, sophistication, and mobility may carry more weight in determining when, where, and why they will commit crimes.

Suburban Crime

Although the suburbs are considered an integral part of the greater metropolitan area of most large cities, much less attention is given to the spatial and dimensional characteristics of suburban crime than city crime. Because of the metropolitan nature of most suburbs, one would expect rates of suburban crime to be nearer to city crime rates than to the rates in rural areas. This holds true, according to official statistics. In 1986, the "suburban areas" (including cities less than 50,000 in population along with counties within MSAs) Crime Index rate for offenses the police knew of was 4,683.6 per 100,000 population compared to 7,363.2 for cities and 2,053.6 for rural counties.[25] The suburban rate was more than twice that of the rural counties. Under a different classification, "suburban cities," the Crime Index rate was even closer to the cities' rate of 5,289.2 and further from the rate in rural counties. Property crime accounted for the bulk of suburban crime in 1986, with the highest rate recorded for larceny-theft. Every Index crime showed an increase over the previous year.

One of the few in-depth studies to address suburban crime produced some surprising results. John Stahura and C. Ronald Huff examined crime between 1960 and 1980 in a cohort of 247 U.S. suburbs with a population of at least 25,000.[26] They divided distance from the center of the city into 4 ten-mile increments (e.g., 0-10 miles, 10-20 miles). Their findings contradicted the traditional inverse relationship between crime rates and distance from the center of the city.

In the years studied (1960, 1970, and 1980), the lowest crime rates were in the 0-10 mile zones, or those closest to the city, for both violent and property crime. Although the crime rates were inconsistent for successive ten-mile zones, they generally were highest the further away from the central city. In 1980, the highest violent and property crime rates were in the 20-30 and 30+ distances from the city. Overall, the study demonstrated a substantial increase in suburban crime rates since 1960.

The authors attributed this increase and the relationship between suburban crime and distance from the central city to population density, census region, percentage of black population, suburban age, the percentage of high-income inhabitants, and industrial/commercial concentration. Specifically, they proposed that

suburbs that are denser and more employment oriented tend to attract people who are less concerned with the social control of behavior within the community; this lack of social control is, in turn, associated with higher rates of crime. If the people who are attracted to denser, employing suburbs are also black, even higher crime rates may be expected.[27]

There are some problems with these conclusions, most notably their lack of support. Further, the correlate of blacks and suburban crime seems to be flawed, and may be biased, since no comparison of other racial/ethnic groups and their effect on suburban crime was used. Nevertheless, it is a useful study which suggests that more research is needed on crime in suburbia.

Rural Crime

Perhaps the one place left in the United States that most people perceive to be relatively crime-free is the countryside or rural America. Certainly, as we have pointed out, the crime rate per 100,000 in rural counties is well below that of metropolitan areas and, for the most part, suburban areas. There are, of course, variations in law enforcement practices, detection and investigation techniques, police department resources, and other factors that may influence to some extent the urban-rural differential in rates of crime. Whether such geographical disparities in crime rates are exaggerated or not, it is evident that rural crime is on the rise in a dramatic way. Between 1960 and 1984 the national rate of rural crime jumped 430 percent, compared to an increase of 360 percent in urban areas.[28] More recently, the total incidence of Index crimes for rural counties rose 4 percent from 1985 to 1986—a smaller rise than for metropolitan or suburban areas during the same period, but an indication of the direction of rural crime.[29]

Italian criminologist Cesare Lombroso once described rural criminality as "barbarous" and motivated primarily by brutality and revenge, as opposed to urban crime, which he considered to be more intellectual by nature.[30] Although there is no real evidence to support his claim that rural crime is more violent than city or suburban crime, statistics show that the crime rate for murder is closer for these geographical areas than the rate for any other crime. In fact, in 1986, the rural counties murder rate of 5.4 was higher than that of suburban areas, which registered a rate of 4.8 (although the "suburban counties" murder rate was slightly higher at 6.1).[31]

Recently, the Rural Crime Prevention Center at Ohio State University presented the following data on rural crime:

- Ten to 15 percent of rural households nationwide will be vandalized in a given year
- Seven to 10 percent of all rural households will be the victims of yard theft
- Three to 5 percent of all rural households will experience break-ins
- Farms have a 25 percent greater chance of being broken into than nonfarm homes
- Ten percent of all farmers will be victimized by fraud
- Eighty percent of all rural crimes are perpetrated by community residents
- Boys, ages 17 to 19, make up the largest group of persons arrested for rural crimes[32]

The rise in rural crime is related to several factors, including the increase in crime committed by suburban and rural juveniles, the increased inventory of farm and other operational equipment, easier access through interstate highways, improvements in transportation, and growth of the rural population largely because of the relocation of industry. Accordingly, this has led to more fear of crime by longtime rural residents than ever before.[33]

What this means is that rural life today no longer fits the misconception that nonrural residents have of it. This is made all too clear by National Rural Crime Prevention director Joe Donnermeyer, who admits, "It's no longer a separate way of living. We're quite dependent on urban areas. All the things that explain rural crime have to do with that growing interdependence between rural areas and urban areas."[34]

TEMPORAL DISTRIBUTION OF CRIME

Ecological patterns of crime can not only be observed through geographical variations, but also through temporal variations as reflected by the place and time of occurrence, the day of the week, and monthly, seasonal, and yearly patterns.

Variations in Place of Occurrence

Where do crimes tend to take place most often? There is little data on locations of criminality. The NCS provides the most detailed breakdown of the distribution of criminal incidents by place of occurrence (see Table 3.7). In 1985, streets were the most common scene for personal crimes of violence, being the place where over one-fourth of all violent crime occurred. Only 13 percent of the violent crimes during the year were committed inside the victim's home, other building, or property. However, among selected crimes, rape took place as often at home as on the street,

Table 3.7
Percentage Distribution of Incidents, by Type of Crime and Place of Occurrence, 1985

Place of Occurrence	Crimes of Violence (4,981,700)	Rape (132,920)	Robbery (878,810)	Assault (3,969,970)	Personal Larceny w/Contact (446,220)	Motor Vehicle Theft (1,270,170)
Total	100.0	100.0	100.0	100.0	100.0	100.0
Inside own home, other building on property	12.9	25.5	13.5	12.3	2.6[a]	2.2
Near own home	12.8	6.3[a]	10.8	13.5	4.3	38.0
Inside restaurant, bar	6.0	0.0[a]	2.3	7.1	11.6	0.3[a]
Other commercial buildings	6.7	2.3[a]	4.5	7.3	22.4	0.6[a]
On public transportation, inside station	1.2	1.3[a]	3.2	0.8	15.0	0.0[a]
On the street	27.0	26.3	37.5	24.7	22.9	13.8
In a parking lot	8.5	10.0[a]	12.5	7.5	5.2	33.9
In a park, field, or playground	2.3	1.8[a]	1.7[a]	2.5	1.3[a]	0.5[a]
Inside school, on school property	9.1	4.4[a]	6.1	9.9	3.7	1.7
Friend's, relative's, or neighbor's home	7.8	19.4	5.9	7.8	2.5[a]	6.9
Other location	5.8	2.6[a]	2.0	6.7	8.4	2.1

Note: Detail may not add to total shown because of rounding. Number of incidents shown in parentheses.

[a]Estimate is based on about 10 or fewer sample cases.

Source: U.S. Department of Justice, *Criminal Victimization in the United States, 1985: A National Crime Survey Report* (Washington, D.C.: Government Printing Office, 1987), p. 50.

while personal larceny with contact was committed equally as often in commercial buildings as on the street. Motor vehicle theft occurred most frequently near the home.

NCS data for 1985 also revealed the following about the place of crime occurrence:

- Armed and unarmed robberies and assaults occurred most frequently on the street
- Violent crimes involving strangers took place most often on the street
- Crimes involving nonstrangers were most likely to occur in the victim's place of residence or a building on their property
- The greatest proportion of stranger rape victimizations occurred on the street
- Seventy percent of the nonstranger rapes took place on the victim's property or in the homes of friends or relatives[35]

Variations in Time of Occurrence

Law enforcement data reveals that violent crimes, particularly murder and forcible rape, and property crimes such as burglary, are most likely to be perpetrated during the evening and night, and least likely to occur during morning and early afternoon hours.[36]

NCS data for 1985 gives a somewhat different version of time variations in crime. As shown in Table 3.8, crimes of violence are split almost evenly between daytime and nighttime, while crimes of theft occurred most often during the daytime. However, household crimes tended to be most frequent in the night hours.

Table 3.8
Percentage Distribution of Crime, by Type and Time of Occurrence, 1985[a]

Type of Crime	Daytime		Nighttime				Not Known and not Available
	Total	6 am – 6 pm	Total	6 pm – Midnight	Midnight – 6 am	Not Known	
Crimes of violence	100.0	49.1	50.5	36.7	13.3	0.6	0.4
Crimes of theft	100.0	46.6	35.2	18.7	8.8	7.7	18.2
Household crimes	100.0	28.2	43.7	13.7	17.1	12.9	28.0

[a]Totals may not add up due to rounding.

Source: U.S. Department of Justice, Criminal Victimization in the United States, 1985: A National Crime Survey Report (Washington, D.C.: Government Printing Office, 1987), p. 48.

According to the NCS, time-of-day patterns for crimes in 1985 were most pronounced for the following offenses:

Nighttime crime:

- Three-quarters of the rapes
- More than 70 percent of the robberies with injury from serious assault
- Over 80 percent of the attempted robberies with injury from serious assault
- Two-thirds of the motor vehicle thefts

Daytime crime:

- Seventy percent of the purse snatching
- More than 60 percent of the pocket picking
- Over half of the personal larceny without contact and completed with less than $50

Day-of-Week Variations

There is really no reliable data to ascertain day-by-day variations in crime. Some studies indicate that violent and property crime are more likely to be perpetrated during weekends than weekdays. However, at least one study reported that aggressive crimes were more apt to occur on Sunday and Monday.[37]

Seasonal Variations

A relationship between climate and crime has been established through a number of studies. One recent study of crime in Houston and Chicago found a positive link between hot weather and violent crimes.[38] Another study, based on data from 858 U.S. cities with a population over 25,000, found that hot, dry weather was a significant factor in forecasting the likelihood of crimes of violence.[39]

Although official data indicate that the seasonal variances in crimes are not great, they do support studies that show crime to occur most frequently during the summer months. Table 3.9 breaks down the percentage of Index crimes in 1986 by month. We can see that the peak month for every crime is in the summer, and that most crimes occurred in the greatest number during the summer months. This is particularly true for forcible rape, murder, aggravated assault, and motor vehicle theft. Robbery is the one crime that appears to happen just as often in the colder months as in the summer, since the January and December percentages are among the highest for robbery.

Victimization data also corroborate seasonal fluctuations in crime. Recent NCS research found that most types of personal and household crimes are

Table 3.9

Percentage Distribution of Crime Index Offenses, by Type of Crime and Month, 1986[a]

Month	Murder	For- cible Rape	Robbery	Aggra- vated Assault	Burglary	Larceny- Theft	Motor Vehicle Theft
Jan.	7.7	7.1	8.7	6.8	8.4	7.8	7.9
Feb.	7.0	6.7	7.7	6.3	7.5	7.2	7.1
March	8.3	7.9	8.2	8.0	8.3	8.3	8.1
April	8.0	8.1	7.6	8.1	7.9	8.2	7.8
May	8.2	8.8	7.7	9.1	8.1	8.4	8.0
June	8.3	9.2	8.0	9.7	8.1	8.6	8.2
July	9.4	9.8	8.4	10.0	8.9	9.1	8.9
Aug.	9.4	10.2	9.3	10.0	9.0	9.3	9.5
Sept.	9.1	9.1	8.6	8.8	8.5	8.4	8.7
Oct.	8.3	8.4	8.7	8.3	8.4	8.5	9.0
Nov.	8.0	7.8	8.3	7.6	8.1	7.9	8.5
Dec.	8.4	7.0	9.0	7.4	8.8	8.3	8.3

[a]Arson figures for month-to-month are not available.

Source: U.S. Federal Bureau of Investigation, Crime in the United States: Uniform Crime Reports 1986 (Washington, D.C.: Government Printing Office,1987).

more likely to take place during the warmer months. The exception to this is the personal crime of robbery.[40]

While temporal variations in crime rates have yet to be explained adequately, the more popular assumptions are that (1) more people are outdoors during the warm weather season and thus are more vulnerable to crime, and (2) lax precautionary measures during the summer, such as leaving windows open, makes it easier for property criminals to strike.

CRIME TRENDS

Trends in the spatial incidence and nature of crime are important in helping us to track directional crime patterns, formulate theories, and assess effectiveness in crime control and preventive measures. Official and victimization data consistently have shown that the crime rate is highest in urban areas, with suburban areas experiencing the second highest rate of crime, and rural areas the lowest rate. However, there are indications that suburban and rural areas are closing the gap somewhat as the character and inhabitants of these areas change.

Regional variations in crime rates have also remained steady for a number of years. The highest rates for major crimes have been in the West and South, with the lowest in the Northeast.[41] This, in turn, reflects to some degree the trend toward a higher incidence of crime in warmer weather. The short-term percentage changes in regional crime rates from 1985 to 1986 show that the Crime Index rate increased the most in the South (9 percent), followed by the West and Midwest (4 percent) and the Northeast (2 percent). The West experienced the greatest increase in the rate of violent crime (15 percent) in the one-year period. However, the rate for murder rose the most in the Northeast (11 percent), while in the South the robbery rate increase (15 percent) nearly doubled that of the second highest robbery rate increase (in the Midwest).[42]

In terms of the amount of crime by community size, UCR data show that compared to 1985, the 1986 Crime Index total increased the same in cities, suburban counties, suburban areas, and suburban cities—by 6 percent— and by 4 percent in rural counties. Violent crime during the period rose 12 percent in cities and suburban regions and 6 percent in rural counties. Property crime climbed 6 percent in cities and suburban areas, compared to 4 percent in rural counties.[43] Although examining absolute crime figures is not as effective as looking at crime rates, there is value in tracking growth trends in crime ecologically, which can then be related to per capita figures.

There are important ecological variations in the spatial distribution of crime that criminological theory must adequately account for. Most crime, both in volume and relative to population size, tends to occur in the West and South, in warmer temperatures, and in metropolitan and densely populated areas. Temporal dimensions of crime are less predictable, but violent crimes generally tend to occur most frequently during the evening or night and take place on the street.

Today there is much less emphasis on the ecology of crime, as criminal behavior is expressed most often in terms of the influences of culture. However, given an ecological influence in prominent theories of criminality and an established spatial dimension to crime, the significance of ecology in the study and resolution of crime cannot easily be dismissed.

NOTES

1. Louis Mirth, as cited in Brian J. L. Berry, *Comparative Urbanization* (New York: St. Martin's Press, 1981), pp. 14-15.

2. See Berry, *Comparative Urbanization*, pp. 9-14. See also David A. Jones, *History of Criminology: A Philosophical Perspective* (Westport, Conn.: Greenwood Press, 1986), pp. 164-68.

3. André Michel Guerry, *Essai sur la Statistique Morale de la France* (Paris, 1833).

4. Henry Mayhew and John Binney, *The Criminal Prisons of London* (London: A. M. Kelly, 1968).

5. Adolphe Quetelet, *Sur l'homme et la Développement de ses Facultés ou Essai de Physique Sociale* (Paris, 1835).

6. Enrico Ferri, *Criminal Sociology* (New York: Little, Brown, 1917).

7. Clifford R. Shaw and Henry D. McKay, *Juvenile Delinquency and Urban Areas*, rev. ed. (Chicago: University of Chicago Press, 1969).

8. Calvin F. Schmid, "Urban Crime Areas: Part I," *American Sociological Review* 25 (1960): 527-42; idem, "Urban Crime Areas: Part II," *American Sociological Review* 25 (1960): 655-78.

9. See Stephen Schafer, *Introduction to Criminology* (Reston, Va.: Reston Publishing Company, 1976), pp. 87-88.

10. Marvin E. Wolfgang and Franco Ferracuti, *The Subculture of Violence: Towards an Integrated Theory in Criminology* (Beverly Hills: Sage Publications, 1967).

11. U.S. Department of Justice, *BJS Data Report, 1986* (Washington, D.C.: Government Printing Office, 1987), p. 12.

12. U.S. Department of Justice, *Criminal Victimization in the United States, 1986: A National Crime Survey Report* (Washington, D.C.: Government Printing Office, 1988), p. 4.

13. Studies, for example, in England, Canada, and the Netherlands indicate that the highest crime rates are recorded in the largest metropolitan areas. See also Richard Block, ed., *Victimization and Fear of Crime: Worldwide Perspectives* (Washington, D.C.: Government Printing Office, 1984).

14. Louise I. Shelley, "Crime in Moscow in 1923 and 1968" (Mimeographed); idem, "The Current Dynamics of Soviet Criminality and the Constitutional Response" (Mimeographed); idem, "Urbanization and Crime: The Soviet Case in Cross-Cultural Perspective," in Louise I. Shelley, ed., *Readings in Comparative Criminology* (Carbondale: Southern Illinois University Press, 1981), pp. 150-151.

15. Jonathan L. Freedman, *Crowding and Behavior* (New York: Viking, 1975), pp. 55-69; Alan Booth, Susan Welch, and David Johnson, "Crowding and Urban Crime Rates," *Urban Affairs Quarterly* 11 (1976): 291-307.

16. Robert C. Schmitt, "Density, Delinquency and Crime in Honolulu," *Sociology and Social Research* 41 (1957): 274-76; Kenneth R. Mladenka and Kim Quaile Hill, "A Reexamination of the Etiology of Urban Crime," *Criminology* 13 (1976): 491-506.

17. Ronald W. Beasley and George Antunes, "The Etiology of Urban Crime: An Ecological Analysis," *Criminology* 11 (1974): 439-61.

18. R. E. Park and Ernest W. Burgess, *The City* (Chicago: University of Chicago Press, 1925).

19. See, for example, Louise I. Shelley, *Crime and Modernization: The Impact of Industrialization and Urbanization on Crime* (Carbondale: Southern Illinois University Press, 1981); G. K. Jarvis and H. B. Messinger, "Social and Economic Correlates of Juvenile Delinquency Rates: A Canadian Case," *Canadian Journal of Criminology and Corrections* 16 (1974): 361-72.

20. U.S. Federal Bureau of Investigation, *Crime in the United States: Uniform Crime Reports 1986* (Washington, D.C.: Government Printing Office, 1987), pp. 42, 147-48.

21. John M. Stahura and C. Ronald Huff, "Crime in Suburbia, 1960-1980," in Robert M. Figlio, Simon Hakim, and George F. Rengert, eds., *Metropolitan Crime Patterns* (Monsey, N.Y.: Willow Tree Press, 1986), pp. 55-56.

22. See, for example, Robert A. Gordon, "Issues in the Ecological Study of Delin-

quency," *American Sociological Review* 32 (1967): 927-44; David J. Bordua, "Juvenile Delinquency and 'Anomie': An Attempt at Replication," *Social Problems* 6 (1958-59): 230-38.

23. See, for example, Sarah L. Boggs, "Urban Crime Patterns," *American Sociological Review* 30 (1965): 899-908.

24. See R. Clyde White, "The Relation of Felonies to Environmental Factors in Indianapolis," *Social Forces* 10 (1932): 498-509.

25. *Uniform Crime Reports 1986*, pp. 147-48.

26. Stahura and Huff, "Crime in Suburbia," pp. 55-70.

27. Ibid., p. 67.

28. Bob Trebilcock, "Crime Comes to the Country," *Country Journal* 13 (1986): 62-71. See also Timothy J. Carter, G. Howard Phillips, Joseph F. Donnermeyer, and Todd N. Wurschmidt, *Rural Crime: Integrating Research and Prevention* (Totowa, N.J.: Allanheld, Osmun, 1982).

29. *Uniform Crime Reports 1986*, pp. 141-42.

30. Cesare Lombroso, *Crime, Its Causes and Remedies*, H. P. Horton, trans. (Boston: Little, Brown, 1918).

31. *Uniform Crime Reports 1986*, p. 148. Rural counties are areas outside MSAs, while suburban areas include suburban counties within MSAs and cities with fewer than 50,000 inhabitants.

32. As cited in Trebilcock, "Crime Comes to the Country," p. 62.

33. Ibid.

34. Joe Donnermeyer, as quoted in Trebilcock, "Crime Comes to the Country," p. 62.

35. U.S. Department of Justice, *Criminal Victimization in the United States, 1985: A National Crime Survey Report* (Washington, D.C.: Government Printing Office, 1987), pp. 6, 50-53.

36. See Menachem Amir, *Patterns in Forcible Rape* (Chicago: University of Chicago Press, 1971); Marvin E. Wolfgang, *Patterns in Criminal Homicide* (Philadelphia: University of Pennsylvania Press, 1958).

37. As cited in "When Tempers and Temperatures Flare," *Science News* 125 (1984): 38.

38. Ibid.

39. As cited in "Climate and Crime," *New York Times* (September 3, 1985): C5(L).

40. U.S. Department of Justice, Bureau of Justice Statistics, *Report to the Nation on Crime and Justice: The Data* (Washington, D.C.: Government Printing Office, 1983), p. 11.

41. Recent trends in the regional arrest rate suggest that the rate of total crime in the Northeast is second only to the West (see Table 3.3).

42. *Uniform Crime Reports 1986*, pp. 44-50. Official data for 1987 indicates that, compared to 1986, regional Crime Index rates rose 3 percent in the South, 2 percent in the Northeast and Midwest, and declined 3 percent in the West.

43. *Uniform Crime Reports 1986*, pp. 141-43.

II

DEMOGRAPHIC CORRELATES
OF CRIME

4

Age and Criminality

The demographic correlate most strongly associated with crime is age. Virtually every form of crime data has shown an inverse relationship between age and criminality; that is, crime perpetration and victimization occur largely among youth, and decrease with age. This has generally proven to be true even when other correlates of crime—such as race, gender, socioeconomic status—are taken into consideration.

OFFICIAL ARREST STATISTICS

The most important sources of information about the correlation of crime and age are official statistics on arrests. UCR data for 1986 reveal that 49 percent of the persons arrested nationwide were under the age of 25, 31 percent were younger than 21, 17 percent were under age 18, and 5 percent of the arrestees were under 15. The 25-and-under age group accounted for 50 percent of those arrested in cities, 45 percent of the suburban arrests, and 41 percent of the arrests in rural counties.

Arrestees under the age of 25 constituted an even larger share—60 percent—of the total arrests for Crime Index offenses; 45 percent of the arrestees were younger than 21, and 30 percent were under the age of 18. For violent crime arrests, persons under the age of 25 made up 48 percent of the total (31 percent were under the age of 18). Sixty-four percent of those arrested for property crime fell into the under-25 age group.[1]

Age-Specific Arrest Figures

A more comprehensive breakdown of Index crime arrests by age in 1986 can be seen in Table 4.1. The data reflects the percentage distribution of total, violent crime, property crime, and Crime Index arrests for several age

Table 4.1

Percentage Distribution[a] of Total[b] and Crime Index Arrests, by Age, 1986

Age	OFFENSE CHARGED			
	Total Arrests	Crime Index Total	Violent Crime	Property Crime
Total all ages	100.0	100.0	100.0	100.0
Under 10	0.4	1.0	0.2	1.2
10-12	1.2	2.9	0.9	3.5
13-14	3.5	7.1	3.0	8.2
15	3.2	5.8	3.0	6.5
16	4.0	6.5	3.9	7.2
17	4.4	6.4	4.4	6.9
18	4.8	5.8	4.5	6.2
19	4.7	5.1	4.5	5.2
20	4.6	4.4	4.6	4.4
21	4.6	4.2	4.8	4.0
22	4.5	3.9	4.7	3.7
23	4.4	3.7	4.7	3.4
24	4.2	3.4	4.5	3.1
25-29	17.9	14.5	19.6	13.1
30-34	12.4	10.0	13.1	9.1
35-39	8.1	6.2	8.2	5.7
40-44	4.7	3.3	4.5	3.0
45-49	2.9	2.0	2.7	1.8
50-54	2.0	1.3	1.6	1.2
55-59	1.4	1.0	1.1	0.9
60-64	0.9	0.7	0.7	0.7
65 and over	0.9	0.9	0.7	0.9

[a]The percentages may not add to total due to rounding.

[b]Based on 10,743 agencies; 1986 estimated population 198,488,000.

Source: U.S. Federal Bureau of Investigation, Crime in the United States: Uniform Crime Reports 1986 (Washington, D.C.: Government Printing Office,1987), pp. 174-75.

categories. Although the distribution is not uniform, it gives us a better picture of arrest variations between specific age groups for total crime and for the most serious crimes. The peak age for arrests varies with the crime category. For total crimes, arrests peak at age 18 and decline for each age group thereafter, with the exception of ages 20 and 21 where arrests level off briefly. The bulk of the arrests fall into the 16-24 age group. Violent crime arrests peak at the age of 21, level off for ages 22 and 23, and decrease for each later age. The peak age group for arrests for crimes of violence is ages 17-24. Arrests for property crimes show a peak at age 16 and decrease with each succeeding age group. The greatest percentage of property crime arrests comes in the 15-20 age group. For the Crime Index totals, arrests peak at age 16 and decline thereafter. Most of the Index crime arrests are concentrated in the ages 15-21. These figures and other data to be presented in this chapter should be viewed with caution, for they may reflect differential arrest patterns or other methodological limitations (see Chapter 1).

Research Using Official Data

Analysis of official arrest statistics and patterns has further supported evidence that a disproportionate number of young people are involved in criminal activity. Hugh Cline's examination of official records revealed that most serious crimes occur in the late teens and early to mid twenties, and gradually decrease with age.[2] An FBI analysis of arrest data from its Computerized Criminal History File of 62,236 men who were released from incarceration showed that the percentage of those rearrested decreased linearly from 64 percent of those under the age of 20 when released from custody to 32 percent who were in the 50 and over age group upon release.[3] Other studies have reached similar conclusions.[4]

SELF-REPORT STUDIES

Evidence of an inverse relationship between age and criminality can be found through self-report studies. In a survey of persons aged 15 and over covering three states, Alan Rowe and Charles Tittle examined the patterns of crimes that had been committed in the past five years.[5] They found that thefts, assaults, and marijuana use declined steadily with age. On the other hand, such crimes as illegal gambling and income tax fraud increased between the 15-24 age group and the 25-44 age group before declining.

Prisoner self-report research has yielded similar results. Joan Petersilia, Peter Greenwood, and Marvin Lavin's study of 49 California prisoners convicted of armed robbery and serving at least their second term in prison revealed that the number "of self-reported offenses committed per month of street time noticeably declined as the sample grew older."[6]

Interviewing more than 600 male inmates of five California penitentiaries, Mark Peterson, Harriet Braiker, and Suzanne Polich examined how the prevalence and incidence of crimes varied with age.[7] Their research concluded that the prevalence of crime generally declined with age, though they found no consistent pattern in the incidence figures.

VICTIMIZATION DATA

Perceived Age of Offenders

Victimization survey findings reflect an age distribution of offenders that parallels official arrest figures in favoring younger people as the peak group for violent and property crime. Table 4.2 presents NCS data for the age of

Table 4.2

Percentage Distribution of Victimizations, by Type, Category of Crime, and Age of Offenders, 1986[a]

SINGLE-OFFENDER VICTIMIZATIONS

Type of Crime	Total[b]	Perceived Age of Offender				
		Under 12	12-20	21-29	30 & Over	Not Known Nor Available
Crimes of violence	100.0	0.1	29.7	31.9	33.9	4.3
Rape	100.0	0.0	20.8	41.3	36.1	1.8
Robbery	100.0	0.0	30.8	36.3	25.9	7.0[c]
Assault	100.0	0.2	29.8	30.8	35.2	4.0

MULTIPLE-OFFENDER VICTIMIZATIONS

Type of Crime	Total[b]	Perceived Age of Offender					
		Under 12	12-20	21-29	30 & Over	Mixed Ages	Not Known Nor Available
Crimes of violence	100.0	0.4[c]	33.7	16.4	6.8	32.8	8.5
Rape	100.0[c]	0.0[c]	10.2	24.5	24.9[c]	18.8[c]	21.7[c]
Robbery	100.0	0.9[c]	35.5	18.5	5.8[c]	28.2	10.6
Assault	100.0	0.2[c]	33.4	15.2	6.8	35.3	7.3

[a]The age range of offenders is based on the perception of the victims.

[b]Totals may not add up due to rounding.

[c]Estimate is based on 10 sample cases or less.

Source: U.S. Department of Justice, Criminal Victimization in the United States, 1986: A National Crime Survey Report (Washington, D.C.: Government Printing Office, 1988), pp. 44, 48.

offenders as perceived by victims in single- and multiple-offender victimizations in 1986. Sixty-two percent of the single-offender crimes of violence were perceived as being committed by offenders between the ages of 12 and 29. Although the bulk of the victimizations are shown to be perpetrated by offenders in the 21-29 age group, when using a greater breakdown in age NCS data reveals that the highest percentage of single-offender crimes of violence were perceived to have occurred in the 18-20 age group. This is supported by a recent comparison of victimization reports and demographic data that found for personal crimes in which victims saw their offender, those aged 18 to 20 had the highest rates of crime.[8] Of the multiple-offender victimizations reflected in Table 4.2, 34 percent were perceived to have been committed by offenders in the 12-20 age group, with mixed ages accounting for the next highest percentage at 33 percent.

Victimization research shows that victims believe offenders aged 18 to 20 are about three times more likely to commit crimes than offenders aged 21 and over, and that offenders aged 12 to 17 are twice as likely to perpetrate crimes as those aged 21 or more. An analysis of offender characteristics has shown this perception to be consistent since the early 1970s.[9]

Victimization and Age

The relationship between age and criminal involvement reveals that the offender and victim tend closely to resemble one another. This is documented through victimization data that generally show a higher rate of victimization for young people and declining victimization rates with increasing age. According to the UCR, the peak age group for murder victimization in 1986 was 20-29.[10] The murder figures indicate that the number of murder victims decreased significantly with age until age 75 and over, when they inexplicably rose. However, the total number of murders was still well below those of younger age groups.

NCS research shows a similar pattern of age and victimization for other crimes. As we see in Table 4.3, persons in the 12-24 age bracket had the highest victimization rates for violent crimes and crimes of theft in 1985. The rate of crimes of violence and theft for victims over the age of 24 decreased with age. Household crime victimization was also generally found to be highest for the youngest heads of household, while declining as age increased. The only exception is the slight rise in motor vehicle theft from the 12-19 group to the 20-34 age group.

Elderly persons show the lowest victimization rates for all crime types. However, some research suggests that were victimization rates calculated relative to time at risk, the elderly rate of victimization could match that of younger persons or even surpass it.[11]

The strong age correlation between the victims and offenders of crimes of violence can be seen in Table 4.4. In 1986, 7 out of 10 victims aged 12-19 of single-offender victimizations believed that the perpetrator fell within the 12-20 age group. Similarly, over half the 12- to 19-year-old victims of multiple-offender crimes perceived their assailants to be between the ages of 12 and 20. The same patterns hold true when broken down into robbery and assault victimizations. The data in Table 4.4 largely supports the youthful nature of criminals and victims.

PATTERNS OF ARREST AND AGE

Given the established relationship between age and criminal activity, it might be useful to examine the frequency of arrests for Index crimes. Table 4.5 ranks from most to least frequent, arrests for selected age groups in 1986. This interesting comparison reveals that although youthful offenders may be the most likely to commit violent and property crimes, the types of

Table 4.3

Victimization Rates for Persons Aged 12 and Over, by Type of Crime and Age of Victims, 1985
(Rate per 1,000 Population Aged 12 and Over)

Type of Crime	A G E							
	12-15	16-19	20-24	25-34	35-49	50-64	65 & over
Crimes of violence	54.1	67.2	60.2	37.4	19.9	9.9	4.5
Rape	0.5[a]	2.3	1.9	1.0	0.3[a]	0.0[a]	0.1[a]
Robbery	9.1	9.5	10.4	6.1	3.2	2.2	1.6
Assault	44.6	55.4	47.9	30.2	16.3	7.7	2.9

Type of Crime	A G E							
	12-15	16-19	20-24	25-34	35-49	50-64	65 & over
Crimes of theft	108.6	122.1	107.6	82.7	62.9	40.0	18.6
Personal larceny with contact	2.9	2.8	4.5	2.5	2.4	2.2	2.7
Personal larceny without contact	105.4	119.4	103.1	80.2	60.5	37.8	15.9

Type of Crime	A G E				
	12-19	20-34	35-49	50-64	65 & over
Household crimes	455.1	241.4	194.5	136.6	78.1
Burglary	213.4	83.1	69.0	48.5	32.7
Household larceny	223.5	137.5	110.2	75.3	40.7
Motor vehicle theft	18.2	20.8	15.3	12.9	4.7

[a]Estimation is derived from about 10 cases or less.

Source: U.S. Department of Justice, *Criminal Victimization in the United States, 1985: A National Crime Survey Report* (Washington, D.C.: Government Printing Office, 1987), pp. 15, 29.

Table 4.4

Percentage Breakdown of Violent Crime Victimizations, by Type, Offense, Age of Victims, and Offenders, 1986[a]

SINGLE-OFFENDER VICTIMIZATIONS

Type of crime and age of victim	Total[b]	Under 12	12-20	21-29	30 & Over	Not Known Nor Available
Crimes of violence[c]						
12-19	100.0	0.5[d]	71.3	14.1	11.6	2.5
20-34	100.0	0.0[d]	15.7	45.2	35.6	3.5
35-49	100.0	0.0[d]	9.6	24.8	57.8	7.8
50-64	100.0	0.0[d]	16.6	32.6	44.5	6.3[d]
65 and over	100.0	0.0[d]	5.7[d]	20.9	60.6	12.8[d]
Robbery						
12-19	100.0	0.0[d]	76.7	18.9	1.6[d]	2.9[d]
20-34	100.0	0.0[d]	21.0	47.1	27.1	4.8[d]
35-49	100.0	0.0[d]	8.1[d]	26.4	49.9	15.6[d]
50-64	100.0	0.0[d]	21.7[d]	39.7	31.2	7.4[d]
65 and over	100.0	0.0[d]	7.3[d]	30.9[d]	39.1[d]	22.7[d]
Assault						
12-19	100.0	0.6[d]	72.2	12.7	11.9	2.6
20-34	100.0	0.0[d]	14.8	44.9	37.0	3.4
35-49	100.0	0.0[d]	9.9	24.3	59.3	6.5
50-64	100.0	0.0[d]	15.1	29.2	49.8	5.9[d]
65 and over	100.0	0.0[d]	5.2[d]	17.5[d]	67.7	9.6[d]

MULTIPLE-OFFENDER VICTIMIZATIONS

Type of crime and age of victim	Total[b]	Under 12	12-20	21-29	30 & Over	Mixed Ages	Not Known Nor Available
Crimes of violence[c]							
12-19	100.0	1.2[d]	53.0	4.4	1.7[d]	31.8	6.0
20-34	100.0	0.0[d]	22.4	24.2	8.1	37.4	6.7
35-49	100.0	0.0[d]	33.9	9.1[d]	13.4	25.8	16.6
50-64	100.0	0.0[d]	5.6[d]	39.6	10.2[d]	20.5[d]	24.2[d]
65 and over	100.0	0.0[d]	30.2[d]	31.8[d]	13.5[d]	12.1[d]	12.5[d]
Robbery							
12-19	100.0	3.5[d]	53.2	0.0[d]	1.6[d]	38.2	1.3[d]
20-34	100.0	0.0[d]	30.3	27.4	7.2[d]	28.1	7.0[d]
35-49	100.0	0.0[d]	35.2	7.7[d]	4.1[d]	30.2	22.9
50-64	100.0	0.0[d]	6.0[d]	45.1[d]	7.6[d]	0.0[d]	41.3[d]
65 and over	100.0	0.0[d]	32.1[d]	32.8[d]	17.8[d]	8.4[d]	8.9[d]
Assault							
12-19	100.0	0.5[d]	52.7	5.8	1.7[d]	30.0	7.5
20-34	100.0	0.0[d]	19.6	22.5	8.1	42.1	5.9
35-49	100.0	0.0[d]	32.9	10.2[d]	20.3	22.6	11.9[d]
50-64	100.0	0.0[d]	5.4[d]	35.8[d]	8.0[d]	43.7[d]	7.1[d]
65 and over	100.0[d]	0.0[d]	24.3[d]	28.5[d]	0.0[d]	23.5[d]	23.7[d]

[a]Age categories for offenders are based on the perception of the victims.

[b]Totals may not add due to rounding.

[c]Includes data on rape, not shown separately.

[d]Estimate is based on 10 sample cases or less.

Source: U.S. Department of Justice, Criminal Victimization in the United States, 1986: A National Crime Survey Report (Washington, D.C.: Government Printing Office, 1988), pp. 45, 49.

Table 4.5
Frequency of Crime Index Arrests for Selected Age Groups, by Offense, 1986

Rank	AGE RANGE					
	16	18	21	30–34	40–44	65 and Over
1 · ·	Larceny-theft	Larceny-theft	Larceny-theft	Larceny-theft	Larceny-theft	Larceny-theft
2 · ·	Burglary	Burglary	Burglary	Aggravated assault	Aggravated assault	Aggravated assault
3 · ·	Motor vehicle theft	Aggravated assault	Aggravated assault	Burglary	Burglary	Burglary
4 · ·	Aggravated assault	Motor vehicle theft	Robbery	Robbery	Robbery	Murder
5 · ·	Robbery	Robbery	Motor vehicle theft	Motor vehicle theft	Motor vehicle theft	Robbery
6 · ·	Forcible rape	Forcible rape	Forcible rape	Forcible rape	Forcible rape	Forcible rape
7 · ·	Arson	Murder	Murder	Murder	Murder	Motor vehicle theft
8 · ·	Murder	Arson	Arson	Arson	Arson	Arson

Source: U.S. Federal Bureau of Investigation, Crime in the United States: Uniform Crime Reports 1986 (Washington, D.C.: Government Printing Office, 1987), pp. 174-75.

Crime Index offenses for which persons are most frequently arrested are fairly constant across all age groups. Property crimes predominate among arrests for Index offenses, with larceny-theft the most frequently committed crime for all the age groups of arrestees. The implication here, in contrast to some findings, is that age is less correlated with the type of crime (particularly Index crimes) than it is with the incidence of criminality.[12]

LONGITUDINAL RESEARCH

Age and Crime

The findings of longitudinal studies of crime and age are key indicators of the inverse age-crime correlation. Sheldon and Eleanor Glueck were among the first to conduct longitudinal research using official records. Their findings of a few decades ago generally indicated that most crime was concentrated in the 15-29 age group, though the type of offense tended to vary according to age.[13]

More recent longitudinal research has used both official and self-report data with varied results. Stuart Miller, Simon Dinitz, and John Conrad found in a retrospective study of the arrest histories of 1,600 violent male offenders that violent crimes generally peaked in the 20-24 age group.[14] A cohort study of nearly 29,000 males in Copenhagen found the peak ages for crime to be 17 and 18, with violent crime peaking at ages 20 to 21.[15]

David Farrington's longitudinal study using self-reports revealed that the majority of offenses peaked between the ages of 15 and 18, with burglary and shoplifting peaking earlier.[16] Another self-report survey found that robbery, burglary, and shoplifting each declined with age.[17]

The existence of an age-crime curve is virtually indisputable; however, differences in types of offenses, periods of time, sample groups, and other factors in long-term studies require that we do less generalizing about the nature and correlation of crime and age and gain a better understanding of their symmetry and relationship to influencing variables.

Trends in the Criminality-Age Relationship

Recently demographers have pointed toward a declining crime rate and have attributed it to changes in the age distribution of the population. Explains one sociologist: "Crime is very age sensitive and there are smaller proportions of young or high risk crime people in the population, offering us the prospect of a more crime-free society into the 21st century."[18] As the baby boomers dramatically increased the proportion of the 15-24 age group relative to the remainder of the population in the 1960s and 1970s, so did the rate of crime show a significant rise. However, because the population is getting older, it has been suggested that a lower rate of crime should result as we head into the 1990s.

The indicators to this effect have been inconsistent. NCS victimization data shows that overall criminal victimization dropped 18 percent between 1981 and 1986. Victimization declined during this period by 16 percent for violent crimes, 17 percent for personal theft, and 19 percent for household crimes.[19]

However, UCR data reveals that crime has been on the increase since the early to mid-1980s when it showed a decline. Index crimes jumped 2 percent from 1982 to 1986. Violent crimes increased 12 percent and property crimes rose 1 percent. A more dramatic rise in Crime Index offenses can be seen in the 10-year period from 1977 to 1986 when Index crimes increased more than 20 percent. For crimes of violence the jump was 44 percent, and property crimes grew by 18 percent.[20]

Arrest figures show an increase in total arrests of 7 percent from 1982 to 1986 and of 27 percent between 1977 and 1986. Hence official data suggests that, demographic changes in the population notwithstanding, more people are committing crimes and being arrested. The implication here is that age may not be as important a singular predictor of crime as it is in conjunction with other factors such as unemployment, substance abuse, and subcultural influence.

Ironically, crime among younger people seems to be on the decline. As we see in Table 4.6, persons arrested under the age of 18 decreased for all crime in both the 5-year and 10-year periods. Contrarily, total arrests of persons aged 18 and over showed a dramatic increase of 39 percent from 1977 to 1986 and increased for every other crime category during the 5-year and 10-year periods. The biggest drop for juvenile crime came in property crime arrests, which decreased by 18 percent from 1977 to 1986. This is noteworthy considering property crime arrests in 1986 peaked at age 16. This may reflect population changes that are lowering the proportion of youthful high-risk property crime groups.

Overall, these percentage changes in arrests are difficult to interpret relative to age and crime, since the UCR does not present data that breaks down 5- and 10-year crime trends by other high-crime-rate ages, such as 18, 21, and 24. However, the evidence suggests that, for whatever reason, people older than the age of majority are committing more crimes, while juveniles are committing fewer.[21]

EXPLANATIONS FOR THE AGE-CRIME RELATIONSHIP

Several explanations have been given for the inverse relationship between age and crime. Some have linked the age-crime curve with biological factors such as menopause, testosterone levels, and physical ability.[22] Others have focused on the environment as a more influential factor in criminality with respect to age, pointing to relationships with family, peer groups, and schooling.[23] Self-report studies have revealed that the desire for excitement and thrills also tend to influence youthful offenders.[24]

Table 4.6
Percentage Change in Arrest Trends, by Age

	PERSONS ARRESTED					
	Under 18 Years of Age			18 Years of Age and Over		
	1977	1986	Percent Change	1977	1986	Percent Change
Total..........	1,824,712	1,603,497	-12.1	5,700,225	7,922,892	+39.0
Violent Crime....	67,376	66,134	- 1.8	253,297	361,623	+42.8
Property Crime....	635,584	521,609	-17.9	726,101	1,041,874	+43.5
Crime Index Total....	702,960	587,743	-16.4	979,398	1,403,497	+43.3
	1982	1986	Percent Change	1982	1986	Percent Change
Total..........	1,544,933	1,531,956	- 0.8	7,114,031	7,695,586	+ 8.2
Violent Crime....	67,232	65,518	- 2.5	327,271	361,830	+10.6
Property Crime....	518,559	498,823	- 3.8	974,864	1,009,066	+ 3.5
Crime Index Total....	585,791	564,341	- 3.7	1,302,135	1,370,896	+ 5.3

Source: U.S. Federal Bureau of Investigation, *Crime in the United States: Uniform Crime Reports 1986* (Washington, D.C.: Government Printing Office, 1987), pp. 168, 170.

Economic factors—ranging from poor parents to the limited funds of juveniles for their social needs—have also been proposed as explanations for the crime-age curve.[25] Some researchers have held that crime is associated with changes in moral reasoning as one ages. This approach assumes that young people do not fully understand or respect the law until they are older, and that they are underdeveloped in terms of moral principles, thereby leading to higher crime rates.[26]

The criminal justice system is blamed by some for the age-crime relationship as it establishes minimum ages of criminal responsibility and differences between juvenile and adult responsibility. This approach argues that because children under certain ages are not deemed responsible or able to understand crime, they are in a sense encouraged or allowed to develop delinquent habits that may become much more serious later in life. Others suggest that differences in processing and the imposition of penalties between juvenile and adult courts favor juveniles and do not deter the commission of crimes.[27]

Some theories of the age-crime curve prefer to focus on why young offenders cease committing crimes as they grow older. This "aging-out process" is believed to result from many things, including socialization and different social roles, employment, education, and family. These factors may "eliminate major sources of criminogenic frustration and at the same time supply informal social control," reinforce the lack of opportunity due to long-term incarceration, and instill greater fear of the legal consequences of criminal conduct.[28]

Although, generally speaking, the relationship between age and crime seems invariant or not dependent upon other variables, evidence provided by studies of crime trends, types of offenses, and other factors (such as gender) indicate that there is indeed variation in patterns of crime when age is related to other variables.

Whether independently or in conjunction with other variables, age has been shown to have a direct causal effect on criminality. Young people tend to commit more crimes and are more often victimized than older people. The age curve for criminal involvement generally peaks in the late teens to mid-twenties and decreases thereafter with age. Changes in the age composition of the population would suggest that the crime rate will begin to drop in the future, though current statistics give contradictory signals on the direction of crime in this country.

NOTES

1. U.S. Federal Bureau of Investigation, *Crime in the United States: Uniform Crime Reports 1986* (Washington, D.C.: Government Printing Office, 1987), p. 163.
2. Hugh F. Cline, "Criminal Behavior Over the Life Span," in Orville G. Brim

and Jerome Kagan, eds., *Constancy and Change in Human Development* (Cambridge, Mass.: Harvard University Press, 1980).

3. As cited in Neal Shover, *Aging Criminals* (Beverly Hills: Sage Publications, 1985), p. 21; see also U.S. Federal Bureau of Investigation, *Crime in the United States: Uniform Crime Reports 1975* (Washington, D.C.: Government Printing Office, 1976).

4. See, for example, David P. Farrington, "Longitudinal Research on Crime and Delinquency," in Norval Morris and Michael Tonry, eds., *Crime and Justice: An Annual Review of Research*, vol. 1 (Chicago: University of Chicago Press, 1979).

5. Alan R. Rowe and Charles R. Tittle, "Life Cycle Changes and Criminal Propensity," *Sociological Quarterly* 18 (1977): 223-36.

6. Joan Petersilia, Peter Greenwood, and Marvin Lavin, *Criminal Careers of Habitual Felons* (Washington, D.C.: National Institute of Justice, 1978), p. vii.

7. Mark A. Peterson, Harriet B. Braiker, and Suzanne M. Polich, *Who Commits Crimes?* (Cambridge, Mass.: Oelgeschlager, Gunn & Hain, 1981).

8. Michael J. Hindelang, "Variations in Sex-Race-Age-Specific Incidence Rates of Offending," *American Sociological Review* 46 (1981): 461-74.

9. John Laub, "Juvenile Criminal Behavior in the United States: An Analysis of Offender and Victim Characteristics," Working paper 25, Michael J. Hindelang Criminal Justice Research Center, Albany, N.Y., 1983, p. 25.

10. *Uniform Crime Reports 1986*, p. 9.

11. See, for example, John H. Lunquist and Janice M. Duke, "The Elderly Victim at Risk: Explaining the Fear-Victimization Paradox," *Criminology* 29 (1982): 115-26.

12. See, for example, James Q. Wilson and Richard J. Hernstein, *Crime and Human Nature* (New York: Simon & Schuster, 1985). The authors' examination of patterns of offenses with age includes all UCR offenses.

13. Sheldon Glueck and Eleanor T. Glueck, *Juvenile Delinquents Grown Up* (New York: Commonwealth Fund, 1940); Sheldon Glueck and Eleanor T. Glueck, *Delinquents and Nondelinquents in Perspective* (Cambridge, Mass.: Harvard University Press, 1968).

14. Stuart J. Miller, Simon Dinitz, and John P. Conrad, *Careers of the Violent* (Lexington, Mass.: D. C. Heath, 1982).

15. Katherine T. VanDusen and Sarnoff A. Mednick, *A Comparison of Delinquency in Copenhagen and Philadelphia: Final Report to the National Institute of Justice* (Washington, D.C.: National Institute of Justice, 1983).

16. David P. Farrington, "Offending From 10 to 25 Years of Age," in Katherine T. VanDusen and Sarnoff A. Mednick, eds., *Prospective Studies of Crime and Delinquency* (Boston: Kluwer-Nijhoff, 1983).

17. James J. Collins, "Alcohol Careers and Criminal Careers," in James J. Collins, ed., *Drinking and Crime* (New York: Guilford Press, 1981).

18. Miles D. Harer, as quoted in "Felonies Decline as Population Ages," *USA Today* (August 1987): 4.

19. U.S. Department of Justice, *Bureau of Justice Statistics Bulletin: Criminal Victimization 1986* (Washington, D.C.: Government Printing Office, 1987), p. 1.

20. *Uniform Crime Reports 1986*, p. 41.

21. Uniform Crime Reports data for 1987 show the same patterns to be true. During the time frame, 1978-1987, total arrests of persons over age 18 increased by 35 percent, compared to a decrease of 8 percent in arrests of persons under 18.

22. See David P. Farrington, "Age and Crime," in Michael Tonry and Norval Morris, eds., *Crime and Justice: An Annual Review of Research*, vol. 7 (Chicago: University of Chicago Press, 1986), pp. 189-250.

23. Ibid.; Delbert S. Elliot, David Huizinga, and Suzanne Ageton, *Explaining Delinquency and Drug Use* (Beverly Hills: Sage, 1985).

24. Petersilia, Greenwood, and Lavin, *Criminal Careers of Habitual Felons*.

25. David F. Greenberg, "Age and Crime," in Sanford H. Kadish, ed., *Encyclopedia of Crime and Justice* (New York: Free Press, 1983).

26. Lawrence Kohlberg, "Moral Stages and Moralization: The Cognitive-Developmental Approach," in Thomas Lickona, ed., *Moral Development and Behavior* (New York: Holt, Rinehart & Winston, 1976).

27. Charles B. Keasey and Bruce D. Sales, "Children's Conception of Intentionality and the Criminal Law," in Bruce D. Sales, ed., *Psychology in the Legal Process* (New York: Spectrum, 1977); David F. Greenberg, "Delinquency and the Age Structure of Society," in Sheldon Messinger and Egon Bittner, eds., *Criminology Review Yearbook* (Beverly Hills: Sage, 1979).

28. Farrington, "Age and Crime," p. 232.

5

Gender and Crime

The variable of gender and its relation to criminality has been given much attention over the years. The evidence indicates that sex is a significant factor in crime, and that males commit considerably more criminal acts than females. Male-female differences in crime rates are seen largely as a product of biological determinism, the socialization process of males and females, and the social classifications of masculinity and femininity that are not only responsible for personality and behavioral differences between males and females but are also influential in the processes of criminal law and justice. The study of gender and crime has yielded varying and often contradictory results. In this chapter we will examine the role of gender in crime statistics and theory.

ARREST DATA

Official statistics reveal that 8 out of every 10 persons arrested in the United States during 1987 were males (Table 5.1). Men were responsible for 78 percent of the Crime Index offense arrests, 89 percent of the arrests for violent crimes, and 76 percent of those for property crimes. The crime for which males were arrested most often was driving under the influence, accounting for 14 percent of their total arrests.

Larceny-theft represented the offense for which females were most often arrested in 1987. This crime accounted for 80 percent of their arrests for Index crimes and 20 percent of the total female arrests. The only crimes for which females were arrested more often than males were prostitution, where female arrestees nearly doubled male arrestees, and the status offense of runaways.

Table 5.1

Total Arrests, Percentage Distribution, by Sex, 1987 (10,616 Agencies;
1987 Estimated Population, 202,337,000)

Offense Charged	Total	Percent Male	Percent Female
TOTAL..	10,795,869	82.3	17.7
Murder and nonnegligent manslaughter...........	16,714	87.5	12.5
Forcible rape.................................	31,276	98.8	1.2
Robbery.......................................	123,306	91.9	8.1
Aggravated assault...........................	301,734	86.7	13.3
Burglary......................................	374,963	92.1	7.9
Larceny-theft................................	1,256,552	68.9	31.1
Motor vehicle theft..........................	146,753	90.3	9.7
Arson..	15,169	86.3	13.7
Violent crime[a]	473,030	88.9	11.1
Property crime[b].............................	1,793,437	75.6	24.4
Crime Index total[c]........................	2,266,467	78.4	21.6
Other assaults...............................	671,938	84.9	15.1
Forgery and counterfeiting...................	78,817	65.6	34.4
Fraud..	280,809	56.5	43.5
Embezzlement.................................	10,639	61.9	38.1
Stolen property; buying, receiving, possessing..	119,048	88.4	11.6
Vandalism....................................	230,088	89.4	10.6
Weapons; carrying, possessing, etc............	165,650	92.4	7.6
Prostitution and commercialized vice...........	100,950	35.2	64.8
Sex offenses (except forcible rape and prostitution).................................	85,627	92.2	7.8
Drug abuse violations........................	811,078	85.1	14.9
Gambling.....................................	22,762	86.5	13.5
Offenses against family and children...........	48,002	82.6	17.4
Driving under the influence...................	1,410,397	88.3	11.7
Liquor laws..................................	505,021	82.1	17.9
Drunkenness..................................	700,662	90.8	9.2
Disorderly conduct...........................	599,622	81.3	18.7
Vagrancy.....................................	32,518	88.4	11.6
All other offenses (except traffic)...........	2,430,913	84.4	15.6
Suspicion....................................	11,670	85.5	14.5
Curfew and loitering law violations...........	77,556	75.0	25.0
Runaways.....................................	135,635	42.8	57.2

[a]Violent crimes are offenses of murder, forcible rape, robbery, and aggravated assault.

[b]Property crimes are offenses of burglary, larceny-theft, motor vehicle theft, and arson.

[c]Includes arson.

Source: U.S. Federal Bureau of Investigation, Crime in the United States: Uniform Crime Reports 1987 (Washington, D.C.: Government Printing Office,1988), p. 181.

ADULT PATTERNS OF ARRESTS

The role gender plays in crime can best be analyzed by examining adult and juvenile arrest data separately. In absolute terms, the disparity in the ratio of men-to-women arrests is greater than gender differences in total arrests of males and females. In 1986, 5.1 males aged 18 and over were

Table 5.2
Most Frequent Arrests of Adults, by Sex and Offense, 1986

Rank	M A L E	Rank	F E M A L E
1	All other offenses (except traffic)[a]	1	All other offenses (except traffic)[a]
2	Driving under the influence	2	Larceny-theft
3	Drunkenness	3	Driving under the influence
4	Larceny-theft	4	Fraud
5	Drug abuse violations	5	Drug abuse violations
6	Other assaults	6	Disorderly conduct
7	Disorderly conduct	7	Other assaults
8	Liquor laws	8	Drunkenness
9	Aggravated assault	9	Prostitution & commercialized vice
10	Burglary	10	Liquor laws

[a]"All other offenses" refers to crimes that are violations of local and state laws and ordinances.

Source: Compiled from U.S. Federal Bureau of Investigation, Crime in the United States: Uniform Crime Reports 1986 (Washington, D.C.: Government Printing Office,1987), pp. 176, 178.

arrested for every female 18 and over. Although the absolute and relative rates of adult arrests by sex have shown some inconsistency in recent years, numerous examinations of official arrest data have consistently supported the conclusion that men commit considerably more crimes than women.[1]

Women are arrested much less often than men for violent, property, and most non-Index crimes. Table 5.2 lists the 10 offenses for which adult males and females were most often arrested in 1986. Aside from the category "all other offenses," which represents the most frequent cause of arrest for both sexes, the patterns differ. Men were arrested second most often for driving under the influence. However, 3 of their top 10 arrests were for Index crimes. Women, on the other hand, were arrested second most often for larceny-theft. This is the only Index crime that ranked among the top 10 in arrests of women. Most of these property offenses are believed to be petty, such as shoplifting. Their other arrests tend to follow traditional patterns of female criminality, such as fraud, drug abuse violations, and prostitution. Both sexes were overrepresented in arrests for substance abuse–related offenses.

Long-Term Adult Arrest Trends

Long-term trends in adult arrest patterns reflect similar differences in the male-female incidence and nature of arrests. For most offenses, men are arrested at a ratio several times greater than that of women. However, while the absolute figures of arrest rates show men continuing to far outdistance women, there is evidence that, in relative terms, the gap is getting smaller. For instance, between 1978 and 1987, total female arrests grew by 33 percent compared to a 23 percent increase in male arrests.[2] Arrests of females for violent and property crimes during this period rose 39 percent and 21 percent respectively; male arrests for crimes of violence increased by 33 percent, and property crimes, 13 percent.

Despite this apparent narrowing of the gap between men and women in arrest trends, most of the increase in female arrests from 1978 to 1987 has occurred in traditional female crimes such as larceny-theft (21 percent), fraud (77 percent), prostitution (51 percent), and drug abuse violations (37 percent).[3] This data is consistent with earlier studies of arrest trends. For example, Rita Simon's examination of arrest statistics from 1932 to 1972 showed that the bulk of the increase in female arrest rates for serious crimes was the result of greater women's involvement in property crimes such as larceny.[4] Darrell Steffensmeier argued on the basis of his analysis of sex differences in UCR arrest figures of adults from 1965 to 1977 that "masculine" crimes remain primarily a male preoccupation and women's crimes continue to be traditional in nature.[5]

JUVENILE PATTERNS OF ARRESTS

Juvenile crime differs from adult crime in that delinquency comprises both crimes that are violations of criminal statutes and status offenses that are applicable only to minors (such as runaways). As a result of this broad range of juvenile crime, one can expect gender differences in criminality to be mitigated somewhat due to role convergence and the socialization process common to adolescents.

Arrest statistics tell us that the volume of juvenile arrests favors males by a wide margin. However, the male-to-female juvenile arrests indicates that juveniles may be closer in their incidence and patterns of crime than adults. In 1986, males under the age of 18 were arrested 3.5 times for every female arrestee under the age of 18. The ratio was closer for property crimes (3.9) than for violent crimes (8.0). The only crimes for which female juveniles had a higher ratio of arrests were prostitution and commercialized vice (1.9) and runaways (1.4).[6]

The 10 crimes for which male and female juveniles were most often arrested in 1986 can be seen in Table 5.3. Both boys and girls were arrested most frequently for larceny-theft. Two of the top three male arrests were for property crimes, with most of the other offenses of the petty or status crime variety.

Females were arrested second most often for running away. Ironically, females placed two forms of assault in their 10 most frequent arrests; only

Table 5.3
Most Frequent Arrests of Juveniles, by Sex and Offense, 1986[a]

Rank	M A L E	Rank	F E M A L E
1	Larceny-theft	1	Larceny-theft
2	All other offenses (except traffic)[b]	2	Runaways
3	Burglary	3	All other offenses (except traffic)[b]
4	Liquor laws	4	Liquor laws
5	Vandalism	5	Other assaults
6	Disorderly conduct	6	Curfew & loitering law violations
7	Other assaults	7	Disorderly conduct
8	Runaways	8	Drug abuse violations
9	Drug abuse violations	9	Vandalism
10	Curfew & loitering law violations	10	Aggravated assault

[a]Juvenile arrest statistics may be less accurate than adult arrest data as a barometer of crime, since the former may not reflect actual arrests (such as police clearances), actual crimes committed (such as prostitution instead of running away), records that have been sealed or destroyed, etc.
[b]"All other offenses" are crimes that violate state and local laws and ordinances.

Source: Compiled from U.S. Federal Bureau of Investigation, *Crime in the United States: Uniform Crime Reports 1986* (Washington, D.C.: Government Printing Office,1987), pp. 176, 178.

the less serious "other assaults" category appeared among the top 10 arrests of males. Although this could seem to reflect a greater penchant for violence among girls who do commit crimes, the absolute numbers are so low as to be of limited significance other than as a predictor for adult crime. Most juvenile female arrests are minor violations of the law and status offenses.

Long-Term Juvenile Arrest Trends

Recent trends show that male juvenile arrests are decreasing and arrests of female juveniles are on the increase. For the 10-year period 1978 to 1987, arrests of males under the age of 18 dropped 14 percent, while arrests of females under 18 rose 21.[7] This suggests that, in a relative sense more than in absolute trends, female juveniles are gaining on their male counterparts in their level of criminal involvement and arrests.

Females under age 18 increased their incidence of arrests for violent crimes over the 10 years by 18 percent, compared to a 10 percent decline among male juveniles. Most of the narrowing of the differential, however, occurred in arrests for property crimes, minor assaults, and typical juvenile crimes such as vandalism and substance abuse–related offenses. Females continue to be far outpaced in aggregate arrests by males, particularly for violent and serious crimes. Several studies of official data have reached the same conclusion.[8]

COMPARISON OF ARREST RATIOS BY GENDER AND AGE

Overall, the male-to-female ratio of arrests is higher for adults than for juveniles or total arrests (Table 5.4). Men aged 18 and over were arrested 5.1 times for every woman arrested in 1986. This compares to a 4.7 ratio of arrests for all males to females and a 3.5 ratio favoring juvenile males over females. The male-to-female ratio of arrests is inconsistent from offense to offense and between age groups. For instance, males 18 and over are 100 times as likely to be arrested for rape as females, but arrest for rape is only 53 times more likely for those under age 18.

Table 5.4
Male-to-Female Ratio of Arrests for Selected Crimes, by Age, 1986

Offense Charged	Ages 17 and under	Ages 18 and over	All Ages
TOTAL UCR OFFENSES....................	3.5	5.1	4.7
Murder & nonnegligent manslaughter...	14.0	6.8	7.1
Forcible rape........................	53.0	100.6	88.4
Robbery..............................	13.4	11.3	11.7
Aggravated assault...................	5.5	6.8	6.6
Burglary.............................	12.2	11.3	11.7
Larceny-theft.......................	2.8	2.1	2.3
Motor vehicle theft.................	8.2	10.7	9.6
Arson...............................	9.0	5.2	6.3
Violent crime......................	8.0	8.2	8.1
Property crime.....................	3.9	2.9	3.2
Crime Index total.................	4.1	3.6	3.7
Forgery & counterfeiting............	2.1	1.9	1.9
Fraud...............................	3.0	1.2	1.3
Embezzlement........................	1.5	1.8	1.7
Vandalism...........................	10.0	7.7	8.5
Weapons; carrying, possessing, etc...	14.6	12.2	12.5
Prostitution & commercialized vice...	1.9[a]	1.9[a]	1.9[a]
Sex offenses (except forcible rape & prostitution......................	12.8	11.4	11.6
Drug abuse violations...............	5.9	5.9	5.9
Driving under the influence.........	6.5	7.7	7.7
Runaways............................	1.4[a]	--	1.4[a]

[a]These ratios are for female-to-male arrests.

Source: Compiled from U.S. Federal Bureau of Investigation, Crime in the United States: Uniform Crime Reports 1986 (Washington, D.C.: Government Printing Office,1987), pp. 176, 178.

The gender gap is much closer in each age category for property crimes and fraud, indicating that in these areas female crime is more likely to be comparable in the degree of commission and type to male crime.

SELF-REPORT SURVEYS

Self-report findings have generally supported arrest statistics on the male nature of criminality, but they have also suggested that the differential between males and females is smaller than that found in official data. Because most self-report research focuses on juveniles, it may not be as useful for overall gender differences in rates of crime.

Much of the self-report findings have shown gender ratios of crime to be under 3.0, a lower ratio than in official reports. Earlier studies by F. Ivan Nye and James Short[9] and Nancy Wise[10] found the sex ratio of juveniles who admitted to criminal involvement to be 2.42 and 2.30 respectively. More recently, studies by Peter Kratcoski and J. Kratcoski[11] and by Steve Cernkovich and Peggy Giordano[12] yielded a differential between male and female juveniles of 2.00 and 2.18.

Some self-report research points toward a variation in the male-to-female ratio of crime, depending on the particular offense, class, and race.[13] On the whole, self-report studies indicate that females are moving nearer to males in minor criminality and delinquency but are not yet equally represented in the more serious crimes. Due to the limitations on self-report data (see Chapter 1), their results must be looked upon accordingly.

VICTIMIZATION STUDIES

Perceived Sex of Offender

Victimization surveys also provide evidence that males commit more crime than females. The NCS for 1985 reveals that most victims of violent crimes identified their assailant as a male (Table 5.5). Eighty-seven percent of the crimes of violence were attributed to male offenders. Females were perceived as offenders most often (14 percent of the time) for simple assaults. These findings have been consistently reported in victimization surveys over the years.[14]

Victimization and Gender

Males not only commit more crimes, but they are also most often the victim of criminal acts. The primary exception to this is forcible rape, which is predominantly the victimization of females. According to the UCR, three out of every four murder victims in the United States in 1986 were males.[15]

Violent crime rates in 1985 were 77 percent greater for males than

Table 5.5

Percentage Distribution of Single-Offender Victimizations, by Type of Crime
and Sex of Offender, 1985[a]

Type of Crime	Total[b]	Perceived Sex of Offender		
		Male	Female	Not known and not available
Crimes of violence (4,134,540)...	100.0	87.2	12.0	0.9
Completed (1,378,800).........	100.0	86.1	13.4	0.5 [c]
Attempted (2,755,740).........	100.0	87.8	11.2	1.0
Rape (124,600)...............	100.0	97.5	1.1 [c]	1.5 [c]
Robbery (500,880)............	100.0	91.4	7.3	1.3 [c]
Completed (297,130).........	100.0	91.7	7.6 [c]	0.7 [c]
With injury (88,200)........	100.0	91.6	8.4 [c]	0.0 [c]
Without injury (208,930).....	100.0	91.7	7.3	1.0 [c]
Attempted (203,750).........	100.0	91.0	6.8 [c]	2.2 [c]
With injury (57,140)........	100.0	93.4	6.6 [c]	0.0 [c]
Without injury (146,610).....	100.0	90.1	6.8 [c]	3.1 [c]
Assault (3,509,060)	100.0	86.2	13.0	0.8 [c]
Aggravated (1,108,630).......	100.0	88.7	10.9	0.4
Simple (2,400,430)	100.0	85.1	14.0	0.9

[a]The sex data on the offender is derived through the victim's perception.

[b]Detail may not add to total shown because of rounding. Number of victimizations shown in parentheses.

[c]Estimate is based on about 10 or fewer sample cases.

Source: U.S. Department of Justice, Criminal Victimization in the United States 1985: A National Crime Survey Report (Washington, D.C.: Government Printing Office, 1987), p. 14.

females, as reflected in Table 5.6. Males were also more likely to be victimized by crimes of theft, though the differential is not as great. In fact, the male and female rates for personal larceny with contact were basically equal. However, this is largely due to the subclassification of purse snatching, which is statistically insignificant.

OTHER DATA SOURCES

The gender discrepancy in criminal behavior has been further established through private agency studies and other sources. For example, in a study of employee theft in a large retail organization, it was found that male employees committed most of the thefts even though female employees comprised the majority of workers.[16] The study also noted that the more value the stolen item had, the greater the likelihood the theft was committed by a male.

Other studies have supported the notion of the "traditional" character of female criminality even when female crime has been shown to be on the

Table 5.6

Victimization Rates for Persons Aged 12 and Over, by Type of Crime
and Sex of Victims, 1985 (Rate per 1,000 Population Aged 12 and Over)

Type of Crime	Male	Female
Crimes of violence..................	38.8[a]	21.9
Rape.............................	0.1	1.3
Robbery..........................	6.8	3.5
Assault..........................	31.9	17.2
Crimes of theft....................	74.7	64.6
Personal larceny with contact.....	2.6	2.7
Personal larceny without contact..	72.0	61.8

[a]Estimate is based on 10 or less sample cases.

Source: U.S. Department of Justice, *Criminal Victimization in the United States 1985: A National Crime Survey Report* (Washington, D.C.: Government Printing Office, 1987), p. 14.

rise. In his study of street gangs, Walter Miller noted that female gang members continue to be in largely supportive roles.[17]

THE MYTH OF THE NEW FEMALE CRIMINAL

Much controversy has ensued in recent years over a supposedly "new," more violent and aggressive female criminal, or one that is becoming more or less equal to male criminals in their types and prevalence of criminal activity. The feminist movement is largely responsible for this perspective, with the works of Freda Adler and Rita Simon receiving the lion's share of the attention. Both authors have pointed to "an explosion" in the total incidence of female crime and "nontraditional crime," parallel to the entry of women into nontraditional fields in the workplace, with the result being a movement toward parity with men in the incidence and nature of crime.

Adler's research particularly has come under attack. She argues that a "new feminism" and assertiveness by women are responsible for their growing violent crime, which is showing "yearly rates of increase now running as high as six or seven times faster than males."[18] These findings were derived largely from UCR data from the early 1950s to the early 1970s. There is virtually no substantiation for Adler's claims. Numerous proponents have disproven the notion that the rate of violent crime by females is approaching that of males.[19] On the contrary, it has been shown that the male rate of violent crime has continued to rise faster than the rate for females.[20] Even the notion of the "liberated" female criminal has been called into question.[21] Actually, UCR arrest data from 1960 to 1985 reveal that female arrests for violent crimes increased 166 percent, compared to 159 percent for male arrestees.[22] However, the differential is somewhat misleading considering the gains made by females have been almost entirely relative while males continue to maintain a considerable quantitative advantage.

Simon's work focuses more on a growth in property crime by women. In fact, she contends that should present trends in these crime rates continue, "approximately equal numbers of men and women will be arrested for larceny and for fraud and embezzlement by the 1990s; and for forgery and counterfeiting the proportions should be equal by the 2010s."[23] From a relative standpoint, there appears to be more merit for Simon's position. Females have shown a steady proportional gain since the 1930s in arrests for property crimes. Between 1960 and 1985, for example, female arrests for property crimes grew by 447 percent, whereas male arrests for property crimes declined by 109 percent.[24] More recently, females have shown greater relative gains in aggregate property crime arrests than males, as reflected in Table 5.7. Larceny-theft is the only property crime for which males show a higher relative increase in arrests than females between 1977 and 1986. The female aggregates rose for every major and minor property crime during the 10-year period. Relative and absolute differentials between male and female arrestees narrowed for such crimes as fraud and embezzlement, which showed gains for females at 77 percent and 176 percent respectively, compared to 29 percent and 39 percent for males arrested.

Notwithstanding, these increases in property crime arrests for females, the volume of arrests for property offenses still favors male arrestees by a considerable margin, thereby giving little indication that females could approach males in their number of arrests by the turn of the century.[25]

Table 5.7
Property Crime Arrest Trends, by Sex, 1977-1986

Offense Charged	MALE			FEMALE		
	TOTAL		Percent Change	TOTAL		Percent Change
	1977	1986		1977	1986	
Burglary	359,497	315,448	-12.3	23,910	27,224	+14.3
Larceny-theft	575,771	754,332	+31.0	276,209	335,340	+21.4
Motor vehicle theft	103,404	106,059	+2.6	9,208	11,131	+20.9
Arson	12,248	12,024	-1.8	1,539	1,925	+25.1
Property crime total[a]	1,050,920	1,187,863	+13.0	310,765	375,620	+20.9
Forgery & counterfeiting	38,629	46,817	+21.2	16,211	24,067	+48.5
Fraud	118,366	152,336	+28.7	65,450	115,711	+76.8
Embezzlement	4,403	6,101	+38.6	1,298	3,577	+175.6
Stolen property; buying, receiving, possessing	78,267	92,880	+18.7	9,449	12,169	+28.8
Vandalism	150,338	181,341	+20.6	13,989	21,388	+52.9

[a]Includes only the Index property crimes of burglary, larceny-theft, motor vehicle theft, and arson.

Source: U.S. Federal Bureau of Investigation, Crime in the United States: Uniform Crime Reports 1986 (Washington, D.C.: Government Printing Office, 1987), p. 169.

Much of the proportional gains for females in property crime arrest data tend to be for traditional female criminality such as petty theft, fraud, and vandalism—a reflection of changes toward *younger* female involvement in crime. White-collar property crimes such as embezzlement actually only represent a fraction of female arrests.[26]

Some other research has also supported, if not a "new" female criminal, then one more equal to male criminals. For example, Cernkovich and Giordano's study of archival records of arrests in Toledo, Ohio, from 1890 to 1975 concluded that: females are being arrested for crimes increasingly similar to those of male arrestees, female arrest rates are rising faster than male arrest rates, and the male-to-female ratio of arrests is decreasing for many crimes.[27] Such a study is limited by the time period examined. The conclusions reached can be expected considering the greater proportional involvement of females in crime and opportunities to commit offenses since the late nineteenth century. However, this does not alter the fact that the absolute percentage of female involvement in crime has remained low and figures to continue that way.

THEORIES OF THE GENDER GAP IN CRIMINALITY

Explanations for gender differences in crime and crime rates tend to focus on two different points of view: (1) why males commit more crimes than females, and (2) why females are not recognized as committing as many crimes as males.

The first theoretical school explains that male criminality is a product of a socialization process that differs for males and females and that creates divergent roles and expectations in their behavioral patterns.[28] This socialization process, in conjunction with the socially assigned classifications of masculinity and femininity, are believed to be primarily responsible for gender-specific personality and character traits that influence crime variations between males and females. In other words, the socialization of males is thought to explain their much higher rate of crime.

A related theory is that males have more opportunities than females to commit crimes because they are more likely to be involved in social settings (for example, the workplace) or social situations that make crime conducive or desirable (such as unemployment).[29] This would seem to be less true today than in past years; however, the socialization of males and the sex-status assigned to them continues to provide males with more legitimate and illegitimate opportunities than females.

Biological theorists point to biological differences between the sexes as a reason for more aggressive, violent behavior by males than females.[30] This difference could particularly account for male-to-female criminality where the males' greater physical strength gives him a distinct advantage in crimes such as rape.

The second prominent theoretical perspective of crime relative to gender tends to suggest that females commit as many crimes as males, or at least considerably more than is known, but are the beneficiaries of their gender, the hidden nature of their crime, and favorable treatment by the system of criminal justice. Cesare Lombroso, believed to be the founder of criminology, and William Ferrero postulated that if the full magnitude of prostitution were known and if it were considered a criminal act, the frequency of crimes between males and females would be virtually equal.[31] Napoleone Colajanni, another eighteenth-century researcher, contended that males and females would commit a like incidence of crime were they equally subject to social forces.[32]

In the 1940s, Otto Pollak also posited that male crime and female crime are comparable but that the "masked" nature of the crime committed by women, in conjunction with an intrinsic deceitfulness, enabled them to avoid detection.[33] More recent studies have furthered this argument, citing the low reportability rate of such crimes as infanticide, prostitution, and illegal abortions.[34] Critics have rejected the hidden crime approach by pointing out that as many male crimes (such as family violence and rape) go undetected or unreported as female crimes.[35]

The other major contention of this school of thought is that females tend to be the beneficiaries of more lenient treatment than is afforded to males at every stage of the criminal justice process, resulting in fewer arrests, less prosecution, shorter sentences, and a lower rate of incarceration of female offenders. Numerous studies have presented evidence of a chivalrous and paternalistic criminal and juvenile justice system.[36] However, other findings refute this belief, contending that in some instances women and girls are treated harsher by the system of justice than are their male counterparts.[37] Overall, it appears that females do fare better than males in the criminal justice system. However, this tends to be mitigated when variables such as race and class are considered. Furthermore, any such advantages still cannot account for the significant discrepancy between male and female crime rates.

Gender plays a strong role in crime. Males are involved in considerably more crime as offenders and victims than are females. The gender differential is greater for adults than for juveniles. Boys and girls tend to be more alike in the nature of their criminality than are men and women. Although the absolute relationship between male and female offenders has remained consistent for some time, there are indications that females are gaining ground on male offenders, most notably in such property crimes as larceny-theft and fraud. Overall, female criminality continues to follow traditional patterns. There is evidence that females receive more lenient treatment in the juvenile and criminal justice systems. However, regardless of this and other variables such as unreported crime, males are much more likely to commit criminal acts than are females.

NOTES

1. See, for example, Carol Smart, *Women, Crime and Criminology* (London: Routledge and Kegan Paul, 1977); Ilene H. Nagel and John Hagan, "Gender and Crime: Offense Patterns and Criminal Court Sanctions," in Michael Tonry and Norval Morris, eds., *Crime and Justice: An Annual Review of Research*, vol. 4 (Chicago: University of Chicago Press, 1983), pp. 91-144.

2. U.S. Federal Bureau of Investigation, *Crime in the United States: Uniform Crime Reports 1987* (Washington, D.C.: Government Printing Office, 1988), p. 169.

3. Ibid.

4. Rita Simon, *The Contemporary Woman and Crime* (Washington, D.C.: Government Printing Office, 1976).

5. Darrell Steffensmeier, "Sex Differences in Patterns of Adult Crimes, 1965-77: A Review and Assessment," *Social Forces* 58 (1980): 1080-1108.

6. U.S. Federal Bureau of Investigation, *Crime in the United States: Uniform Crime Reports 1986* (Washington, D.C.: Government Printing Office), pp. 176, 178.

7. Ibid., p. 169.

8. See, for example, Nagel and Hagan, "Gender and Crime"; Darrell Steffensmeier and Renee Steffensmeier, "Trends in Female Delinquency: An Examination of Arrest, Juvenile Court, Self-Report and Field Data," *Criminology* 18 (1980): 62-85.

9. F. Ivan Nye and James F. Short, "Scaling Delinquent Behavior," *American Sociological Review* 22 (1958): 326-32.

10. Nancy Wise, "Juvenile Delinquency Among Middle-Class Girls," in Edmund Vaz, ed., *Middle Class Juvenile Delinquency* (New York: Harper & Row, 1967).

11. Peter Kratcoski and J. Kratcoski, "Changing Patterns in the Delinquent Activities of Boys and Girls: A Self-Reported Delinquency Analysis," *Adolescence* 10 (1975): 38-91.

12. Steve A. Cernkovich and Peggy C. Giordano, "A Comparative Analysis of Male and Female Delinquency," *Sociological Quarterly* 20 (1979): 131-45.

13. See Suzanne S. Ageton, "The Dynamics of Female Delinquency, 1976-1980," *Criminology* 21 (1983): 555-84.

14. U.S. Department of Justice, *Criminal Victimization in the United States, [1973-]1986: A National Crime Survey Report* (Washington, D.C.: Government Printing Office, 1975-1988 [various reports]).

15. *Uniform Crime Reports 1986*, p. 8.

16. Alice Franklin, "Criminality in the Workplace: A Comparison of Male and Female Offenders," in Freda Adler and Rita Simon, eds., *The Criminology of Deviant Women* (Boston: Houghton Mifflin, 1979).

17. Walter Miller, "The Molls," *Society* 11 (1973): 32-35.

18. Freda Adler, *Sisters in Crime: The Rise of the New Female Criminal* (New York: McGraw Hill, 1975), p. 15.

19. See, for example, E. B. Leonard, *Women, Crime, and Society: A Critique of Theoretical Criminology* (New York: Longman, 1982); Steven Box, *Power, Crime and Mystification* (London: Tavistock, 1983).

20. Steffensmeier and Steffensmeier, "Trends in Female Delinquency."

21. Leonard, *Women, Crime and Society*; J. G. Weis, "Liberation and Crime: The Invention of the New Female Criminal," *Crime and Social Justice* 6 (1976): 17-21.

22. Ronald B. Flowers, *Women and Criminality: The Woman as Victim, Offender, and Practitioner* (Westport, Conn.: Greenwood Press, 1987), pp. 78-81.

23. Rita Simon, *Women and Crime* (Lexington, Mass.: D. C. Heath, 1975), p. 42.

24. Flowers, *Women and Criminality*, p. 79.

25. See also, Steffensmeier, "Sex Differences."

26. In 1986, less than 1 percent of the aggregate female arrests were for embezzlement. See also, *Uniform Crime Reports 1986*, p. 178.

27. Cernkovich and Giordano, "A Comparative Analysis."

28. See John Conklin, *Criminology*, 2d ed. (New York: Macmillan, 1986); Jeanne Gregory, "Sex, Class and Crime: Towards a Non-Sexist Criminology," in Roger Matthews and Jock Young, eds., *Confronting Crime* (Beverly Hills: Sage, 1986), pp. 53-71.

29. See Stephen Shafer, *Introduction to Criminology* (Reston, Va.: Reston, 1976), pp. 101-103.

30. See Flowers, *Women and Criminality*, pp. 91-93; Sarnoff A. Mednick et al., "Biology and Violence," in Marvin E. Wolfgang and Neil Alan Weiner, eds., *Criminal Violence* (Beverly Hills: Sage, 1982), pp. 21-80.

31. Cesare Lombroso and William Ferrero, *The Female Offender* (New York: Appleton, 1900).

32. Napoleone Colajanni, *La Sociologia Criminals* (Catania: 1889).

33. Otto Pollak, *The Criminality of Women* (Philadelphia: University of Pennsylvania Press, 1950).

34. See, for example, A. Campbell, *Girl Delinquents* (Oxford: Blackwell, 1981).

35. See, for example, Rebecca Emerson Dobash and Russell Dobash, *Violence Against Wives* (New York: Free Press, 1979).

36. See Nagel and Hagan, "Gender and Crime."

37. See, for example, Carol Engel Temin, "Discriminatory Sentencing of Women Offenders: The Argument of ERA in a Nutshell," *American Criminal Law Review* 11 (1973): 355-72; Meda Chesney-Lind, "Judicial Enforcement of the Female Sex Role: The Family Court and the Female Delinquent," *Issues in Criminology* 8 (1973): 51-69.

6

Race, Ethnicity, and Criminal Involvement

Race and, to a lesser extent, ethnicity are among the strongest predictors of crime involvement. The relationship between crime, race, and ethnicity has consistently held up in arrest and victimization data. In short, by volume, whites are most likely to be both offenders and victims of crime. However, minority group members, specifically blacks and Hispanics, have the highest rate of criminal involvement. Racial and ethnic variations in crime generally reflect several themes, including cultural, social, economic, and biological differences, as well as differential treatment within the criminal justice system. This chapter will focus on the statistical disparity in the crime of racial and ethnic groups.

ARREST STATISTICS

Arrest and Race

The racial distribution of total arrest figures in the United States in 1986 generally reflected the racial composition of the country (Table 6.1). Whites, who constitute the largest racial group, accounted for 71 percent of the arrestees, 68 percent of those arrested for property crimes, and 52 percent of the violent crime arrestees. The second most populous race in the country, blacks, was responsible for 27 percent of the aggregate arrests, 47 percent of those for violent crimes, and 30 percent of the property crime arrestees. The black arrest figures are much more noteworthy, considering that blacks represent only 12 percent of the nation's population, compared to about 85 percent for whites. Blacks were disproportionately arrested for every UCR offense in 1986, with the exception of driving under the influence and liquor law violations. Their arrest percentage for robbery was more than five times their national percentage. Native Americans and

Table 6.1
Total Arrests, Distribution by Race, 1986[a]

Offense Charged	Percent Distribution[b]				
	Total	White	Black	American Indian or Alaskan Native	Asian or Pacific Islander
TOTAL	100.0	71.3	27.0	1.0	0.7
Murder & nonnegligent manslaughter ..	100.0	50.3	48.0	0.9	0.8
Forcible rape.....................	100.0	52.0	46.6	0.8	0.5
Robbery......................	100.0	37.0	62.0	0.5	0.5
Aggravated assault	100.0	58.8	39.8	0.9	0.6
Burglary......................	100.0	69.1	29.5	0.8	0.6
Larceny-theft	100.0	67.8	30.1	1.1	1.0
Motor vehicle theft...............	100.0	63.6	34.7	0.9	0.9
Arson	100.0	75.5	23.6	0.5	0.5
Violent crime[c]	100.0	52.2	46.5	0.7	0.6
Property crime[d]	100.0	67.8	30.2	1.0	0.9
Crime Index total[e]...............	100.0	64.5	33.7	1.0	0.8
Other assaults...................	100.0	65.7	32.7	1.0	0.7
Forgery & counterfeiting	100.0	66.4	32.6	0.5	0.5
Fraud	100.0	66.2	33.0	0.4	0.4
Embezzlement	100.0	70.1	28.8	0.4	0:7
Stolen property; buying, receiving, possessing	100.0	61.6	37.4	0.6	0.5
Vandalism.....................	100.0	78.5	19.9	0.9	0.7
Weapons; carrying, possessing, etc. .	100.0	64.5	34.4	0.5	0.7
Prostitution & commercialized vice..	100.0	59.9	38.8	0.5	0.9
Sex offenses (except forcible rape & prostitution)	100.0	78.1	20.4	1.0	0.6
Drug abuse violations.............	100.0	67.3	31.8	0.4	0.5
Gambling......................	100.0	50.7	46.1	0.1	3.1
Offenses against family & children..	100.0	66.1	32.3	1.1	0.5
Driving under the influence........	100.0	88.7	9.7	1.1	0.6
Liquor laws	100.0	87.6	9.8	2.0	0.6
Drunkenness	100.0	79.7	17.7	2.3	0.2
Disorderly conduct	100.0	67.9	30.7	1.1	0.3
Vagrancy......................	100.0	66.9	29.4	3.1	0.6
All other offenses (except traffic) .	100.0	64.7	33.6	0.8	0.9
Suspicion......................	100.0	76.1	22.9	0.6	0.4
Curfew & loitering law violations...	100.0	75.9	21.9	0.7	1.5
Runaways......................	100.0	84.3	13.4	1.0	1.4

[a]10,699 agencies; 1986 estimated population 197,663,000.

[b]Due to rounding, the percentages may not add up to total.

[c]Violent crimes are offenses of murder, forcible rape, robbery, and aggravated assault.

[d]Property crimes are offenses of burglary, larceny-theft, motor vehicle theft, and arson.

[e]Includes arson.

Source: U.S. Federal Bureau of Investigation, *Crime in the United States: Uniform Crime Reports 1986* (Washington, D.C.: Government Printing Office,1987), p. 182.

Table 6.2
Total Arrests, Distribution by Ethnic Origin, 1986[a]

Offense Charged	TOTAL ALL AGES		
	Percent Distribution		
	Total	Hispanic	Non-Hispanic
TOTAL...............................	100.0	12.7	87.3
Murder & nonnegligent manslaughter..	100.0	15.7	84.3
Forcible rape.......................	100.0	11.5	88.5
Robbery.............................	100.0	13.9	86.1
Aggravated assault..................	100.0	15.3	84.7
Burglary............................	100.0	14.7	85.3
Larceny-theft.......................	100.0	12.0	88.0
Motor vehicle theft.................	100.0	16.3	83.7
Arson...............................	100.0	7.8	92.2
Violent crime......................	100.0	14.7	85.3
Property crime.....................	100.0	12.9	87.1
Crime Index total.................	100.0	13.3	86.7

[a]9,597 agencies; 1986 estimated population 176,840,000.

Source: U.S. Federal Bureau of Investigation, Crime in the United States: Uniform Crime Reports 1986 (Washington, D.C.: Government Printing Office,1987), p. 185.

Asians, who represent two of the nation's smallest racial groups, each accounted for about 1 percent of the aggregate arrests nationwide in 1986.

Arrest and Ethnic Origin

Official data on ethnic origin are tabulated independently and limited only to Hispanic and non-Hispanic arrests. There are no official figures for arrests of white ethnic groups such as Italians, Irish, and Jews. In 1986, 87.3 percent of the aggregate arrests were of non-Hispanics. Although Hispanics represent only 7.9 percent of the total population, they accounted for 12.7 percent of the arrests for all crimes, 13.3 percent of the Crime Index arrests, and 14.7 percent of the arrests for crimes of violence. Table 6.2 shows the percentages of Crime Index offense arrests by ethnic origin in 1986. Non-Hispanics were arrested most often for arson, whereas Hispanic arrests were highest for motor vehicle theft, at 16.3 percent, at a level nearly twice their population.

Arrest and Age

Variations in arrest figures with respect to race and ethnic origin also exist when comparing arrests of those under and over the age of 18 (Table 6.3). Three-quarters of the persons under 18 arrested in 1986 were white. White

Table 6.3
Percentage Distribution of Arrests, by Age, Race, and Ethnic Origin, 1986[a]

R A C E

Offense	Arrestees Under 18					Arrestees 18 and Over				
	Total	White	Black	American Indian or Native Alaskan	Asian or Pacific Islander	Total	White	Black	American Indian or Native Alaskan	Asian or Pacific Islander
Total UCR Offenses	100.0	74.8	23.3	0.8	1.1	100.0	70.6	27.7	1.1	0.6
Violent Crime	100.0	46.5	52.2	0.6	0.8	100.0	53.3	45.4	0.8	0.5
Property Crime	100.0	72.2	25.5	1.0	1.3	100.0	65.6	32.6	1.0	0.7
Crime Index Total	100.0	69.3	28.5	1.0	1.2	100.0	62.4	35.9	0.9	0.7
Non-Crime Index Total	100.0	77.9	20.3	0.7	1.0	100.0	72.4	26.0	1.1	0.6

E T H N I C   O R I G I N

Offense	Arrestees Under 18			Arrestees 18 and Over		
	Total	Hispanic	Non-Hispanic	Total	Hispanic	Non-Hispanic
Total UCR Offenses	100.0	11.8	88.2	100.0	12.9	87.1
Violent Crime	100.0	14.5	85.5	100.0	14.7	85.3
Property Crime	100.0	11.8	88.2	100.0	13.5	86.5
Crime Index Total	100.0	12.1	87.9	100.0	13.8	86.2
Non-Crime Index Total	100.0	11.6	88.4	100.0	12.7	87.3

[a]Percentages may not add up due to rounding.

Source: Compiled from U.S. Federal Bureau of Investigation, Crime in the United States: Uniform Crime Reports 1986 (Washington, D.C.: Government Printing Office, 1987), pp. 183-84, 186-87.

youths accounted for 77.9 percent of the arrests for non-Index crimes. Blacks, who constitute roughly 13 percent of the nation's juvenile population, made up nearly one-fourth of all juvenile arrests and more than half the arrests for violent crimes. Other ethnic group members under age 18 had very low arrest percentages.

These patterns are virtually replicated among racial groups for those aged 18 and over. Although adult blacks show a higher percentage of arrest than juveniles for all crimes, they were arrested at a lower percentage for violent crimes. Yet the percentage of 45.4 for violent crime was still well in excess of their representation in the population.

Non-Hispanics under age 18 accounted for nearly 90 percent of the juvenile arrests. Hispanic youths nevertheless are overrepresented in arrest figures. They comprise some 6 percent of the juvenile population, but nearly double that percentage of the juvenile arrests. The disproportion is even higher for violent crime arrests.

The ethnic origin distribution for arrestees aged 18 and over reveals a similar pattern. Although non-Hispanics accounted for the vast majority of arrests, adult Hispanics formed a higher percentage of the aggregate adult arrests than did juvenile Hispanics among all persons under age 18.

The Rate of Arrests

The most useful measure for examining race and ethnic origin differentials in arrest patterns is through expressing arrest rates per 100,000 population. Table 6.4 compares the rates and ratios of arrest of racial groups and Hispanics for Crime Index offenses in 1986. It should be noted that Hispanics may also be included in the data of racial groups; the comparisons, however, are still informative.

Blacks showed the highest overall arrest rate and Crime Index arrest rate, while Asians had the lowest rate of arrest for all crime categories. The probability of a black person being arrested for an Index offense is much higher than it is for whites or Asians. For example, in 1986 blacks were arrested for crimes of violence at a rate 6 times as often as whites and nearly 10 times as often as Asians. The black arrest rate for robbery was 14 times greater than the rate for Asians and almost 12 times the rate for whites.

While whites and Asians show the lowest arrest rates, Native Americans and Hispanics have high rates of arrest relative to the size of their populations. The Native American total arrest rate was second only to that of blacks, two times the rate for whites, and 3.7 times greater than the Asian rate. Hispanics had the second highest arrest rate for violent crimes. For all UCR offenses, Hispanics were arrested at a rate nearly twice that of whites and three times greater than Asians.

Researchers examining official data have reached similar conclusions in documenting racial and ethnic differentials in crime and arrest rates.[1] Even

Table 6.4
Rates of Arrest per 100,000 Population, by Race and Ethnic Origin, 1986

Offense Charged	RACE/ETHNIC ORIGIN					RATIO OF ARRESTS					
	White	Black	Native American[a]	Asian[b]	Hispanic	Black/ White	Black/ Asian	Native American/ White	Native American/ Asian	His- panic/ White	His- panic/ Asian
TOTAL UCR OFFENSES	3640.7	9640.3	7539.6	2021.7	6240.6	2.6	4.8	2.1	3.7	1.7	3.1
Murder & nonnegligent manslaughter	4.0	26.5	10.3	3.5	11.6	6.6	7.6	2.6	2.9	2.9	3.3
Forcible rape	7.9	49.6	16.9	4.9	16.2	6.3	10.1	2.1	3.4	2.0	3.3
Robbery	22.6	265.0	40.7	18.9	79.8	11.7	14.0	1.8	2.2	3.5	4.2
Aggravated assault	85.1	403.4	176.1	49.7	206.3	4.7	8.1	2.1	3.5	2.4	4.1
Burglary	127.6	381.9	203.0	69.8	252.6	3.0	5.5	1.6	2.9	2.0	3.6
Larceny-theft	395.1	1225.3	929.6	347.2	659.0	3.1	3.5	2.4	2.7	1.7	1.9
Motor vehicle theft	40.1	153.2	79.5	32.3	98.3	3.8	4.7	2.0	2.5	2.4	3.0
Arson	5.7	12.6	5.4	2.1	5.7	2.2	6.0	1.0[c]	2.6	1.1[c]	2.7
Violent crime	119.5	744.5	244.1	76.9	313.9	6.2	9.7	2.0	3.2	2.6	4.1
Property crime	568.6	1773.0	1217.6	451.4	1015.6	3.1	3.9	2.1	2.7	1.8	2.2
Crime Index total	688.1	2517.5	1461.7	528.4	1329.5	3.7	4.8	2.1	2.8	1.9	2.5

[a]Uniform Crime Reports define Native Americans as American Indian or Alaskan Native. The 1980 Bureau of the Census identifies 99 percent of the Native American population as American Indian and Eskimo, and 1 percent as Aleut.

[b]Also includes Pacific Islanders.

[c]The ratio of these figures is reversed with respect to the racial or ethnic groups compared.

Source: Arrest rates are computed for each race and ethnic origin from 1980 Census of Population data, 1987 Current Population Survey, and U.S. Federal Bureau of Investigation, Crime in the United States: Uniform Crime Reports 1986 (Washington, D.C.: Government Printing Office, 1987), pp. 182, 185.

when such background variables as class have been taken into consideration, studies have shown that disparities in criminality between certain groups still exist.[2] More detailed study of the relationship between race, ethnicity, and crime can be found in *Minorities and Criminality*, the third volume of this series.

Patterns of Arrests

There are also racial and ethnic differences in the types of crimes for which particular groups are most often arrested. Table 6.5 reflects the top ten incidences of arrest by race or ethnic origin in 1986. The only common ranking among all groups is arrests for "all other offenses," or violations of local and state laws and ordinances. This accounted for the most frequent incidence of arrest. Other patterns may be a reflection of cultural differences, differential law enforcement, opportunity, and/or an unexplainable fluctuation. Nevertheless, the arrest patterns do provide us with some indication of the offenses that individual groups are most likely to be arrested for. For instance, Native American arrests are mostly for alcohol-related crimes (this is supported by the fact that the Native American arrest rate for alcohol-related offenses is the highest of any racial or ethnic group). Studying these patterns can help us to better understand differences in the occurrence of crime and possible reasons to attribute to them.

Long-Term Arrest Trends

Trends in arrest patterns over several years indicate that there is a solid relationship between race, ethnicity, and crime.[3] The volume of crime has been shown consistently to parallel population figures. That is, whites are arrested most often, followed by blacks, Hispanics, and other racial groups. However, relative to their populations, blacks, Hispanics, and Native Americans are habitually overrepresented in long-term statistical trends. Blacks regularly comprise almost half of all arrests for crimes of violence, even though they represent only 12 percent of the U.S. population.

SELF-REPORT STUDIES

Self-report studies offer some support for differences in rates of crime with respect to race. However, they are limited as a means of measuring the racial distribution of crime because of their almost sole focus on juveniles. Furthermore, most such studies are concerned entirely with black-white crime differentials, while ignoring the criminality of other racial or ethnic groups. The results of self-report research have been inconclusive. Generally, they indicate that the disparity found in official data with respect to race is unsubstantiated.

Table 6.5
Crimes Most Often Arrested For, by Race and Ethnic Origin, 1986

RACE/ETHNIC ORIGIN

Rank	WHITE	Rank	BLACK	Rank	HISPANIC	Rank	NATIVE AMERICAN	Rank	ASIAN
1	All other offenses (except traffic)	1	All other offenses (except traffic)	1	All other offenses (except traffic)	1	All other offenses (except traffic)	1	All other offenses (except traffic)
2	Driving under the influence	2	Larceny-theft	2	Driving under the influence	2	Drunkenness	2	Larceny-theft
3	Larceny-theft	3	Drug abuse violations	3	Drunkenness	3	Driving under the influence	3	Driving under the influence
4	Drunkenness	4	Other assaults	4	Larceny-theft	4	Larceny-theft	4	Other assaults
5	Drug abuse violations	5	Disorderly conduct	5	Drug abuse violations	5	Liquor laws	5	Drug abuse violations
6	Liquor laws	6	Driving under the influence	6	Other assaults	6	Disorderly conduct	6	Liquor laws
7	Other assaults	7	Drunkenness	7	Disorderly conduct	7	Other assaults	7	Burglary
8	Disorderly conduct	8	Aggravated assault	8	Burglary	8	Drug abuse violations	8	Runaways
9	Burglary	9	Burglary	9	Liquor laws	9	Burglary	9	Disorderly conduct
10	Fraud	10	Fraud	10	Aggravated assault	10	Aggravated assault	10	Aggravated assault

Source: Compiled from U.S. Federal Bureau of Investigation, *Crime in the United States: Uniform Crime Reports 1986* (Washington, D.C.: Government Printing Office, 1987), pp. 182, 185.

Early studies by Leroy Gould[4] and William Chambliss and Richard Nagasawa[5] found that in contrast to the significantly higher official rate of delinquency among blacks than among whites, self-report studies revealed that white juveniles had a slightly higher rate of delinquency than did black youths. More recent studies, such as that done by Michael Hindelang, Travis Hirschi, and Joseph Weis, show that blacks report more serious delinquent offenses, but black and white juveniles tend to be more similar in their rates of petty delinquent behavior.[6] Other evidence points toward a higher frequency of delinquency among blacks than whites,[7] while some researchers report that any such differential between black and white youths is negligible.[8]

VICTIMIZATION SURVEYS

Perceived Race of Offender

Victimization research provides another corroborating measurement of the racial distribution of criminal offenders. As shown in Table 6.6, victims of crime reported to the NCS in 1986 that in 7 out of 10 single-offender crimes of violence, the offender was perceived to be white. This perception rose to nearly three out of four for assaultive crimes. The identification of blacks as the offender in single-offender violent crimes is somewhat lower than in UCR figures, yet well in excess of the black percentage of the general population. Blacks were perceived to be the offender in nearly half of all robberies. Other racial groups were believed to be responsible for only a small percentage of single-offender crimes.

Victim perceptions of multiple-offender crimes generally followed similar patterns. Around 50 percent of the multiple-offender victimizations were identified as being perpetrated by all white offenders. However, all black offenders were disproportionately believed to be involved in multiple-offender crimes. Although the NCS data does not identify all other or "mixed" races, the data shows that these groups were perceived to be the offenders in 15 percent of the multiple-offender victimizations, including 42 percent of the rapes.

Victimization data also reflect the largely intraracial nature of violent crime. In 1986, 80 percent of the crimes of violence against whites were perpetrated by white offenders, whereas black offenders were responsible for 84 percent of the violent victimizations of blacks. However, black offenders were found to commit more than half their violent crimes against white victims.[9]

Victimization, Race, and Ethnicity

When race and ethnicity are considered in victimization studies, minorities are also shown to be disproportionately victimized by crime (Table 6.7).

Table 6.6
Percentage Distribution of Single- and Multiple-Offender Victimizations, by Type of Crime and Race of Offenders, 1986[a]

Type of Crime	PERCEIVED RACE										
	Single-Offenders					Multiple-Offenders					
	Total[b]	White	Black	Other	Unknown	Total	All White	All Black	All Other	Mixed Races	Unknown
Crimes of violence....	100.0	70.7	24.0	3.7	1.6	100.0	49.8	32.4	5.5	9.4	2.9
Rape................	100.0	72.9	25.2	1.8[c]	0.0[c]	100.0	25.2[c]	21.9[c]	0.0[c]	41.9[c]	11.0[c]
Robbery.............	100.0	49.0	44.6	3.6	2.8[c]	100.0	34.8	45.2	7.2	9.5	3.2[c]
Assault.............	100.0	74.3	20.5	3.7	1.4	100.0	57.4	26.6	4.9	8.6	2.6

[a]The race of offender is based on the victim's perception.

[b]Totals may not add up due to rounding.

[c]Estimate is derived from 10 or fewer samples.

Source: U.S. Department of Justice, Criminal Victimization in the United States: A National Crime Survey Report 1986 (Washington, D.C.: Government Printing Office, 1988), pp. 44, 49.

Table 6.7
Victimization Rates for Persons Aged 12 and Over, by Type of Crime, Race, and Ethnicity of Victims, 1985

Type of crime	RACE			ETHNICITY	
	White	Black	Other[b]	Hispanic	Non-Hispanic
Crimes of Violence	29.1	38.2	25.0	30.1	30.1
Rape	0.6	1.8	0.7[a]	0.2[a]	0.8
Robbery	4.2	10.9	6.9	8.1	4.9
Assault	24.2	25.5	17.4	21.8	24.4
Crimes of Theft	70.1	63.4	72.5	60.5	70.0
Personal larceny with contact	2.3	4.8	5.5	3.4	2.6
Personal larceny without contact	67.8	58.5	67.1	57.1	67.4
Household Crimes	168.5	225.8	150.1	235.7	171.0
Burglary	60.5	83.4	45.2	85.4	61.5
Household larceny	94.9	120.1	87.9	126.8	95.8
Motor vehicle theft	13.1	22.3	17.0	23.4	13.7

[a]Estimate is calculated from around 10 cases or less.

[b]Includes Asians, Pacific Islanders, and Native Americans.

Source: U.S. Department of Justice, Criminal Victimization in the United States: A National Crime Survey Report 1985 (Washington, D.C.: Government Printing Office, 1987), pp. 16, 18, 28.

NCS data reveals that in 1985 blacks were victims of crimes of violence and household crimes at a higher rate than whites and other racial minority groups. Other racial minorities collectively had the highest rate of theft victimization, followed by whites.

The data on ethnicity show that Hispanics and non-Hispanics had similar rates of violent crime victimization, while non-Hispanics were more likely to be victimized by crimes of theft. Hispanics had the highest rate of victimization for total and individual household crimes of any ethnic or racial group.

NCS findings for 1985 show further that black males are disproportionately more likely to be the victims of violent crime than any other group when race and sex are combined. Even when other factors are considered, such as income and educational level, blacks and other minority groups are still generally shown to have higher rates of victimization than whites.[10] These trends in victimization have held true for several years.[11]

THEORIES OF RACIAL-ETHNIC DISPARITIES
IN CRIMINALITY

There have been many attempts to explain variations in crime rates with regard to racial or ethnic background. Among the weakest of them are the theories of biological difference.[12] Atavistic theories, genetic theories, and brain dysfunction theories all purport to explain crime differentials as a matter of physiological, anatomical, or constitutional differences between criminals and noncriminals. These differences are applied to crime variations of racial and ethnic groups either as a singular explanation or as a key correlate in combination with other variables of crime. The major fault with biological theories is that they seek to explain something (racial and ethnic differences) that is representative of socially defined groupings rather than of biological classifications. Furthermore, no reliable evidence has surfaced to indicate that high or low crime rates are the result of biological determinants.

Other significant theories about the relationship between race or ethnicity and crime include historical oppression theories, conflict theories, and economic theories. Historical oppression hypotheses propose that certain groups' past experiences in this country—subjugation, discrimination, and victimization—have had a cause-and-effect role in determining their disposition and, hence, rate of crime.[13] Such theories tend to be limited because they fail to account for extreme variations in the crime rates of certain applicable racial groups (for instance, blacks and Asians).

Conflict theories posit that only certain types of behavior are defined legally as crimes, and that those who wield power and resources determine what is to be considered criminality and what is not.[14] Thus the criminal law is viewed as a reflection of the best interests of the wealthy and powerful members of society and biased against those who are in the least power-ful position to influence public policies—minorities and lower-class members. Conflict theorists argue that, as a result, certain groups (such as blacks and Hispanics) are more likely than whites to face greater police scrutiny, be arrested, be tried, and receive severe sentences.

The economic deprivation approach postulates that minority groups are more likely to be poor and face a greater shortage of economic opportuni-ties than whites, and hence are more likely to resort to crime out of their resentment of poverty or because of unequal access to desired goals.[15] No one theoretical formula seems to be adequate to explain variations in crime rates among racial and ethnic groups. Rather, differences in crime patterns are more likely a combination of individual, social, and economic correlates.

A relationship between criminal participation and racial and ethnic corre-lates has been firmly established. Although the volume of arrests favor whites by a large margin, blacks, Hispanics, and Native Americans are arrested out of proportion to their numbers in the population. Race or ethnicity is also strongly related to victimization. Minorities are over-represented as crime victims, while most victimization is intraracial. Under-standing disparities in the crime patterns of racial and ethnic groups has proven difficult. Despite many theories, we are still searching for answers that can adequately account for these unexplained variations in criminality.

NOTES

1. See, for example, Marvin E. Wolfgang, *Patterns in Criminal Homicide* (Phila-delphia: University of Pennsylvania Press, 1958); Menachem Amir, *Patterns in Forcible Rape* (Chicago: University of Chicago Press, 1971).

2. Ibid.; Marvin E. Wolfgang, Robert M. Figlio, and Thorsten Sellin, *Delin-quency in a Birth Cohort* (Chicago: University of Chicago Press, 1972).

3. U.S. Federal Bureau of Investigation, *Crime in the United States: Uniform Crime Reports [1970-]1987* (Washington, D.C.: Government Printing Office, 1971-1988 [various reports]).

4. Leroy Gould, "Who Defines Delinquency: A Comparison of Self-Reported and Officially-Reported Indices of Delinquency for Three Racial Groups," *Social Problems* 16 (1969): 325-36.

5. William Chambliss and Richard Nagasawa, "On the Validity of Official Statis-tics: A Comparative Study of White, Black, and Japanese High School Boys," *Journal of Research in Crime and Delinquency* 6 (1969): 71-77.

6. Michael J. Hindelang, Travis Hirschi, and Joseph G. Weis, "Correlates of Delinquency: The Illusion of Discrepancy Between Self-Report and Official Mea-sures," *American Sociological Review* 44 (1979): 995-1014.

7. Delbert S. Elliot and Suzanne S. Ageton, "Reconciling Race and Class Differ-ences in Self-Reported and Official Estimates of Delinquency," *American Socio-logical Review* 45 (1980): 90-110.

8. See, for example, Jay R. Williams and Martin Gold, "From Delinquent Behavior to Official Delinquency" *Social Problems* 20 (1972): 209-29.

9. U.S. Department of Justice, *Criminal Victimization in the United States, 1986: A National Crime Survey Report* (Washington, D.C.: Government Printing Office, 1988), p. 7.

10. Ibid.

11. Ibid., *National Crime Survey, 1975-1988.*

12. See Ronald B. Flowers, *Minorities and Criminality* (Westport, Conn.: Greenwood Press, 1988).

13. Ibid.

14. Richard Quinney, *The Social Reality of Crime* (Boston: Little, Brown, 1970); Jeffrey H. Reiman, *The Rich Get Richer and the Poor Get Prison: Ideology, Class, and Criminal Justice* 2d ed. (New York: Wiley, 1984).

15. Willem A. Bonger, *Criminality and Economic Conditions*, trans. Henry P. Horton (Boston: Little, Brown, 1916); Belton Fleisher, *The Economics of Delinquency* (Chicago: Quadrangle Books, 1966).

7

Social Class and Criminality

Criminologists have given much attention to the relationship between social class and crime. Traditional wisdom would have us believe that the lower and working classes are responsible for the bulk of criminality, especially the more serious crimes, and that, by correlation, they are the most likely to be victimized by crime. This perspective assumes that people at the lowest level of the social structure are more apt to engage in criminality because of their greater inability to obtain desired goods and services through legitimate means and because of their rage and resentment against those who can. The link between crime and the lower class is bolstered by official data that not only define "crime" primarily as conventional street crime but indicate that crime is higher in urban, impoverished areas.

In this chapter, we will examine the conclusions and criticisms of social class research. The following chapter will then explore specific factors generally related to class and crime such as employment and income.

ADULT CRIME AND SOCIAL CLASS

Research Using Official Statistics

Only a scant number of studies have examined the relationship between adult crime and class. Most have relied on official arrest statistics. UCR data do not supply information on the class differences of arrested suspects. However, studies that use aggregate arrest statistics have uniformly found crime rates to be higher in lower-class areas than among the higher classes.

An inverse correlation has been found between social class and adult street crime.[1] In a review of 46 studies that used official arrest data, it was established that lower-class adults had consistently higher crime rates than their middle- and upper-class counterparts.[2] A recent study found that social class and adult criminality were strongly related to a person's social status, as defined by employment stability and educational attainment.[3] The study found no relationship between adult crime and the socioeconomic status of the person's family of origin. The association between social class and adult criminality was found to be strongest when using official arrest statistics, although the relationship was present also when using self-report studies.

Research Using Self-Report Data

In the limited amount of research on the adult crime–social class link that has relied on self-report surveys, criminologists have generally found that the relationship between class and crime is not as strong as it is when official arrest data are used. Most self-report surveys have found either that the adult rate of crime is higher in the lower class or that class differences in the crime rate are insignificant. In any event, no self-report study of adult criminality has shown the middle or upper classes to have a higher rate of crime than the lower class.[4]

JUVENILE DELINQUENCY AND SOCIAL CLASS

Research Using Official Records

Studies of official data have indicated that delinquency is disproportionately a product of the lower class. A review of studies examining the relationship between juvenile delinquency and class found that in 44 of the 53 studies that had used official data, juveniles of the lower class had higher rates of delinquency than their middle-class counterparts.[5] Another review of class-delinquency research found a consistent, though small, inverse association between class and street crime by juveniles when official statistics were used.[6] Some research, employing both official data and self-report surveys, has found that socioeconomic class was related to delinquency when using official statistics, though not when self-report data were the criteria.[7]

Research Using Self-Report Measures

Most research into the class-crime relationship has been conducted with juveniles, using self-report data. Early self-report studies found no relationship between social class and delinquency. Research by James Short and F. Ivan Nye found that, although there was no class-delinquency association when using self-report surveys, a distinct relationship emerged when juvenile incarceration was the basis of examination. They also found that correlates often associated with lower-class existence, such as fragmented homes or families, were related to institutionalization but not to self-reported delinquency.[8] Short and Nye, along with Virgil Olsen, also explored socioeconomic status and delinquent behavior by focusing on the father's occupation as a measurement of social class. This research corroborated the conclusion that there was no relationship between self-reported delinquent conduct and social class,[9] as did a study by Robert Dentler and Lawrence Monroe.[10] In most instances, however, these researchers have found that lower-class youths were more apt to be given official attention and labeled delinquents by the system of justice than were non-lower-class juveniles, thereby giving the appearance of overrepresentation among official delinquents.

More recent self-report research into social class and juvenile delinquency has yielded inconsistent results. Perhaps the most influential work opposing a class-crime relationship was that undertaken by Charles Tittle, Wayne Villemez, and Douglas Smith. The authors reviewed 35 studies that included 363 separate estimates regarding the association between class and crime. They concluded that social class status is not related to crime or delinquency.[11]

However, others have questioned the findings of Tittle and associates. John Braithwaite, for example, has argued that the researchers' review of the literature was incomplete, and that in many instances those studies reporting no relationship between class and crime failed to differentiate between various subgroups within the lower or working classes.[12] Others have criticized the inclusion of relatively trivial offenses in many self-report instruments, suggesting that were only serious crimes considered, lower-class juveniles would be found more delinquent. Thus there would exist a real class-crime relationship.

Albert Reiss, Jr., and Albert Rhodes have documented that there is a socio-economic-class variation in delinquency rates when self-report data are relied on. They cited various studies that indicate more frequent and severe delinquent conduct among lower-class youth and their middle-class counterparts.[13]

The self-report findings of Delbert Elliot and Suzanne Ageton offer the most prominent support for this perspective. From a sample group of 1,726 juveniles aged 11 to 17, they found that lower-class youths admitted to much more serious crimes (such as assault and robbery) than "working"- or middle-class youths and were much more likely than middle-class youths to have participated in numerous serious personal and property offenses.[14] As a result of these findings, the authors concluded that self-report data on crime and class are similar to official indicators. Later research by Elliot and David Huizinga supported the conclusion that class differences exist in the incidence and prevalence of serious criminality.[15] This is contrary to the recent work of Michael Hindelang, Travis Hirschi, and Joseph Weis, who found that there was no relationship between social class and crime whether one used self-report or official data.[16]

In spite of these apparently opposite conclusions, the preponderance of the most recent self-report findings indicate that class differences do appear to be strong with respect to serious crimes, whereas for the least-serious crimes class differences are minimal at best. There continues to be a significant disparity between self-report and official data as they relate to class and crime.

Race, Class, and Crime

Another aspect of social class and delinquency concerns the factor of race. Although black youths are disproportionately represented in arrest data compared to whites, many experts believe that the *actual* relationship between race, social class, and crime is far less pronounced (see also Chapter 6). Travis Hirschi's study of delinquency, using self-report and arrest data, concluded that there was no relationship between social class and delinquency, and only a slight race-delinquency correlation.[17]

However, in the Elliot and Ageton study, the authors found significant race-class differences between blacks and whites in the commission of serious offenses.[18] A cohort study of class, race, and delinquency using official data found an association between social class and being stopped by the police for juvenile delinquency. The race-class relationship was unclear since both whites and blacks in the higher class were less likely to be stopped by the police than blacks and whites in the lower class.[19] A study of adult criminality and class found that the relationship was stronger for blacks than whites.[20]

In short, when race is considered along with social class, it appears that there exists a relatively strong parallel between social class and race in the likelihood of criminality.

VICTIMIZATION AND SOCIAL CLASS

Victimization data, such as that provided by NCS reports do not measure social class per se, though they do tabulate related class characteristics, for example, annual income and education for personal and household crime victims (see Chapter 8). These data indicate that crimes of violence are strongly related to income: victimization rates are highest at the lowest income level and decline with rising income. For crimes of theft, the opposite is true: victimization rates increase the higher the income. However, for personal larceny with contact, the victimization rate is highest at the lowest income levels. Overall, household victimization rates tend to be highest at the lowest levels of income, but they are higher among persons making $50,000 or more annually than among people in some moderate-income brackets.[21]

The relationship between income and victimization seems to be most pronounced for violent crimes. In 1985, the victimization rate was more than twice as high for persons with incomes below $7,500 than for those with incomes of $50,000 or more. Assault victimization had the highest rate of victimization for crimes of violence among all income levels, but was twice as high among the lowest income group as it was among the highest. Despite the positive association between crimes of theft and income, the victimization rate for personal larceny with contact in 1985 was better than twice as high for persons with incomes of less than $10,000 as compared to persons with incomes of $50,000 or more.[22]

Total household crime rates are more evenly distributed across income levels than other crimes, though households with family incomes below $7,500 had higher victimization rates in total household crimes in 1985 and 1986 than households in any other income brackets.[23] The negative association between income and household crimes is greatest for burglary. However, there is a positive relationship between income and the household crime of motor vehicle theft. In 1985, the rate of motor vehicle theft for households with an income of $50,000 or more was nearly twice as high as for households with incomes of less than $7,500.

Educational attainment as a factor in social class also appears to be associated with crime. Violent crime victimization rates are lowest for persons with less than four years of education, followed by those with four years or more of college. The educational variable and its positive association with income is most related to crimes of theft. In 1986, persons with some college education had considerably higher rates of victimization than individuals with lower educational achievement.[24]

In sum, it can be concluded that susceptibility to violent criminal victimization increases as one's income becomes lower. However, other crimes such as theft and household victimization are positively and negatively associated with income or social class, depending upon the type of crime.

EXPLANATIONS OF SOCIAL CLASS–CRIME DISPARITIES

Although some self-report data suggest a correlation between crime and social class, the differences overall are not as strong as is seen in official data. Why is this? To many, it is clear evidence that law enforcement and judicial agencies exaggerate social class disparities in crime because of the biases operating in the criminal and juvenile justice systems.[25] These biases manifest themselves in the partiality toward classifying and labeling more youths of the lower classes as delinquents than juveniles of other class groups, which results in an exaggeration of class disparities in delinquency rates. Such a class bias in official estimates of delinquency is fairly evident when one considers that many self-report studies show similarities in the admitted incidence and range of criminal activities between different classes, yet official data reflect a disproportionate involvement of the lower class in crime and delinquency. This means that lower-class offenders are more likely to be arrested, find themselves in court, and be incarcerated than offenders of other classes. If the lower-class member is a minority, the bias is even more evident. This view then proposes that middle- and upper-class crimes occur much more often than is officially indicated, but remain hidden.

Another explanation for social class disparities in criminality takes a radical or critical approach.[26] These theorists regard class differences in crime rates as resulting primarily from definitions of crime that generally favor the ruling class and victimize the working or lower classes. Crimes are defined as socially harmful acts that violate basic human rights and include both crimes common to the lower class ("street crimes") and ruling-class crimes such as unemployment and exploitation. Because the law is a "tool" of the ruling class, its socially harmful acts are generally not defined as crimes by the official system of criminal justice. Critics of radical criminology point toward its predictability and disregard for objective reality. Nevertheless, this approach certainly is useful in explaining the conflict between classes on issues of basic values, and thus must be considered sound when discussing theories of class disparity in rates of crime.

There are some who suggest that class biases by the criminal justice system cannot solely account for the strong relationship between social class and official crime. One explanation for this is that the lower class may actually underreport criminal involvement in self-report surveys more often than the middle class, thereby implying that lower-class criminality is of lesser incidence than it really is.[27] The problem with this approach is that it can not determine the degree to which the middle and upper classes underreport crime less than the lower class, or for that matter why the lower class would admit to less crime than other classes.

Methodological problems in self-report research as well as differences, sometimes significant ones, from one study to another also may help to explain self-report/official data differentials with regard to the relationship between social class and crime. Such problems include lack of uniformity in what constitutes class and incompatible measurement of various types of crimes. Equal problems exist with the validity of official data, which only underscores the difficulty in getting reliable data from which to make sound conclusions (see also Chapter 1). Also used to explain social class–crime differentials are such traditional approaches as relative deprivation, poverty, and unequal access to opportunity.

The relationship of social class to crime has led to a number of sociological theories of crime and delinquency. There continues to be controversy as to what exact role class plays in crime involvement, however, a few sound observations can be made from the research:

- Crime is not class-specific
- There is no significant class variation in minor forms of criminality
- Lower-class members are disproportionately involved in serious crimes
- The relationship between racial status and crime is as strong as or stronger than that between social class and crime
- Middle- and upper-class crime remains largely hidden
- Class biases exist in the official processing of criminals and delinquents
- Victims of violent crimes are more likely to be of the lower class, while property crime victimization rates rise parallel to income level

The relationship between class and crime may be better approached when examined in association with other variables such as racial and ethnic status, marital status, and educational level.

NOTES

1. Michael J. Hindelang, "Class and Crime," in Sanford H. Kadish, ed., *Encyclopedia of Crime and Justice*, vol. 1 (New York: Free Press, 1983), pp. 175-81.

2. John Braithwaite, "The Myth of Social Class and Criminality Reconsidered," *American Sociological Review* 46 (1981): 36-57.

3. Terence P. Thornberry and Margaret Farnworth, "Social Correlates of Criminal Involvement: Further Evidence on the Relationship Between Social Status and Criminal Behavior," *American Sociological Review* 47 (1982): 505-18.

4. John Braithwaite, *Inequality, Crime, and Public Policy* (London: Routledge & Kegan Paul, 1979).

5. Ibid.

6. Hindelang, "Class and Crime."

7. See, for example, James Short and F. Ivan Nye, "Reported Behavior as a Criterion of Deviant Behavior," *Social Problems* 5 (1958): 207-13; Charles Tittle, Wayne Villemez, and Douglas Smith, "The Myth of Social Class and Criminality: An Empirical Assessment of the Empirical Evidence," *American Sociological Review* 43 (1978): 643-56.

8. Short and Nye, "Reported Behavior."

9. F. Ivan Nye, James Short, and Virgil Olsen, "Socioeconomic Status and Delinquent Behavior," *American Journal of Sociology* 63 (1958): 381-89.

10. Robert Dentler and Lawrence Monroe, "Social Correlates of Early Adolescent Theft," *American Sociological Review* 63 (1961): 733-43.

11. Tittle, Villemez, and Smith, "The Myth of Social Class and Criminality." See also Richard Johnson, "Social Class and Delinquency," *Criminology* 18 (1980): 86-93.

12. Braithwaite, "The Myth of Social Class and Criminality Reconsidered."

13. Albert J. Reiss, Jr., and Albert L. Rhodes, "The Distribution of Juvenile Delinquency in the Social Class Structure," *American Sociological Review* 26 (1961): 720-32.

14. Delbert S. Elliot and Suzanne S. Ageton, "Reconciling Race and Class Differences in Self-Reported and Official Estimates of Delinquency," *American Sociological Review* 45 (1980): 95-110.

15. Delbert Elliot and David Huizinga, "Social Class and Delinquent Behavior in a National Youth Panel, 1976-1980," *Criminology* 21 (1983): 149-77.

16. Michael Hindelang, Travis Hirschi, and Joseph Weis, *Measuring Delinquency* (Beverly Hills: Sage, 1981).

17. Travis Hirschi, *Causes of Delinquency* (Berkeley: University of California Press, 1968), pp. 66-81.

18. Elliot and Ageton, "Reconciling Race and Class Differences."

19. Marvin E. Wolfgang, Robert M. Figlio, and Thorsten Sellin, *Delinquency in a Birth Cohort* (Chicago: University of Chicago Press, 1972).

20. Thornberry and Farnworth, "Social Correlates of Criminal Involvement."

21. U.S. Department of Justice, *Criminal Victimization in the United States, 1985: A National Crime Survey Report* (Washington, D.C.: Government Printing Office, 1987), pp. 24-25, 30-31.

22. Ibid, pp. 24-25.

23. Ibid, pp. 30-31; U.S. Department of Justice, *Criminal Victimization in the United States, 1986: A National Crime Survey Report* (Washington, D.C.: Government Printing Office, 1988), p. 5.

24. *National Crime Survey, 1986*, pp. 3-4.

25. Tittle, Villemez, and Smith, "The Myth of Social Class and Criminality"; Martin R. Haskell and Lewis Yablonsky, *Juvenile Delinquency*, 2d ed. (Chicago: Rand McNally, 1978), pp. 221-29.

26. Thomas Bernard, "The Distinction Between Conflict and Radical Criminology," *Journal of Criminal Law and Criminology* 72 (1981): 366-70; Gresham M. Sykes, "The Rise of Critical Criminology," *Journal of Criminal Law and Criminology* 65 (1974): 206-13.

27. Braithwaite, *Inequality, Crime, and Public Policy.*

8

Employment, Income, Education, Marital Status, and Crime

The evidence suggests that there exists a strong correlation between involvement in crime and the variables of employment, income, education, and marital status. Much of what we know about these sociodemographic characteristics comes from prisoner and victimization data. Despite their shortcomings, these sources provide us with meaningful detailed information about demographic correlates of crime.

OFFENDER CHARACTERISTICS

Employment

The majority of offenders tend to be disproportionately unemployed, working unsteadily or part-time, or in unskilled jobs. A recent survey of jail inmates found that 47 percent were unemployed prior to arrest. Of the 53 percent who were working, 12 percent had only part-time jobs.[1] By comparison, about 84 percent of the males aged 18 to 54 in the general population (males make up 92 percent of the persons in jail) are employed, with only around 3 percent part-time. While more than two out of every five males in jail were out of work before their incarceration, the proportion is even higher for females. Two out of every three jailed women were unemployed before entering jail; less than half of the women in the general population are unemployed. That offenders tend to lack a stable employment history can be seen in a study of adult felons, which found that approximately half had no work experience, while the other half had held a wide range of short-term jobs.[2]

Table 8.1 distributes by percentage of race and sex the employment status of inmates in 1978. About one-third of the male and female inmates not working at the time of arrest were actively seeking employment. A compar-

Table 8.1
Employment Status of Inmates, by Race and Sex

PERCENT DISTRIBUTION

Employment Status	All Races[b]		White		Black	
	Male	Female	Male	Female	Male	Female
Total[a]	100	100	100	100	100	100
Working	58	33	58	37	58	28
Full-time	46	26	48	32	43	21
Part-time	12	6	11	5	15	7
Not Working	42	66	41	62	42	71
Seeking work	27	31	25	26	29	36
Not seeking work	15	35	16	36	13	35
Not Reported	0	1	0	1	0	1

[a]Detail may not add to total because of rounding.
[b]Includes data on members of races other than white and black.

Source: U.S. Department of Justice, Profile of Jail Inmates: Sociodemographic Findings from the 1978 Survey of Inmates of Local Jails (Washington, D.C.: Government Printing Office, 1980), p. 6.

able percentage of white and black males were working before being incarcerated, however, a higher percentage of blacks were working part-time. Black females had the highest percentage of unemployment (71 percent), and were more likely than white females to be seeking a job.

Prisoner statistics also confirm the overrepresentation of unemployment among offenders. Recent data show that the highest rate of incarceration for males between the ages of 16 and 64 belonged to those who were unemployed before entering prison.[3] A profile of inmates found that of the offenders who had been working over 60 percent were employed in blue-collar occupations, 13 percent were in farm and service work, and only 15 percent were in white-collar fields.[4]

Income

Offenders generally have poor levels of income. The high percentage of criminals out of work, working part-time, or in unskilled occupations is reflected in the low income of most offenders. In 1983, the median income of jail inmates before their arrest was $5,486.[5] A survey of prison inmates found that 6 of every 10 had incomes of less than $6,000 in the year prior to arrest.[6]

These income levels are low, but somewhat higher than the data derived from the more detailed 1978 survey of jail inmates. The median pre-arrest annual income at the time of the survey was only $3,714—near poverty-level as determined by the U.S. government.[7] A breakdown of income levels by total, sex, and race can be seen in Table 8.2 (see also Chapter 12).

Table 8.2
Annual Income of Jail Inmates, by Race and Sex

	Total Inmates	White		Black	
		Male	Female	Male	Female
TOTAL	100	100	100	100	100
Without Income	7	6	9	7	8
With Income[a]	93	90	85	87	85
Under $3,000	46	35	47	42	52
$3,000 - $9,999	36	38	30	35	27
$10,000 +	13	17	8	10	6
Median Income	$3714	$4288	$2594	$3158	$2254
Not Reported[b]	5	4	6	6	7

[a]Percentages may not add due to rounding.

[b]These percentages are included in without-income totals.

Source: U.S. Department of Justice, *Profile of Jail Inmates: Sociodemographic Findings from the 1978 Survey of Inmates of Local Jails* (Washington, D.C.: Government Printing Office, 1980), pp. 6-7, 14-15.

Of the 93 percent of inmates who reported income, 46 percent had incomes of less than $3,000, and 82 percent under $10,000. As in the general population, blacks had lower incomes than whites, and females had lower incomes than males. When combining sex and race, black females showed the lowest income, with more than 50 percent of the inmates making less than $3,000 before arrest.

Approximately one out of every four inmates either had no source of income prior to arrest or depended on welfare, social security, unemployment benefits, or family support.

		Percent	
Primary Income Source	Total	Male	Female
Wages and salaries	70	72	38
Welfare and other government aid	26	25	56
Illegal income	4	4	6

For 7 out of 10 inmates, the primary income source was through wages or salary. About 4 percent of the prisoners said their main income source was obtained by illegal means.

The proportion of women depending primarily on welfare, social security, or unemployment compensation was roughly three times that of men, and the number of females relying on family or friends' support was twice as high as the number of males. Black women were more likely than white women to need income other than wages or salaries; their reliance on unemployment and welfare payments was nearly twice as high.[8]

Education

The level of education of offenders is considerably lower than that of the general population. In 1983, 59 percent of jail inmates failed to complete high school.[9] A comparison of two surveys of the educational level of jail and prison inmates can be seen below:[10]

Prison Inmates		Jail Inmates	
Education	Percent	Education	Percent
0-6 years	5	0-8 years	19
7-8 years	11	9-11 years	42
9-11 years	5	12 years	30
12 years	23	13 or more years	10
More than 12 years	11		
		Median	10.2
Median	10.4		

The median grade of schooling completed by prison and jail inmates is grade 10. The highest educational level reached by most inmates is grades 9 to 11. Nearly one-fifth of the jail inmates and more than 16 percent of the prison inmates do not go beyond the eighth grade. Only about one-tenth of persons incarcerated have any college education.

Inmate data indicate that, on the average, female offenders have a slightly higher educational attainment than male offenders. Female criminals are more likely than male criminals to have at least one year of college. Black offenders are more likely than white offenders to have no high school diploma and a lower level of educational advancement in general. However, members of other races tend to have a slightly higher median grade completion than blacks or whites. When considering race and sex, white female offenders have been shown to have the highest rate of graduating from high school.[11]

The Bureau of Justice Statistics recently reported the following relationships between offenders and educational level:

- Three times as many high school dropouts as nondropouts are incarcerated
- Six percent of all prisoners have no education; their incarceration rate is three times greater than that of high school dropouts
- The rate of incarceration for college graduates is extremely low
- Among whites, property crimes and drug offenses are more typical of those with a high school diploma than of those with less than eight years of school
- Incarceration for public order crimes is more likely for offenders with lower educational attainment
- Imprisonment for robbery or drug offenses is more associated with graduates from high school
- Inmates with some prior college background are more likely to be imprisoned for nonviolent offenses and less likely to have had a past criminal record than prisoners with less education[12]

Marital Status

Offenders are most likely to be nonmarried. Seventy-nine percent of the jail inmates in 1983 were unmarried.[13] Survey data of the marital status of jail and prison inmates found the following:[14]

Marital Status	Jail Inmates (Percent)	Prison Inmates (Percent)
Married	21	26
Separated/Divorced/Widowed	25	22
Never Married	54	53

More than half of the jail and prison inmates at the time of the surveys had never married, while about one-fourth were either separated, divorced, or widowed. Only 26 percent of the prison inmates and 21 percent of the jail inmates were married.

Male offenders are more likely than female offenders to be married or never married, and female inmates are separated, divorced, or widowed at a higher percentage than are male prisoners. Black male and female offenders are more likely to be never married; however, white male and female inmates have a much higher separation or divorce rate than do whites in the general population. White female inmates have the highest rate of separation or divorce when race and sex are combined.[15]

VICTIM CHARACTERISTICS

The National Crime Survey program provides sociodemographic data on crime victims that, when combined with offender data, provide a more complete picture of the characteristics of crime.

Income

Victimization data for 1985 reveals that, for crimes of violence, victimization rates are highest among low-income persons, whereas for crimes of theft, victimization rates generally tend to rise as income levels do (Table 8.3). For persons aged 12 and over, the highest rate of overall violent crime victimization and the highest rate for the individual crimes of rape, robbery, and assault occurred among those with annual incomes of less than $7,500; they were followed by persons in the $7,500-$9,999 income bracket.

Theft victimization rates were highest for persons in the $50,000 and over income level, followed by those making between $30,000 and $49,999. Although there is a strong relationship between crimes of theft and income level, persons with the lowest annual incomes had the highest rates for personal larceny with contact, and victims with incomes below $7,500 actually were victimized by theft at a greater rate than persons in the next two income brackets.

Households with annual family incomes of under $7,500 had the highest total rate of victimization and the highest rate for burglary. However, the motor vehicle theft rate was highest for persons in the $50,000 and over income level, and larceny rates generally rose with income.

Race does not appear to be a strong factor in the relationship between income and crimes of violence. Whites and members of minority groups generally display higher rates of victimization the lower the level of income, though the second highest rate of violent crime victimization among blacks in 1985 was for those making between $25,000 and $29,000 yearly. For crimes of theft, blacks making annual incomes of $50,000 or more had higher victimization rates than whites in the same income bracket. How-

Table 8.3

Victimization Rates for Persons Aged 12 and Over, by Offense and Annual Family Income of Victims, 1985 (Rate per 1,000 Population Aged 12 and Over)

Type of Crime	Less Than $7,500	$7,500–$9,999	$10,000–$14,999	INCOME $15,000–$24,999	$25,000–$29,999	$30,000–$49,999	$50,000– or more
Crimes of Violence	52.1	33.8	31.7	28.0	29.0	22.3	24.6[a]
Rape	2.2	1.1[a]	0.7	0.1[a]	0.4[a]	0.6	0.4[a]
Robbery	8.8	7.4	5.4	4.7	4.7	3.5	3.2
Assault	41.1	25.4	25.7	23.2	23.9	18.2	21.0
Crimes of Theft	67.5	62.6	64.5	67.8	68.7	76.1	89.7
Personal larceny with contact	4.8	5.5	2.0	2.2	2.1	2.0	2.4
Personal larceny without contact	62.7	57.1	62.5	65.6	66.6	74.1	87.3
Household Crimes	195.1	177.1	182.5	176.3	161.9	172.6	180.5
Burglary	86.3	60.4	67.0	58.7	53.9	58.4	55.9
Household larceny	98.1	101.4	101.4	103.5	95.2	98.5	103.5
Motor vehicle theft	10.7	15.4	14.1	14.0	12.7	15.6	21.1

[a]Estimate is based on 10 or less sample cases.

Source: U.S. Department of Justice, *Criminal Victimization in the United States, 1985: A National Crime Survey Report* (Washington, D.C.: Government Printing Office, 1987), pp. 24-25, 30-31.

ever, whites had a higher rate of theft victimization than blacks for persons making less than $7,500 a year.[16] Blacks have higher victimization rates than whites for all household crimes at the highest and lowest income levels.

Education

NCS data reveals that the highest rates of violent crime victimization for persons aged 12 and over occur among those without a high school diploma (Table 8.4). In 1985, persons with only one to three years of high school had the highest victimization rate for crimes of violence, and were followed by persons with five to seven years of schooling. However, violent crime victimization rates were fairly consistent across educational levels.

For crimes of theft, persons with one or more years of college education had higher victimization rates than did persons with lower educational achievement. This association appears to exist in part because of the positive relationship between education and income, as persons in higher income brackets tend to have higher rates of theft victimization than individuals in lower income categories.

When race is considered, blacks at all educational levels have a higher rate of victimization for crimes of violence than do whites or other minorities. Blacks have a higher theft victimization rate than all other races when the level of educational attainment is completion of high school or some college. Whites have the highest victimization rate of all races for crimes of theft when the educational level is one to three years of high school or less.[17]

Marital Status

The victimization rate is highest for persons who have never married or are divorced or separated. As seen in Table 8.5, the rate of violent crime victimization in 1985 for these individuals (aged 12 and over) was more than seven times greater than that for widowed persons and over three times the rate for those who were married. For crimes of theft, persons never married had the highest victimization rate, followed by those divorced or separated. Unmarried persons were more than five times as likely to be victimized by theft as widowed individuals and better than twice as likely as married persons to be victims of theft.

When gender is considered with marital status, victimization data show that the highest rate of violent crime victimization for males is among those who have never married, while female victims of violent crime have the highest rate when divorced or separated. The theft victimization rate for males is highest among those never married, divorced, or separated. The female rate of theft victimization is highest for those never married.[18]

Table 8.4

Victimization Rates for Persons Aged 12 and Over, by Educational Attainment Level and Offense, 1985 (Rate per 1,000 Population Aged 12 and Over)

Level of Education Completed	Crimes of Violence	Rape	Robbery	Assault	Crimes of Theft	Personal Larceny With Contact	Personal Larceny Without Contact
Elementary School							
0-4 years	13.1	0.4[a]	4.5	8.2	22.5	2.7[a]	19.8
5-7 years	34.8	0.1[a]	6.6	28.1	59.3	2.1	57.2
8 years	34.1	0.7[a]	8.9	24.5	57.3	2.8	54.5
High School							
1-3 years	38.9	0.9	6.2	31.9	71.1	2.8	68.3
4 years	27.3	0.9	4.2	22.2	59.6	2.5	57.1
College							
1-3 years	33.5	0.8[a]	5.2	27.5	87.1	2.9	84.2
4 years or more	22.1	0.3[a]	3.5	18.4	89.0	3.1	85.9

[a]Total is derived from 10 or fewer cases.

Source: U.S. Department of Justice, Criminal Victimization in the United States, 1985: A National Crime Survey Report (Washington, D.C.: Government Printing Office, 1987), pp. 26-27.

Table 8.5
Victimization Rates for Persons Aged 12 and Over, by Type of Offense
and Marital Status of Victims, 1985

Type of Crime	Never Married	Married	Widowed	Divorced or Separated
Crimes of Violence	56.0	15.0	17.4	53.4
Rape	1.4	0.2	0.2[a]	1.9
Robbery	9.6	2.2	2.9	9.3
Assault	45.0	12.6	4.4	42.2
Crimes of Theft	107.5	51.2	22.5	90.7
Personal larceny with contact	3.9	1.7	2.3	4.8
Personal larceny without contact	103.6	49.5	20.2	85.9

[a]Estimate is figured on about 10 or less sample cases.

Source: U.S. Department of Justice, *Criminal Victimization in the United States, 1985: A National Crime Survey Report* (Washington, D.C.: Government Printing Office, 1987), p. 20.

Sociodemographic data of crime involvement reveal that criminals and victims generally have similar characteristics. Offenders and victims of violent crimes tend to be of a lower employment, income, and educational level than nonoffenders and nonvictims, and are predominantly unmarried and male. For crimes of theft, offenders tend to come from the lower socioeconomic levels, however victims are more likely to be in higher income brackets. These typologies appear to be especially true for street crimes. More needs to be known about the demographic profile of perpetrators and victims of white-collar criminality. Although white-collar crime may be more widespread than conventional criminality, it has been difficult to examine in detail.

NOTES

1. U.S. Department of Justice, *BJS Data Report, 1986* (Washington, D.C.: Government Printing Office, 1987), p. 46.

2. The study was conducted by the Rand Corporation and cited in "Predatory Crime: The Offender," in Joseph F. Sheley, ed., *Exploring Crime: Readings in Criminology and Criminal Justice* (Belmont, Calif.: Wadsworth, 1987), p. 128.

3. U.S. Department of Justice, *Prisons and Prisoners* (Washington, D.C.: Government Printing Office, 1982).

4. Law Enforcement Assistance Administration, *Profile of State Prison Inmates: Sociodemographic Findings from the 1974 Survey of Inmates of State Correctional Facilities* (Washington, D.C.: Government Printing Office, 1979).

5. *BJS Data Report, 1986.*

6. Cited in Harry E. Allen and Clifford E. Simonsen, *Corrections in America* (New York: Macmillan, 1986), p. 273.

7. U.S. Department of Justice, *Profile of Jail Inmates: Sociodemographic Findings from the 1978 Survey of Inmates of Local Jails* (Washington, D.C.: Government Printing Office, 1980), p. 6.

8. Ibid., p. 607.

9. *BJS Data Report, 1986.*

10. *Profile of Jail Inmates;* U.S. Department of Justice, *Bureau of Justice Statistics Special Report: Examining Recidivism* (Washington, D.C.: Government Printing Office, 1985), p. 6.

11. *Profile of Jail Inmates,* pp. 4-5, 12.

12. U.S. Department of Justice, Bureau of Justice Statistics, *Report to the Nation on Crime and Justice: The Data* (Washington, D.C.: Government Printing Office, 1983), pp. 30-40.

13. *BJS Data Report, 1986.*

14. *Examining Recidivism; Profile of Jail Inmates.*

15. *Profile of Jail Inmates,* p. 4.

16. U.S. Department of Justice, *Crime Victimization in the United States, 1985: A National Crime Survey Report* (Washington, D.C.: Government Printing Office, 1987), pp. 24-25.

17. Ibid., pp. 26-27.

18. Ibid., pp. 3, 20-21.

9

Substance Abuse/Use
and Criminality

The relationship of drug use/abuse and criminal behavior manifests itself in several ways. Foremost perhaps is the possession and use of drugs and alcohol where prohibited by law. This has a wide-ranging effect, since it can involve both legal and illegal drugs as well as drugs (such as alcohol) that are legal for adult users but illegal for minors. Second, drug use can act as a precipitating correlate of violent or serious behavioral patterns. Third, drug users may resort to economic crime as a means to support their habit. A final association between crime and drug use is drug dealing and the often high financial stakes, violence, and other crimes involved in the illicit drug trade. Because of the complicated demography of casual versus abusive drug use and prescription versus illegal drug use, the primary emphasis in this chapter will be on the demographic characteristics of substance abuse and criminality.

WHO IS THE SUBSTANCE ABUSER?

The characteristics of the substance abuser are heterogeneous. Studies have shown that persons who use and abuse alcohol and drugs are old and young, wealthy and poor, educated and undereducated, and of every racial and ethnic background; in short, the abuse of substances has been shown to touch people of every conceivable character profile. Yet there are clear indications of who is most susceptible to substance abuse. A comparative typology of the demographic characteristics of alcoholics, narcotics abusers, and abusers of both alcohol and narcotics was established by Paul Haberman and Michael Baden, who studied 1,954 adults who initially were believed to have died of unnatural causes in New York City during a twelve-month period from 1974 to 1975.[1]

Their findings are summarized in Table 9.1. Fifty-eight percent of the

Table 9.1

Comparative Demographic Profile of Decedent Substance Abusers

Characteristics[a]	Percentage Distribution		
	Alcoholics	Narcotics Abusers	Abusers of Alcohol & Narcotics
Sex			
Male	78.0	83.5	80.6
Female	22.0	16.5	19.4
Race/Ethnicity			
White	42.6	32.8	21.2
Black	39.0	45.4	50.9
Hispanic	18.4	21.8	27.9
Age (at Decease)			
18 to 29	9.5	72.0	42.3
30 to 49	50.4	26.2	51.4
50 and older	40.1	1.8	6.3
Median age	46	26	32
Education[b]			
Less than high school graduate	46.0	55.7	59.5
High school graduate	25.3	28.9	24.8
Post high school	13.9	13.6	8.1
Marital Status[b]			
Never Married	28.9	63.4	57.7
Married	30.5	20.1	19.8
Divorced/widowed	40.0	16.5	21.3
Primary Activity In Year Prior To Death			
Employment	36.7	37.5	24.3
Illness	21.7	8.3	26.1
Substance abuse, nothing, incarceration	14.4	25.4	27.1
Retired	9.8	0.3	0.5
Other[b]	17.3	28.6	22.1
Cause Of Death			
Substance abuse[c]	47.0	54.6	71.6
Natural	7.2	1.8	0.5
Accidental	17.0	5.0	5.9
Suicide	10.5	7.1	4.5
Homicide	18.2	31.6	17.6

[a]Each classification rounds to 100 percent.

[b]Total includes unknown.

[c]Death was caused either singularly by alcoholism or drug abuse, or in relation to another cause of death.

Source: Paul W. Haberman and Michael M. Baden, *Alcohol, Other Drugs and Violent Death* (New York: Oxford University Press, 1978), pp. 56-57.

sample group was identified as having abused alcohol, narcotics, or both. The typology indicates that in every category male abusers outnumbered female abusers by about four to one. Alcoholic decedents were slightly more likely to be white than black, however the black percentage of narcotics

abusers and substance abusers was about half the totals. In each classification, the black and Hispanic percentages were heavily disproportionate
to their population figures.

The median age of the alcoholics was 46, twenty years older than the
average narcotics abuser and 14 years older than those who abused both
drugs. The authors speculated that this generation gap was most responsible
for the differences in marital status of alcoholics and the other groups at the
time of death. The majority of the narcotics abusers and abusers of both
drugs were never married, compared to less than one-third of the
alcoholics. About six out of ten of the abusers of alcohol and narcotics, and
around half of those in the categories of alcoholic and narcotics abuser,
failed to complete high school. Over half the decedents abusing both substances and more than one-third of those abusing alcohol or narcotics
separately spent their last year ill, abusing drugs or alcohol, doing nothing,
or incarcerated. Seventy-two percent of those with both conditions died as a
result of substance abuse, while 55 percent of the narcotics abusers and 47
percent of the alcoholics did so.

These demographic characteristics of substance abusers support earlier
conclusions reached by the researchers and by other studies.[2] However,
since they were based on decedent abusers, all of whom lived in a large urban
setting before their deaths, the typology should be viewed with caution
when making conclusions about all substance abusers. To more fruitfully
examine the relationship between substance abuse and crime requires that
we explore alcohol abuse and drug abuse separately.

ALCOHOL AND CRIME

Arrest Data

The seriousness of alcohol usage and abuses can be seen in the fact that in
1986 roughly one-third of the 10.3 million arrests made were for alcohol-
related offenses. Table 9.2 reflects the percentage of alcohol-associated
arrests by sex, age, race, and ethnic origin in 1986. For the five offenses
most often related to alcohol abuse, either directly or indirectly, the demographic percentages of arrests heavily favored males, persons aged 18 and
over, whites, and non-Hispanics. Of the arrests for directly related alcohol
offenses (driving under the influence, liquor laws, drunkenness), the percentages were even higher for males, those age 18 and over, and whites,
while only slightly lower for non-Hispanics than their overall percentages.

With respect to sex and age, arrest rates for alcohol-related offenses are
highest for males and persons aged 18 and over. However, the rate of arrest
per 100,000 population by race and ethnic origin find that Native
Americans have the highest rate for alcohol-associated offenses, followed

Table 9.2
Percentage Distribution of Alcohol-Related Arrests, by Sex, Age, Race, and Ethnic Origin, 1986

Offense Charged	Total	SEX		AGE			RACE					ETHNIC ORIGIN		
		Male	Female	Total	Under 18	18 & Over	Total	White	Black	Native American	Asian	Total	Hispanic	Non-Hispanic
TOTAL[a]	3,397,334	86.9	13.1	100.0	7.9	92.1	100.0	80.2	14.9	1.5	0.4	100.0	14.0	86.0
Driving under the influence	1,458,531	88.5	11.5	100.0	1.6	98.4	100.0	88.7	9.7	1.1	0.6	100.0	14.2	85.8
Liquor laws	490,436	83.2	16.8	100.0	27.0	73.0	100.0	87.6	9.8	2.0	0.6	100.0	8.8	91.2
Drunkenness	777,866	91.1	8.9	100.0	3.4	96.6	100.0	79.7	17.7	2.3	0.2	100.0	20.0	80.0
ALCOHOL-RELATED TOTAL	2,726,833	88.3	11.7	100.0	6.7	93.3	100.0	85.1	11.9	1.6	0.5	100.0	14.9	85.1
Disorderly conduct	564,882	81.8	18.2	100.0	14.7	85.3	100.0	67.9	30.7	1.1	0.3	100.0	9.5	90.5
Vagrancy	32,992	88.1	11.9	100.0	7.7	92.3	100.0	66.9	29.4	3.1	0.6	100.0	14.9	85.1

[a]Percentages may not add up due to rounding and differences in aggregate participating agencies in some classifications.

Source: Calculated from U.S. Federal Bureau of Investigation, *Crime in the United States: Uniform Crime Reports 1986* (Washington, D.C.: Government Printing Office, 1987).

by blacks. Moreover, Hispanics have a much higher rate of arrest for alcohol offenses than non-Hispanics.[3]

Trends in arrests between 1971 and 1986 show that these demographic characteristics of arrestees for alcohol-related offenses have been remarkably consistent from year to year, though the arrest rate for females has shown a greater increase than that for males in short- and long-term studies.[4]

Alcohol Abuse and Other Crimes

The relationship between alcohol abuse and other forms of criminality has been well documented and is viewed with greater concern than the abuse of alcohol itself. A California study found that 98 percent of the imprisoned felons had used alcohol and 29 percent reported being intoxicated at the time they committed the offense for which they were sent to prison.[5] A survey by the National Institute of Mental Health revealed that the highest incidence of problem-related alcohol abuse occurs among men, single, separated, and divorced people.[6]

Most research on alcohol and crime has focused on violent criminality. In a study of criminal homicide, Marvin Wolfgang and R. B. Strohm found that, in more than 60 percent of the cases, alcohol was used by either the offender or the victim.[7] In a later writing, Wolfgang found that criminal homicides related to alcohol were commonly the most violent.[8] Similar findings emerged from Harwin Voss and John Hepburn's study of homicides in Chicago. They found that in more than half of the 370 cases examined, alcohol was a correlate.[9]

More recently, a report by the Bureau of Justice Statistics showed that more than 50 percent of the jailed inmates convicted of crimes of violence had been drinking prior to committing the crime.[10] Almost 7 out of 10 people convicted of manslaughter had been drinking before the incident, and over 60 percent of the persons convicted of assault had been drinking. Other studies have indicated that between one-third and two-thirds of male sexual aggression against females occurred when the attacker was intoxicated.[11]

The relationship between alcohol, crime, and aggression has been further supported by some research that shows alcoholics to be imprisoned out of proportion to their numbers in the general population.[12] In a report to Congress, the National Institute on Alcohol Abuse and Alcoholism held that "violence, accidental or intentional, constitutes a substantial part of all mortality, illness and impairment in the United States," and suggested that "alcohol often plays a major role in such violent events as motor vehicle accidents . . . crime; suicide; and family abuse."[13]

Other research has linked alcohol abuse to violent and nonviolent crimes. For example, Herbert Bloch and Gilbert Geis have related alcohol to homicide, aggravated assault, and sexual offenses, as well as to property crimes and writing bad checks.[14]

DRUGS AND CRIME

The relationship between drug use and crime may have even more implications than that between alcohol use and crime, since illicit drug use constitutes a crime in itself, whereas for most of the population alcohol use only technically becomes a crime when its abuse results in detectable offenses, such as driving under the influence, or when it contributes to the commission of another crime. Drug abuse is of alarming proportions in this country. In 1985, the National Institute on Drug Abuse found that nearly one in every four Americans aged 12 and older had used drugs during the prior year.[15] It is estimated that each month approximately 20 million people smoke marijuana, 5 to 10 million use cocaine, and more than 4.5 million use stimulants or depressants.

Arrest Data

By comparison, official arrest figures show that in 1986, 691,882 people were arrested for violations of drug abuse laws. When broken down demographically, as is done in Table 9.3, we can see that the proportions of arrests are similar to those for alcohol-related arrests. Arrestees for drug abuse violations are predominantly aged 18 and over, male, white, and non-Hispanic. Blacks and Hispanics are arrested disproportionately. Arrest trends between 1977 and 1986 show these patterns of arrests and the relative differentials to be fairly consistent.[16] Because of the abuse of prescription drugs and the hidden use and abuse of illicit drugs, the actual number of participants in drug abuse is believed to be much closer to estimates than to official data.

Research on Arrestees, Drug Use, and Other Crimes

Several studies of arrested persons have validated the strong relationship between drug use/abuse and criminality. The National Institute of Justice recently found that more than half of the men and women arrested in Washington, D.C., and New York City for serious crimes had been using one or more illicit drugs.[17] Over one-fourth of the arrestees were using more than one drug prior to arrest. Cocaine was the drug of choice for most of the New York arrestees, whereas phencyclidine (PCP) was the most often used drug of the Washington arrestees.

Another Justice Department study conducted in 1987 reported that from one-half to three-quarters of the men arrested for serious crimes in 12 large cities tested positive for recent use of illegal drugs.[18] The study was the first

Table 9.3

Percentage Distribution of Arrests for Drug Abuse Violations, by Age, Sex, Race, and Ethnic Origin, 1986[a]

Offense Charged	Total[b]	A G E		S E X		
		Under 18	18 & Over	Total	Male	Female
Drug abuse violations	691,882	9.9	90.1	100.0	85.5	14.5

Offense Charged	R A C E					ETHNIC ORIGIN		
	Total	White	Black	Native American	Asian	Total	Hispanic	Non-Hispanic
Drug abuse violations	100.0	67.3	31.8	0.4	0.5	100.0	19.9	80.1

[a]Percentages may not correspond to totals due to rounding.

[b]The total shown is for age and sex; race and ethnic origin totals are slightly different in UCR data because of differences in the number of agencies reporting.

Source: Calculated from U.S. Federal Bureau of Investigation, *Crime in the United States: Uniform Crime Reports 1986* (Washington, D.C.: Government Printing Office, 1987).

to test persons nationwide for the use of drugs at the point of arrest. The results led Attorney General Edwin Meese to observe: "Drug abuse by criminal suspects far exceeds the estimated use in the general population, where it appears to be leveling off."[19]

Heroin and Crime. The traditional measuring stick of criminality and drugs has been the use of heroin, the most powerful narcotic. Most studies suggest that heroin addicts engage in crimes primarily to support their habit. Studies of drug-using arrestees by William Eckerman and colleagues[20] and Nicholas Kozel and Robert DuPont[21] concluded that heroin users were more likely to be arrested for income-producing crimes or drug abuse violations than crimes of violence. In a study of Baltimore street addicts, William McAuliffe and Robert Gordon found that 96 percent of the addicts who used drugs daily committed crimes to support their addiction.[22] These crimes included drug dealing, shoplifting, pickpocketing, con games, gambling, robbery, and prostitution.

A study of urban heroin users also found that the diversity and incidence of their criminality was great. The researchers reported that the average heroin user committed approximately 1,000 offenses a year—ranging from robbery, burglary, and property offenses to drug distribution—and that the worst offenders perpetrated drug dealing and robbery in combination.[23] The typology of the sample revealed that most were black or Hispanic males, ages 24 to 40, unemployed, and neither incarcerated nor receiving drug treatment.

Cocaine and Crime. The link between cocaine and crime has only recently begun to attract much attention with the onset of the highly addictive crack cocaine, which is smoked instead of snorted. Crack abusers can become addicted in anywhere from 4 to 10 weeks, compared to around 3 to 4 years on average for regular cocaine users. The National Cocaine Hotline estimates that more than one million Americans nationwide have tried crack.[24] Experts fear that the rapid spread of crack could result in a new era of cocaine addiction in this country that would rival in severity the heroin addiction of the late 1960s.

Recent studies have attributed crack cocaine addiction to many violent and property crimes as well as the sale of the drug.[25] Much of the crack-related crime occurs in predominantly minority, poor, inner-city areas. A recent survey of cocaine users revealed the following: their average age was 27, 60 percent had incomes under $25,000, 75 percent were multiple drug users, and female users had increased relative to male users.[26]

WOMEN AND DRUG ABUSE

Although men far outnumber women in arrests for substance abuse violations, the severity of substance abuse among women can be seen from the fact that in 1986 nearly one-quarter of all crimes for which females were

Table 9.4
Arrest Trends for Substance Abuse Violations, by Offense and Sex, 1977-1986

Offense Charged	MALE			FEMALE		
	1977	1986	Percent Change	1977	1986	Percent Change
Drug abuse violations	410,577	540,976	+31.8	66,810	91,249	+36.6
Driving under the influence	863,775	1,162,713	+34.6	80,569	150,708	+87.1
Liquor laws	229,913	361,637	+57.3	40,653	72,200	+77.6
Drunkenness	971,196	666,330	-31.4	75,925	65,441	-13.8
TOTAL	2,475,461	2,731,656	+92.3	263,957	379,598	+187.5

Source: Adapted from U.S. Federal Bureau of Investigation, Crime in the United States: Uniform Crime Reports 1986 (Washington, D.C.: Government Printing Office, 1987), p. 169.

arrested were drug- or alcohol-related violations of the law.[27] Furthermore, there is some evidence that women substance abusers are narrowing the gap between themselves and men abusers. As seen in Table 9.4, between 1977 and 1986, female arrests for substance abuse violations rose 187.5 percent, more than double the male increase for such arrests over the same period. The greatest increases in female arrests were for driving under the influence (87.1 percent) and liquor laws (77.6 percent). Although female arrests for drunkenness decreased by nearly 14 percent, the number of males arrested for drunkenness dropped 31.4 percent over the 10-year period.

Studies show that at least 60 percent of women nationwide drink alcoholic beverages, and that women as a group have shown the greatest recent increase in alcohol consumption. Female alcoholics drink on the average 11 times as often as nonalcoholic drinkers.[28] Data on the relationship between female alcohol abuse and other crimes are severely limited. However, there is some evidence that women who abuse alcohol are more likely to be involved in domestic crimes than women who do not.[29]

The most important implications of female substance abuse may lie in women's abuse of drugs. Recent surveys have shown a considerably greater incidence of psychotherapeutic drug use (a combination of medical and nonmedical drug use) among females.[30] Cocaine and Valium are believed to be the drugs abused most often by women. Research findings indicate that female addicts commit a range of crimes in order to support their habits, including prostitution, property crimes, and drug sales.[31]

The demographic characteristics of female drug abusers have been established as follows:

• Minority female drug abusers are younger than white female abusers

- Female addicts are older than their male counterparts, usually starting drug usage in their mid-twenties
- Female abusers are more likely to be separated, divorced, or widowed and to have children than male drug abusers
- Female drug addicts have experienced more financial and family-related problems than male addicts
- Female abusers often fail to graduate from high school and have unsuccessful work records
- Female drug abusers tend to have lower self-esteem than female nonaddicts and male addicts[32]

JUVENILES AND SUBSTANCE ABUSE

Perhaps the most serious implications of substance abuse pertain to the use/abuse of alcohol and drugs among our nation's youth. Consider these figures provided by the National Institute on Drug Abuse and the National Council on Alcoholism:

- The average age of initial alcohol use is 12
- The average age of first-time drug use is 13
- One out of every three 12-17 year olds has tried marijuana
- One out of six in this age group continues to smoke marijuana
- Almost one in every five high school seniors has tried cocaine or crack[33]

Further demographic data on substance abuse among teenagers under-score the severity of the problem. Despite attempts to control adolescent alcohol use through "legal drinking ages," which vary from 18 to 21 depending on the state, a recent survey of teenage drinking found that 74 percent of the teens were drinkers, 79 percent of the boys and 70 percent of the girls.[34] The survey established that 19 percent of the sample were prob-lem drinkers (as determined by six or more episodes of drunkenness or at least two "negative consequences" as a result of drinking), 23 percent of the males and 15 percent of the females.

Studies show that drug use among youth is 10 times greater than parents suspect. The United States has the highest rate of adolescent drug use of any industrialized nation.[35] Over 60 percent of high school seniors have used drugs. Forty-one percent of seniors in 1985 admitted to using marijuana in the past year, 26 percent in the prior month, while 13 percent said they had used cocaine in the past year.[36]

Arrest data show that 14.3 percent of the aggregate arrests for persons under age 18 in 1986 were for substance abuse–related offenses, compared to 23 percent of the arrests for persons under age 21.[37] Long-term arrest figures reveal that arrests of juveniles for substance abuse violations are on the decline. From 1977 to 1986, juvenile arrests for these offenses decreased by nearly 75 percent. For male juveniles, the drop was 83 percent, with only liquor law violations showing an increase (10 percent). However, the decline among female juveniles was only 12 percent; they showed increases over the 10-year period for arrests for driving under the influence (39 percent) and liquor laws (38 percent).[38]

The relationship between adolescent substance abuse and other crimes has been established through a number of studies. A recent survey of juvenile and family court judges estimated that between 60 and 90 percent of all juvenile crime is related to alcohol and drug use.[39] Much of the crime of adolescent drug abusers involves drug selling and distribution.[40] However, some studies report that serious juvenile offenders are generally regular users of alcohol and/or drugs.[41]

Contrary to the belief of many professionals—namely, that juvenile substance abusers commit property crimes, such as theft, primarily to support their habits[42] —a study by Cheryl Carpenter and associates found that, from the viewpoint of delinquents, crimes were perpetrated not to buy drugs but "to have fun, to obtain valued goods, or to get money for a variety of purposes."[43] The delinquents indicated that money for alcohol and drug needs could readily be obtained from their normal allowance for "movies, lunch, and records."

EXPLANATIONS FOR THE SUBSTANCE
ABUSE–CRIME RELATIONSHIP

Many general explanations have been applied to the relationship between substance abuse and crime. One is that substance abuse reduces inhibitions (self-control) and increases criminal behavior and the need for money.[44] A second explanation suggests that persistent criminals may use alcohol or drugs to reduce anxiety or as a means to gain courage for planned acts of criminality.[45] A third reason given for the association of crime and substance abuse is previous criminal tendencies and background factors (such as abuse, delinquency, poverty, peers, and broken homes).[46] A final explanation pertains to group norms about how people under the influence of drugs or alcohol should act. For example, among some groups, drunkenness is tolerated or accepted by convention as a way to relax even if behavior resulting from it is aggressive or criminal.

Many dismiss the idea that there is a direct relationship between substance abuse and other crimes, preferring to believe that criminals, like noncriminals, have the freedom to choose whether or not to commit crimes, regardless of substance use or abuse. There appears to be some merit to this argument, considering the studies that show criminal involvement of alcohol and drug abusers prior to their substance use or addiction.[47] Overall, more study is needed into the causes and effects of substance abuse and its relationship to criminal behavior.

FIGHTING SUBSTANCE ABUSE

Clearly there is a strong relationship between substance abuse as a crime itself and other forms of criminality. This suggests that controlling substance abuse will at once mitigate much of our crime problem. Recent years have seen many legislative attempts to toughen substance abuse laws. In the 1980s, there have been more than 200 new drunken-driving statutes, and many states have sought to control drug abuse by toughening drug laws and considering antiparaphernalia legislation to criminalize the manufacture, distribution, and sale of drug-related paraphernalia.[48] Despite the progress being made, the statistics tell us we still have a long way to go in the fight against drug and alcohol abuse.

Substance abuse is related to crime both as a direct violation of the law and for its association with other crimes. The majority of substance abusers tend to be male, white, unmarried, undereducated, of low income, and have unsteady employment histories. Minority members are disproportionately represented among drug and alcohol abusers. Substance abuse among women is on the rise. However, what may be most unsettling is the epidemic proportions of alcohol and drug use by youth. Crack cocaine is the latest and possibly deadliest drug to hit the country. Its full ramifications, in the form of drug abuse and crime, have yet to be felt. Efforts to contain substance abuse still are falling far short of what is needed.

NOTES

1. Paul W. Haberman and Michael M. Baden, *Alcohol, Other Drugs and Violent Death* (New York: Oxford University Press, 1978).

2. Ibid.

3. Ronald B. Flowers, *Minorities and Criminality* (Westport, Conn.: Greenwood Press, 1988).

4. U.S. Federal Bureau of Investigation, *Crime in the United States: Uniform Crime Reports [1971-]1986* (Washington, D.C.: Government Printing Office, 1971-1986 [various reports]).

5. Cited in Martin R. Haskell and Lewis Yablonsky, *Criminology: Crime and Criminality* (Chicago: Rand McNally, 1974).

6. As cited in Brent Q. Hafen and Molly J. Brog, *Alcohol*, 2d ed. (St. Paul, Minn.: West, 1983), p. 18.

7. Marvin Wolfgang and R. B. Strohm, "The Relationship Between Alcohol and Criminal Homicide," *Quarterly Journal of Studies on Alcoholism* 17 (1956): 411-26.

8. Marvin E. Wolfgang, *Patterns in Criminal Homicide* (Philadelphia: University of Pennsylvania Press, 1958).

9. Harwin L. Voss and John R. Hepburn, "Patterns in Criminal Homicide in Chicago," *Journal of Criminal Law, Criminology, and Political Science* 59 (1968): 499-508.

10. Cited in "U.S. Study Cites Role of Alcohol in Crimes," *New York Times* (November 4, 1985): A12 (L).

11. Paul H. Gebhard, John H. Gagnon, Wardell B. Pomeroy, and Cornelia V. Christenson, *Sex Offenders: An Analysis of Types* (New York: Bantam, 1967); Menachem Amir, *Patterns in Forcible Rape* (Chicago: University of Chicago Press, 1971). See also Erich Goode, "Drugs and Crime," in Abraham S. Blumberg, ed., *Current Perspectives on Criminal Behavior: Essays on Criminology*, 2d ed. (New York: Knopf, 1981), pp. 227-72.

12. D. N. Hancock, "Alcohol and Crime," in G. Edwards and M. Grant, eds., *Alcoholism: New Knowledge and New Responses* (London: Croom Helm, 1977), pp. 264-70; L. W. Gerson, "Alcohol Consumption and the Incidence of Violent Crime," *Journal for the Study of Alcoholism* 40 (1978): 307-12.

13. As quoted in Robert Straus, "The Social Costs of Alcohol," in Edith Gomberg, Helene White, and John A. Carpenter, eds., *Alcohol, Science and Society Revisited* (Ann Arbor: University of Michigan Press, 1982), p. 143.

14. Cited in Joseph F. Sheley, *Exploring Crime: Readings in Criminology and Criminal Justice* (Belmont, Calif.: Wadsworth, 1987), p. 149. See also Herbert A. Bloch and Gilbert Geis, *Man, Crime, and Society* (New York: Random House, 1962).

15. As cited in Rory O'Connor, "Getting High on It: Drug Abuse is Big Business," *Vogue* 177 (January 1987): 209. See also "A 'Rite of Passage' More Young People Avoid," *Scholastic Update* 117 (May 10, 1985): 14.

16. *Uniform Crime Reports, 1986.*

17. Cited in "Wide Drug Use Found in People Held in Crimes," *New York Times* (June 4, 1986): A14.

18. Cited in Peter Kerr, "Study: Drugs Play Key Crime Role," *Sacramento Bee* (January 22, 1988): A19.

19. Cited in Ibid.

20. William C. Eckerman, J. D. Bates, J. Valley Rachal, and W. K. Poole, *Drug Usage and Arrest Charges: A Study of Drug Usage and Arrest Charges Among Arrestees in Six Metropolitan Areas of the United States* (Washington, D.C.: Government Printing Office, 1971).

21. Nicholas J. Kozel and Robert L. DuPont, *Criminal Charges and Drug Use Patterns of Arrestees in the District of Columbia* (Rockville, Md.: National Institute on Drug Abuse, 1977).

22. William E. McAuliffe and Robert A. Gordon, "A Test of Lindesmith's Theory of Addiction: The Frequency of Euphoria Among Long-Term Addicts," *American Journal of Sociology* 79 (1974): 795-840.

23. "Heroin and Crime: A Stronger Link," *Science News* 126 (1984): 343.

24. Cited in "Crack: A Cheap and Deadly Cocaine is a Spreading Menace," *Time* 127 (June 2, 1986): 16-18.

25. Ibid.; "Crack's Deadly Cycle," *Macleans* 99 (1986): 44-45.

26. "Cocaine Survey Shows Poorer, Younger Users," *Jet* (July 15, 1985): 31.

27. *Uniform Crime Reports, 1986,* p. 181.

28. Haberman and Baden, *Alcohol, Other Drugs and Violent Death,* pp. 12-13.

29. Ronald B. Flowers, *Women and Criminality: The Woman as Victim, Offender, and Practitioner* (Westport, Conn.: Greenwood Press, 1987), pp. 107-15.

30. Ibid., p. 142.

31. Ibid., p. 143; James A. Inciardi, "Women, Heroin and Property Crime," in Susan K. Datesman and Frank R. Scarpitti, eds., *Women, Crime, and Justice* (New York: Oxford University Press, 1980).

32. Flowers, *Women and Criminality*, p. 143.

33. Cited in Ken Barun, "How to Help Your Children Stay Off Drugs," *Parade Magazine* (May 1, 1988): 15.

34. Cited in Haberman and Baden, *Alcohol, Other Drugs and Violent Death*, pp. 18-19.

35. "How to Stop Teen Drug Use," *Consumer's Research* 70 (1987): 27-31.

36. Ibid., p. 27.

37. *Uniform Crime Reports, 1986*, p. 180.

38. Ibid., pp. 168-69.

39. Curtis J. Sltomer, "Drugs, Drink and Youth Crime," *Christian Science Monitor* (November 18, 1985): 3.

40. Ibid.; Cheryl Carpenter, Barry Glassner, Bruce D. Johnson, and Julia Loughlin, *Kids, Drugs, and Crime* (Lexington, Mass.: Lexington Books, 1988), p. 9.

41. Carpenter et al., *Kids, Drugs, and Crime*, pp. 10-11, 219; David H. Hirizinga, "The Relationship Between Delinquent and Drug Use Behaviors in a National Sample of Youths," in Bruce D. Johnson and Eric Walsh, eds., *Crime Rates Among Drug Abusing Offenders* (New York: Interdisciplinary Research Center, 1986), pp. 145-94.

42. See, for example, Eric Walsh and Bruce D. Johnson, "The Impact of Substance Abuse on Criminal Careers," in Alfred Blumstein, Jacqueline Cohen, Jeffrey A. Rother, and Christy A. Visher, eds., *Criminal Careers and "Criminal Abusers,"* vol. 2 (Washington, D.C.: National Academy Press, 1986), pp. 52-88.

43. Carpenter et al., *Kids, Drugs, and Crime*, p. 220.

44. H. Abelson, R. Cohen, D. Schrayer, and M. Rappeport, "Drug Experiences, Attitudes and Related Behavior Among Adolescents and Adults," in National Commission on Marijuana and Drug Abuse, ed. *Drug Use in America: Problem in Perspective*, vol. 1. (Washington, D.C.: Government Printing Office, 1973), pp. 488-608.

45. James J. Collins, Jr., *Alcohol Use and Criminal Behavior: An Executive Summary* (Washington, D.C.: National Institute of Justice, 1981).

46. Ronald B. Flowers, *Children and Criminality: The Child as Victim and Perpetrator* (Westport, Conn.: Greenwood Press, 1986).

47. James A. Inciardi, "Heroin Use and Street Crime," *Crime and Delinquency* 25 (1979) 335-46; Duane C. McBride and Richard R. Clayton, "Methodological Issues in the Etiology of Drug Abuse," *Journal of Drug Issues* (Fall 1985): 509-29.

48. "A 'Rite of Passage': Drunk Drivers Turn to the Bar," *Time* 123 (January 16, 1984): 62; "War on Alcohol Abuse Spreads to New Fronts," *U.S. News & World Report* 97 (December 24, 1984): 63.

III

DEMOGRAPHIC CHARACTERISTICS OF DEVIANT GROUPS

10

Chronic Offenders

A variety of terms have been used to refer to the chronic or habitual offender, including "career criminal," "hardened offender," "repeat offender," and, for some, a "born criminal." Where most criminologists agree is that the chronic offender is a person who has been actively involved in criminal participation repeatedly, habitually, and often over a period of time ranging anywhere from years to decades. In recent years the study of chronic offenders and their role in the overall crime problem has intensified and influenced the direction of the criminal justice system and its strategies for crime control. The emphasis in this chapter will be limited primarily to the demographic correlates and characteristics of the chronic offender.

RESEARCH METHODOLOGIES FOR STUDYING CHRONIC OFFENDERS

Before we actually examine the characteristics of habitual offenders, it might be useful briefly to review the most common research strategies used to establish career offender profiles. Most studies of chronic offenders are retrospective studies of officially known offenders (persons arrested or incarcerated). These studies generally rely on official data of criminal careers, but some also use self-report data to obtain information about the past criminal histories of offenders. (Refer to Chapter 1 for the strengths and weaknesses of official and self-report data). Recent retrospective studies of known criminals by the Rand Corporation utilized official records and self-report measures to study the previous criminality of 2,190 male inmates of jails and prisons in three states. The studies, which were primarily interested in discovering the volume of crime committed by the men during the one- to two-year period just before entering prison to serve their current terms, found that the men who were offenders in both adolescence and young adulthood were the most active as criminals during the one- to two-year stretch.[1]

Prospective studies of officially known criminals are the second most common type of study of career criminals. These studies also start with a group of known (arrested or imprisoned) offenders; however, in addition to reviewing previous career-crime patterns, they track offenders' progression in time, generally for a period of several years. Some prospective studies also rely on self-report surveys to obtain a more complete picture of the career criminal. The Justice Department's Office of Juvenile Justice and Delinquency Prevention has announced its sponsorship of three prospective studies—at the University of Colorado, the University of Pittsburgh, and the State University of New York at Albany—to track the development of individual criminals. Various cohorts, beginning with six-year-olds, will be followed up periodically over a minimum of five years. The combined sample groups will total around 6,000.[2] One completed prospective study of known offenders was conducted by the FBI in a follow-up of 4,363 parolees. Within two years of release from prison, almost two-thirds of the sample had been rearrested at least one time. The rearrest rate of young adult parolees was 67 percent, compared to a rate of under 50 percent for middle-aged parolees.[3]

Prospective studies of the general public are a third type of study that analyzes chronic offenders. It is the least utilized type in the research community. The most notable example of such a study is a birth cohort study by Marvin Wolfgang, Robert Figlio, and Thorsten Sellin, in which all the males born in Philadelphia in 1945 who lived in the city between their 10th and 18th birthdays were identified, and their criminal and noncriminal careers were followed from adolescence through young adulthood. This will be discussed later in the chapter; however one important finding of the study was that males who were criminals in adolescence were nearly four times more likely to be criminals in young adulthood than were males who were noncriminals as adolescents.[4]

GENERAL CHARACTERISTICS OF CHRONIC OFFENDERS

Research on repeat offenders has revealed the following:[5]

- One of the strongest predictors of future and continual criminality is the early onset of criminal behavior
- Chronic offenders constitute a relatively small proportion of aggregate offenders, yet are responsible for a very high proportion of the total crime
- The average criminal career is between 5 and 10 years
- Males are considerably more likely to be chronic offenders than females

- Minorities are disproportionately likely to be chronic offenders
- Criminal careers peak in the late teens and decline steadily with successive age groups
- Chronic offenders continuing criminal careers in their 30s tend to be the most persistent offenders
- Habitual offenders commit a disproportionately large amount of urban street crimes
- Substance abuse is strongly related to high-frequency criminal behavior
- Few chronic offenders are "career" offenders in that crime is their full-time or sole occupation or source of income
- Career violent offenders generally begin and remain as violent criminals
- Habitual offenders' crimes tend to vary between misdemeanors and felonies as well as violent and property crimes

A profile of the characteristics of habitual offenders was developed by Joan Petersilia, Peter Greenwood, and Marvin Lavin, based on their study of 49 chronic offender inmates in California whose criminal careers averaged 20 years.[6] The researchers divided the offenders into intensive types (those who regarded themselves as career criminals) and intermittent types (opportunistic, yet did not view themselves as career criminals). Based on these classifications, the following characteristics emerged:

- Intensive offenders were more likely to preplan their crimes
- Burglary was much more profitable to intensive offenders than to intermittent offenders
- As juvenile offenders, most intensives perpetrated crimes alone, whereas most intermittents tended to have accomplices
- A higher percentage of intensive offenders than intermittents committed a serious crime prior to age 13
- A larger percentage of intermittents were incarcerated prior to age 18
- A greater proportion of intensive offenders were involved with drugs and alcohol; intermittents were more likely to be associated with alcohol alone
- Intermittent offenders were more likely to be better employed
- A greater proportion of intensive offenders were violent and had violent backgrounds
- Intermittents were five times as likely to be arrested as adult career criminals; however, overall, intensives were arrested slightly more often than intermittent offenders
- Intermittent criminals had higher conviction and incarceration rates for nondrug arrests

ADULT CHRONIC OFFENDERS

The most comprehensive study of the characteristics of the adult career criminal is a retrospective self-report study conducted by the Census Bureau for the Bureau of Justice Statistics.[7] The survey of state prisoners nation-wide included a sample of 11,397 men and women, representing approximately 275,000 state prisoners who were old enough to have been able to establish a career in criminality covering several decades (age 40 and over). The sample from which most of the results were based was composed of 827 men who entered prison in at least middle age (age 40 or older), and represented approximately 24,398 inmates across the country. The following section contains sociodemographic results of the survey.

Types of Career Criminals

The study identified four career criminal types based on the absence or existence of criminality during three of life's primary stages: adolescence, young adulthood, and middle age (see Table 10.1). Type 1 offenders were criminals in all three stages; Type 2, in adolescence and middle age; Type 3, in young adulthood and middle age; and Type 4, only in middle age. Nearly 47 percent of the men incarcerated in middle age were Type 4 offenders, or career criminals who had no record of imprisonment during adolescence or young adulthood. Thirty-eight percent were Type 3 offenders, those who were criminals in each stage aside from adolescence. Only 1 percent were Type 2 offenders, and 14 percent were Type 1 criminals who were involved in crime over each life stage.

Type 4 criminals were the most likely to be imprisoned for committing violent crimes, with the percentage declining as the offender type lowered. In three of the four types, there was little differentiation in the percentage of those incarcerated currently or previously for a crime of violence, though Type 1 criminals were the most likely by a slight margin.

Table 10.2 provides a more detailed breakdown of the offenses for which career criminals were serving time. The most significant category—violent crimes—reveals that although Type 4 offenders represented 46.6 percent of the prisoners, they constituted more than half of the total for the most serious crimes such as murder, rape, and lewd acts with children. The data show that Type 4 prisoners also committed a disproportionate share of the public order crimes, which some theorize were committed in relation with more serious criminal acts.

Type 3 offenders perpetrated the bulk of the remaining offenses for which career criminals were in prison and for some violent offenses (attempted murder, robbery, and other violent crimes) exceeded the percentage of Type 4 offenders. Type 3 offenders were also imprisoned more often than Type 4 offenders for most property crimes and all drug offenses.

Table 10.1
Four Types of Career Criminals

Adolescence: Ages 7-17	Young Adulthood: Ages 18-39	Middle Age: Age 40+	Type	Middle-aged Inmates	Career Type Percent	
					Presently Imprisoned for a Violent Crime	Presently or Previously Incarcerated for a Violent Crime
Criminal	Criminal →	Criminal	1	14.0	46.6	69.1
	Noncriminal →	Criminal	2	1.2[a]	51.1[a]	60.5[a]
Noncriminal	Criminal →	Criminal	3	38.2	54.1	68.7
	Noncriminal →	Criminal	4	46.6	66.4	67.6

[a]Estimate based on 10 or less cases is statistically unreliable.

Source: U.S. Department of Justice, Bureau of Justice Statistics Special Report: Career Patterns in Crime (Washington, D.C.: Government Printing Office, 1983), pp. 2-3.

Table 10.2
Offenses for Which Offenders Are Imprisoned, by Number and Distribution
of Offenses and Criminal Career Type

Offense	Number of Offenses[a]	Career Type (Percent Distribution)				Total[b]
		1	2	3	4	
Violent	15,494	11.6%	1.0%[c]	35.7%	51.7%	100%
Murder	3,920	6.2	1.6[c]	27.6	64.7	100
Attempted murder	537	16.4	0.0[c]	45.4	38.2	100
Manslaughter	2,382	10.5	1.1[c]	33.7	54.7	100
Kidnapping	315	17.5	0.0[c]	27.1	55.4	100
Rape, sexual assault	1,892	11.8	0.0[c]	30.3	57.9	100
Lewd act with child	554	0.0	0.0[c]	25.5	74.5	100
Robbery	2,763	23.2	0.0[c]	46.6	30.3	100
Assault	2,959	9.0	2.2[c]	41.6	47.2	100
Extortion	57[c]	0.0	0.0[c]	47.4	52.6	100
Other violent	114[c]	24.3	0.0[c]	51.3	24.3	100
Property	7,410	23.9	2.4[c]	44.2	29.5	100
Burglary	2,542	32.9	1.2[c]	37.6	28.3	100
Forgery, fraud	1,721	13.3	1.7[c]	57.1	27.9	100
Larceny-theft	1,792	26.8	4.9[c]	40.1	28.2	100
Arson	279[c]	10.0	10.0[c]	30.1	50.1	100
Other property	1,076	18.4	0.0[c]	50.1	31.9	100
Drug	2,713	16.7	1.0[c]	54.8	27.6	100
Trafficking	1,369	16.4	0.0[c]	48.0	35.6	100
Possession	1,139	20.0	2.5[c]	60.2	17.4	100
Other drug	205	0.0	0.0[c]	69.8	30.7	100
Public order/other	3,776	10.6	0.7[c]	32.4	56.4	100
Weapons	934	13.0	2.9[c]	27.7	56.4	100
Traffic	1,233	4.5	0.0[c]	28.0	67.4	100
Other	1,609	13.8	0.0[c]	38.5	47.9	100

[a]The number of offenses is greater than the number of inmates because some inmates were imprisoned for more than one offense.

[b]Detail may not add to total because of rounding. Estimated values of less than about 300 are based on too few cases to be statistically reliable.

[c]Estimate based on 10 or fewer cases is statistically unreliable.

Source: U.S. Department of Justice, *Bureau of Justice Statistics Special Report: Career Patterns in Crime* (Washington, D.C.: Government Printing Office, 1983), p. 3.

Employment

Type 1 criminals were the most likely, at 30 percent, to have been without employment in the month prior to the crime that led to their imprisonment. In total, 22.5 percent of the prisoners were out of work at the time of their imprisonment crime; this compared to an 8.6 percent unemployment rate for men aged 45 to 54 in the general public at the time of the survey.

Income

In the year prior to the arrest that resulted in their incarceration, Type 1 offenders were the most likely, at 8.5 percent, to have been receiving welfare assistance. Type 1 and Type 3 offenders were the most likely to have been receiving illegal income in the year prior to their arrest and current imprisonment.

Educational Attainment

Forty-one percent of all the prisoners had less than a ninth grade education, with only slight variation between the offender types. By comparison, only around 16 percent of the general public between ages 45 and 54 had less than a ninth grade education during the year of the study.

Marital Status

In total, 15.4 percent of the offenders had never been married. Type 1 and Type 3 inmates were the most likely to have never been married. The aggregate percentage of never-married, middle-aged prisoners is more than three times that of a survey of the males in the general public between the ages of 41 and 50.

Family Dynamics

Of the prisoners who were never married, almost 25 percent had children. Type 1 and Type 3 prisoners were the most likely to have had children outside of marriage. More than one-fourth of the offenders came from families in which at least one family member had a record of imprisonment. Nearly 50 percent of the Type 1 offenders fell into this category, compared to just over 17 percent of the Type 4 inmates.

Substance Abuse

The majority of the inmates, irrespective of career type, had a severe alcohol problem. Nearly two-thirds of the offenders were in an alcohol abuse treatment program at some stage of their lives. About half had been under the influence of alcohol at the time of the offense that led to their arrest and detention, and around one-third were drunk at the time. Drug use was most evident among Type 1 and Type 3 offenders. In combination, they constituted 85 percent of the heroin users and 79 percent of the hashish and marijuana users.

JUVENILE HABITUAL OFFENDERS

The most important work on chronic juvenile offenders has been accomplished by Marvin Wolfgang and his colleagues. The researchers undertook two Philadelphia birth cohort studies. The first, which traced the criminal history of 9,945 males born in 1945 who resided in Philadelphia between ages 10 and 18, found that 6.3 percent of the cohort and 18 percent of the delinquent group were chronic offenders (they had been arrested five times or more).[8] These habitual offenders accounted for nearly 52 percent of the aggregate delinquent offenses perpetrated by the cohort, 19 percent of which were crimes against the person.

The second study was of all the males and females born in Philadelphia in 1958 who lived there from 1968 to 1975.[9] This cohort study found that of the 27,160 children aged 10 to 17, only 7 percent were considered chronically delinquent, yet they accounted for 75 percent of all serious offenses in their age bracket. Although the study revealed that approximately the same percentage of juveniles committed crimes in each generation, habitual offenders in the second study committed more crimes and more serious crimes. The aggregate violent crime rate for the second delinquent group was three times higher and the robbery rate was five times greater.[10]

Males were more than two-and-a-half times more likely than females to be chronic juvenile offenders. No significant differences were shown between white and black delinquents. However, a violent delinquency cohort study of males and females born in Columbus, Ohio, between 1956 and 1960 who had been arrested by Columbus police at least one time for a violent crime and who lived within the surrounding Franklin County during their delinquent years, found that blacks were disproportionately involved in chronic violent delinquency and were more likely than whites to be repeat offenders in robbery. White youths, however, were shown to be arrested slightly more often for rape and assault.[11] The Wolfgang and associates study found that almost half of the juveniles who perpetrated four serious crimes were never incarcerated or placed on probation.

The research indicates that although chronic offenders represent a small proportion of the criminal element, they commit a disproportionate share of total offenses and violent crimes. As a result, the criminal justice system has put more emphasis in recent years on toughening arrest and incarceration policies for this group. There have been inconsistent findings on the primary age range of habitual criminals. Most studies show that criminal careers peak in the late teens or early twenties. However, some studies suggest that many criminal careers are still going strong well into their forties, and that older criminals tend to be the most hardened. Chronic offenders are typically male, unmarried, under- or unemployed, undereducated, and have some involvement with substance use or abuse. Blacks tend to be overrepresented as habitual offenders, yet race does not appear to be a significant determinant of a career in crime or delinquency.

NOTES

1. P. W. Greenwood, *Selective Incapacitation* (Santa Monica, Calif.: Rand Corporation, 1982); J. M. Chaiken and M. R. Chaiken, *Varieties of Criminal Behavior* (Santa Monica, Calif.: Rand Corporation, 1982).

2. Cited in "Growing Focus on Criminal Careers," *Science* 233 (1986): 1377-78.

3. C. M. Kelley, *Crime in the United States: Uniform Crime Reports, 1974* (Washington, D.C.: Government Printing Office, 1975).

4. Marvin E. Wolfgang, Robert M. Figlio, and Thorsten Sellin, *Delinquency in a Birth Cohort* (Chicago: University of Chicago Press, 1972). See also Marvin E. Wolfgang, "From Boy to Man—From Delinquency to Crime," in U.S. Department of Justice, ed., *The Serious Juvenile Offender: Proceedings of a National Symposium* (Washington, D.C.: Office of Juvenile Justice and Delinquency Prevention, 1981).

5. See, for example, Wolfgang, Figlio and Sellin, *Delinquency in a Birth Cohort;* Alfred Blumstein and Jacqueline Cohen, "Characterizing Criminal Careers," *Science* 237 (1987): 985-91.

6. Joan Petersilia, Peter Greenwood, and Marvin Lavin, *Criminal Careers of Habitual Felons* (Washington, D.C.: National Institute of Justice, 1978).

7. U.S. Department of Justice, *Bureau of Justice Statistics Special Report: Career Patterns in Crime* (Washington, D.C.: Government Printing Office, 1983).

8. Wolfgang, Figlio, and Sellin, *Delinquency in a Birth Cohort.*

9. Cited in "Study Tells of Role of Chronic Juvenile Criminals," *New York Times* (December 8, 1985): 61(L).

10. M. E. Wolfgang and P. E. Tracy, "The 1945 and 1958 Birth Cohorts: A Comparison of the Prevalence, Incidence, and Severity of Delinquent Behavior" (Paper presented at the Conference on Public Danger, Dangerous Offenders and the Criminal Justice System, Harvard University, Cambridge, Mass., February 11-12, 1982).

11. John P. Conrad, *The Dangerous and the Endangered* (Lexington, Mass.: Lexington Books, 1985), pp. 44-45.

Family Violence

Unquestionably one of the biggest and most complex problems in the United States today is the problem of family violence. Although this issue has received considerable attention in recent years, the truth is that not nearly enough is known about the variables, range, and incidence of violence in the family. It is known that 11 percent to 52 percent of all assaults are intrafamilial,[1] 12 percent to 18 percent of the murders in the United States each year are spouse murders,[2] and domestic violence calls are among the most frequent and perilous for law enforcement officers.[3]

Estimating the extent of family violence has proven to be particularly frustrating, owing in part to the innumerable, often conflicting data available on the subject. Official statistics give us little information on the incidence of domestic violence since such crimes as marital rape are not broken down in rape statistics, while other crimes, such as nonaggravated assault, are not reported to the FBI.

The closest thing to an official measurement of family violence is the number of persons arrested for "offenses against family and children." In 1986 this total was 47,327.[4] This figure illustrates the unreported nature of family violence, particularly in light of the NCS estimate that its program uncovers 450,000 cases of family violence annually.[5]

In this chapter, we will confine our focus on family violence primarily to the demographic characteristics of its perpetrators and a brief review of theories of family violence.

CHILD ABUSE

Incidence

Child abuse is the most studied form of family violence. Estimates of the incidence of child abuse range from the National Center on Child Abuse and Neglect's estimate[6] that 1 million children are abused annually in the United States to David Gil's approximation that anywhere from 2.5 million to 4 million children are victimized by their parents each year.[7] Studies have shown that between 84 percent and 97 percent of all families engage in spanking, the most common form of family violence.[8] A national study by Murray Straus and his associates of 2,143 American families with children aged 3 to 17 at home during the year of the survey found that, among the families in which the following had "ever happened," 8 percent of the children were kicked, punched, or bitten approximately 9 times per year; 4 percent were beaten about 6 times yearly; and 3 percent were victimized by a knife or gun.[9]

Gender

Research into the gender of abusing parents seems to indicate that mothers are more likely to abuse their children than fathers. Richard Gelles's study revealed that 94 percent of the mothers, compared to only 65 percent of the fathers sampled, physically abused their children at least once.[10] Brandt Steele and C. Pollock found that the mother was the abuser in 50 of the 57 abuse cases studied.[11] However, some data have shown parental abuse to be more evenly distributed.[12] It is important to note that because of definitional variations in child abuse and methodological differences in studies, comparisons of various results are not always reliable.

Age

The majority of child abusers range in age from 20 to 40, the typical child-bearing, child-rearing years. Gil's sample found that 71 percent of the mothers or mother substitutes and 66 percent of the fathers or father substitutes fell into this age bracket.[13] Blair and Rita Justice also found from their research that 75 percent of their sample group was between the ages of 20 and 40.[14]

Race

The relationship between race and child abuse has failed to establish a consistent pattern in the literature. Official data have shown child abuse to be more prevalent among blacks than whites.[15] However, some studies have contended that the rate of child abuse in black and white families is similar.[16] Other research such as the recent National Study of the Incidence and Severity of Child Abuse and Neglect has indicated that child abuse is actually lower in black families than in white families.[17] In addition to the inconsistency of data on race and child abuse, such research often fails to study the relationship between child abuse and other racial/ethnic groups besides blacks and whites, leaving a void in the findings.

Socioeconomics

Most research points toward a higher incidence of child abuse among families of low income, low occupational, and low educational status. A study by E. Bennie and A. Sclare found that 8 out of 10 child abuse cases involved low-income families.[18] Gil's study found that most of the abusive parents were not high school graduates and that nearly half of the abusers were unemployed during some stage of the year preceding the child abuse.[19] Numerous other studies have supported the association between child abuse and socioeconomic variables. Yet most agree that child abuse occurs at all socioeconomic levels and that middle- and upper-class abusers are better able to hide their abuse because they have better resources and there is less reporting of abuse cases.

Intergenerational Child Abuse

There is solid evidence that a cycle of violence exists among most child abusers. That is, it appears that an individual who was abused as a child is more likely to become an abuser in adulthood than an individual whose childhood was not characterized by domestic violence. One study reported that 75 percent of the parents in the sample group who sexually abused their children were themselves sexually abused as children.[20] Vincent Fontana posited that abusive parents are a reflection of parents who were unloving, cruel, and brutal,[21] a contention shared by Christopher Ounsted and colleagues whose sample confirmed the hypothesis that abusive parents often come from families where violence has existed for generations.[22] Although much controversy surrounds this approach, most research indicates that there is some association between child abuse and an abusive history of one form or another.

Substance Abuse and Child Abuse

Several studies have found a relationship between child abuse and substance abuse. D. W. Behling's study of alcohol-related child abuse at a large clinic found that 84 percent of the abused children had at least one parent that abused alcohol, and 65 percent of the suspected child abusers were alcoholics or abused alcohol.[23] Other studies have documented an association between drug abuse and temper tantrums directed at children as well as sexual abuse of children.[24] Brandt Steele reported that chronic alcohol or drug abuse can "cause severe distortions of mental functioning," which may result in child abuse or other forms of violence.[25]

SPOUSE ABUSE

Incidence

Because of vast underreporting and the complex, secretive nature of spouse abuse, no one can be any more certain of its prevalence than one can about child abuse. However, there is every reason to believe that the incidence of spouse or marital violence is high and often severe. Gelles found that 55 percent of his sample of married partners had experienced at least one episode of violence.[26] Murray Straus estimated that 65 percent of all married couples engage in some type of physical violence over the course of the relationship, with 25 percent being of a serious nature.[27]

Wife battering is believed to be the most severe, if not most frequent, form of spouse abuse. According to official statistics, a woman is beaten or abused by her husband every 18 seconds in this country.[28] Sociologists estimate that upwards of two million American women are battered annually.[29] Some suggest it is closer to twice this figure.[30]

Estimates on husband abuse are equally striking. Robert Langley and Richard Levy approximate that 12 million American men are the victims of physical abuse by their wife during some point in their marriage.[31] Suzanne Steinmetz estimates that 280,000 men in this country are battered each year.[32] An extrapolation of an analysis of spouse abuse findings produced a nationwide estimate of 2 million husbands, compared to 1.8 million wives, who had experienced at least one of the more severe forms of spouse violence.[33]

Gender

It has long been generally believed that the typical offender-victim pattern of spousal abuse is that of the male being the aggressor. Gelles found that 47 percent of the husbands in his sample, compared to 32 percent of the wives, had ever been violent.[34] A study of college students revealed that 16.7 percent of their fathers and 10 percent of their mothers had physically abused the other parent during the students' senior year in high school.[35]

Official data support the contention that male partners are more abusive than female partners. Police reports indicate that husband-perpetrated abuse complaints outnumber wife-perpetrated abuse complaints by a ratio of about 12 to 1.[36] Similarly, NCS victimization data found a rate of 13 abused wives for every abused husband.[37] Research by Rebecca Emerson Dobash and Russell Dobash yielded a ratio of male to female spouse violence of 66 to 1.[38]

There are others, however, who have challenged the traditional notions about patterns of marital violence. Straus and associates found approximately equal aggregate rates of marital abuse among men and women, with women perpetrating more serious violent acts than men.[39] Steinmetz published a controversial article which posited that husband abuse was in fact the most underreported form of domestic violence.[40]

Although the ratio of male to female marital violence continues to be a matter of debate, overall the evidence suggests that males inflict the more severe violence in the relationship. For instance, recent studies show that wives constitute about 52 percent of the murdered spouses, with husbands being six to seven times more likely to have initiated the violent dispute resulting in the death.[41]

Marital Status

Conjugal violence is generally expressed in terms of legally married couples. However, as many unmarried couples cohabitate in an otherwise full-fledged relationship, it is important to differentiate the levels of violence of unmarried and married intimates. Studies indicate that nonmarried couples appear to exhibit more violent behavior than do legally married spouses. In examining a sample of couples from a national family violence survey, K. Yllo and M. A. Straus found that cohabitating couples reported more violent incidents than did married couples.[42] Other research has shown that a disproportionate number of cohabitating couples engaged in violence.[43] These studies contradict traditional views that nonmarried couples are less violent owing to the absence of the pressures associated with the legal constraints of the marital contract.

Race

Unlike the sketchy relationship between race and child abuse, there seems to be a more definitive pattern in race and spousal violence research. The findings of Straus and associates show the rate of spouse abuse among black couples to be more than double that among white couples.[44] The rate of wife abuse was three times greater for blacks than whites, and husband abuse was twice as high. These conclusions should be viewed with caution, since they are neither representative of all minority groups nor do they imply that spousal violence among whites is rare. In the latter case, such results could be misleading as whites may be more secretive about their abusive relationships in surveys.

Class

Most of the research into the class status of spouse abusers has shown it to be more a product of the lower and working classes. G. Levinger found in his study of couples seeking divorce that conjugal violence was reported most often among lower-class women.[45] Bulcroft and Straus found spouse abuse among both genders to be consistently higher in the working class than in the middle class.[46] Several researchers have disputed these findings with other data indicating spouse violence to be at least as prevalent, if not higher, in the middle and upper classes.[47] Whether class as a singular variable can be related positively to domestic abuse remains to be seen.

Income

The evidence supports the general belief that the rate of spousal violence lowers as income levels rise. A national survey of family violence revealed that 11 percent of the families with income less than $6,000 reported spouse abuse, compared to only 2 percent of the families with incomes of $20,000 or more.[48] Gelles's study showed a decline in the rate of violence of the second-lowest income group.[49] Some studies have shown a relationship between the satisfaction with a level of income and spouse violence. In O'Brien's sample, the wife displayed serious dissatisfaction with her spouse's income in 84 percent of the violent marriages and in only 24 percent of the nonviolent marriages.[50]

Occupational Status

Studies indicate that violence between couples is more prevalent among blue-collar than white-collar workers. Straus and colleagues found the rate of extreme spousal violence of blue-collar workers to be double that of white-collar workers.[51] Gelles reported that 82 percent of the violent husbands in his sample were of a lower occupational status than their non-violent neighboring male spouses.[52] The highest rates of overall and frequent violence occurred in married couples where the male spouse's occupational status was lower than the female spouse's.

Employment/Unemployment

Employment status appears to be a strong predictor of spousal violence. Numerous studies have shown a higher rate of spouse abuse among the unemployed. Straus and associates' research showed the rate of severe violence to be two to three times greater among families where the male spouse was unemployed or employed only part-time than among families where the male partner had a full-time job.[53] They also found severe violence to be most common when the male partner was disabled, as opposed to employed full time, and least common among married partners when the male spouse was retired. One study found that part-time unemployment was more closely associated with violent families than was unemployment.[54]

Educational Levels

An association between educational level and violence between intimates has been documented through a number of studies, though the results have been mixed. Gelles found rates of wife abuse to be highest among male partners without a high school diploma, with steadily decreasing rates as the level of higher education increased.[55] Ironically, the most violent wives in Gelles's sample were those who had graduated from college. Straus and associates' work produced contrasting results, with male spouses who graduated from high school being the most violent and those men with less than eight years of schooling or with some college but without a bachelor's degree being the least violent spouses.[56] As for gender differences, studies show that the violence rate is greater for both spouses when the husband is less educated than the wife.[57]

Intergenerational Abuse and Spouse Abuse

The intergenerational or cycle theory of spouse abuse is well documented in the literature. Gayford found in a study of 100 battered wives that 51 of the male perpetrators and 23 of the battered women had violent childhoods.[58] Maria Roy's research revealed that 81 percent of the abusive spouses and 33 percent of the abused wives experienced violent family backgrounds.[59] The substantial evidence seems to support the hypothesis that in most cases of domestic violence a link can be established with previous episodes of family violence.

Substance Abuse and Spouse Abuse

The research on spouse abuse and its relationship to substance abuse is both controversial and unclear. Some studies have pointed to a correlation between spousal violence and alcohol or drug abuse.[60] However, most such data are limited because of methodological problems and a lack of empirical research. Nevertheless, the relationship between substance abuse and domestic abuse appears to be at least as solid as it is where other variables influence the propensity to commit violent acts.

PARENT BATTERING

Incidence

Only recently has attention been drawn to another form of family violence that is equally as serious, if not as well documented, as child and spouse abuse—violence directed at parents by their children. Referred to by some as the "battered parent syndrome," an estimated 2.5 million parents in this country are struck by their children each year. Of these, roughly 900,000 are victims of severe violence.[61] A survey of family violence found that nearly 1 in 10 parents reported being physically abused by a child aged 3 to 17 during the year of the survey.[62]

A second branch of parent battering even lesser known is elderly parent abuse or "granny bashing." There are no national figures on its incidence, however, it is believed that this may be the most underreported form of family violence.

Demographic Characteristics

The demographic data on parental batterers largely parallel that for other forms of domestic violence. That is, there is a supportive relationship between violence against parents and lower socioeconomic groups, race, stress, substance abuse, and intergenerational abuse.[63] Teenage sons are the most frequent batterers of parents. One researcher estimated that where nonviolent parents stand only a 1 in 400 chance of being battered parents, for violent parents the probability rises to 200 out of 400.[64]

SIBLING ABUSE

Incidence

Sibling violence has been universally looked upon as "normal," and therefore is given very little attention in the literature. However, there has been some recent research into this branch of domestic violence that suggests that not only is it widespread, but it is not always a matter of fun and games.

Steinmetz found that nearly all of her sample of college students had used verbal aggression to resolve sibling conflicts, while 70 percent had engaged in physical violence with a sibling.[65] Straus and associates' study of family violence revealed that 75 percent of the families surveyed with children aged 3 to 17 reported physical violence among siblings.[66] Extrapolating the findings nationwide, it is estimated that 8.3 million children have been "beaten up" by a sibling at some point during their childhood, while 2.3 million have at one time been the recipient of a sibling knife or gun attack.

Demographic Characteristics

Boys tend to be more violent in sibling confrontations than girls. The findings of Straus and colleagues show that 83 percent of the male siblings exhibited violent behavior compared to 74 percent of the female siblings.[67] All-male siblings had the highest rate of violence, followed by mixed siblings, with all-female siblings demonstrating the fewest episodes of violence. Steinmetz found that siblings aged 8 and under engaged in the highest percentage of violence, with the second highest percentage in the 9-14 age group, and the third, or least, highest among siblings aged 14 and older.[68] Other demographic data on sibling violence reflect the data on family violence in general and its relationship to social and economic factors, race, substance abuse, and the cycle of violence as examined in this chapter.

THEORIES OF FAMILIAL VIOLENCE

Most theoretical advances into the causes of family violence generally fall into one of three categories: (1) psychiatric theories, (2) social-psychological theories, and (3) social-cultural theories.

Psychiatric theories are most concerned with the perpetrator's personality characteristics as they relate to abuse and violence. This approach includes theories that associate family violence with mental illness and drug and alcohol abuse.[69] Such theories, while sound in some cases, are inadequate in most others as primary determinants of violence in the family.

Social-psychological hypotheses consider family violence to be a product of the external and environmental variables that affect family life and focus on the individual daily interactions that are most susceptible to familial violence.[70] Theories utilizing this school of thought include such general theories as exchange theory, frustration-aggression theory, and learning theory, and proposals that attribute family violence to factors such as stress and intergenerational violence. Social-psychological theories on the whole offer more fundamentally sound explanations of family violence than do psychiatric theories relative to the general population.

The same can be said for social-cultural or sociological theories, which examine family violence in terms of socially structured inequality and cultural norms concerning violence, abuse, and family relations.[71] Two influential theories of this perspective are the structural-functional theory and the subculture-of-violence theory.

In recent years, some research has been conducted on family violence and its relationship to genetics and nutrition.[72] Although these studies have yielded some interesting findings (such as a link between PMS and women's violence, and between diet and family violence), methodological limitations have made such data suspect at this time. However, further empirical research in this area could prove to be significant in the study of violence in the family.

Family violence continues to be one of the most difficult forms of violence to assess accurately, for much of it is never made public through official data, surveys, or private research. Relatively speaking, however, available demographic data point toward the following conclusions about the characteristics of violence in the family:

- The actual incidence of family violence is staggering
- Mothers are more likely than fathers to abuse their children

- Spouse abuse is fairly evenly distributed by gender
- Male spouses tend to be more violent than female spouse abusers
- Most child abusers are between ages 20 and 40
- Family abuse is disproportionately associated with the lower socioeconomic groups
- Middle- and upper-class family violence is lesser known, but probably just as prevalent, as lower-class domestic violence
- Such variables as substance abuse and intergenerational violence are likely contributors to violence in the family

NOTES

1. Boudouris, "Homicide and the Family," *Journal of Marriage and the Family* 33, no. 4 (1971).

2. Richard J. Gelles, *The Violent Home* (Beverly Hills: Sage Publications, 1987); Del Martin, *Battered Wives* (San Francisco: Glide Publications, 1976).

3. Martin, *Battered Wives.*

4. U.S. Federal Bureau of Investigation, *Crime in the United States: Uniform Crime Reports 1986* (Washington, D.C.: Government Printing Office, 1987), p. 174.

5. U.S. Department of Justice, *Bureau of Justice Statistics Special Report: Family Violence* (Washington, D.C.: Government Printing Office, 1984), p. 2.

6. D. J. Besharov, "U.S. National Center on Child Abuse and Neglect: Three Years of Experience," *Child Abuse and Neglect: The International Journal* 1 (1977): 173-77.

7. David G. Gil, *Violence Against Children: Physical Abuse in the United States* (Cambridge, Mass.: Harvard University Press, 1970).

8. H. R. Erlanger, "Social Class and Corporal Punishment: A Reassessment," *American Sociological Review* 39 (1974): 68-85; R. Stark and J. McEvoy, "Middle Class Violence," *Psychology Today* 4 (1970): 52-65.

9. Murray A. Straus, Richard J. Gelles, and Suzanne K. Steinmetz, *Behind Closed Doors: Violence in the American Family* (New York: Doubleday, 1980).

10. Gelles, *The Violent Home*, p. 55.

11. Brandt F. Steele and C. Pollock, "A Psychiatric Study of Parents Who Abuse Infants and Small Children," in Ray E. Helfer and C. Henry Kempe, eds., *The Battered Child* (Chicago: University of Chicago Press, 1968), pp. 89-133.

12. S. Zalba, "Battered Children," *Trans-Action* 8 (1971): 58-61.

13. Gil, *Violence Against Children*, p. 109.

14. Blair Justice and Rita Justice, *The Abusing Family* (New York: Human Sciences Press, 1976), p. 90.

15. See Gil, *Violence Against Children*; E. M. Thompson, N. W. Paget, D. Mesch, and T. I. Putnam, *Child Abuse: A Community Challenge* (East Aurora, N.Y.: Henry Stewart, 1971).

16. Straus, Gelles, and Steinmetz, *Behind Closed Doors.*

17. U.S. Department of Health and Human Services, *Study Findings: National*

Study of the Incidence and Severity of Child Abuse and Neglect (Washington, D.C.: Government Printing Office, 1981).

18. E. Bennie and A. Sclare, "The Battered Child Syndrome," *American Journal of Psychiatry* 125, no. 7 (1969): 975-79.

19. Gil, *Violence Against Children.*

20. "Preventing Sexual Abuse of Children," *Parade Magazine* (May 26, 1985): 16.

21. Vincent J. Fontana, *The Maltreated Child: The Maltreatment Syndrome in Children* (Springfield, Ill.: Charles C. Thomas, 1964).

22. Christopher Ounsted, Rhoda Oppenheimer, and Janet Lindsay, "The Psychopathology and Psychotherapy of the Families Aspects Bounding Failure," in A. Franklin, ed., *Concerning Child Abuse* (London: Churchill Livingston, 1975).

23. D. W. Behling, "History of Alcohol Abuse in Child Abuse Cases Reported at Naval Regional Medical Center" (Paper presented at the National Child Abuse Forum, Long Beach, California, June 1971).

24. See G. C. Murdock, "The Abused Child and the School System," *American Journal of Public Health* 60 (1970): 105; Patricia Mrazek and David A. Mrazek, "The Effects of Child Sexual Abuse: Methodological Considerations," in Patricia Mrazek and C. Henry Kempe, eds., *Sexually Abused Children and Their Families* (New York: Pergamon Press, 1981), p. 236.

25. Brandt F. Steele, "Violence Within the Family," in Ray E. Helfer and C. Henry Kempe, eds., *Child Abuse and Neglect: The Family and the Community* (Cambridge: Ballinger, 1976), p. 12.

26. Gelles, *The Violent Home.*

27. Murray Straus, as cited in Jeanne Thornton, "Family Violence Emerges from the Shadows," *U.S. News & World Report* (January 23, 1984): 66.

28. As cited in Frances Patai, "Pornography and Woman Battering: Dynamic Similarities," in Maria Roy, ed., *The Abusive Partner: An Analysis of Domestic Battering* (New York: Van Nostrand Reinhold, 1982).

29. Ibid.

30. Murray Straus, "Wife-Beating: How Common and Why?" *Victimology* 2 (1978): 443-58.

31. Robert Langley and Richard C. Levy, *Wife Beating: The Silent Crisis* (New York: E. P. Dutton, 1977).

32. Suzanne K. Steinmetz, "The Battered Husband Syndrome," *Victimology* 2 (1978): 507.

33. Richard J. Gelles, "The Myth of Battered Husbands," *Ms.* (October 1979): 65-66, 71-72.

34. Gelles, *The Violent Home*, pp. 50-52.

35. M. Bulcroft and M. Straus, "Validity of Husband, Wife, and Child Reports of Conjugal Violence and Power," cited in Lewis Okun, *Woman Abuse: Facts Replacing Myths* (New York: State University of New York Press, 1985), pp. 38, 261.

36. As cited in Steinmetz, "The Battered Husband Syndrome."

37. D. A. Gaquin, "Spouse Abuse: Data from the National Crime Survey," *Victimology* 2 (1977-1978): 632-43.

38. Rebecca Emerson Dobash and Russell Dobash, *Violence Against Wives* (New York: Free Press, 1979).

39. Straus, Gelles, and Steinmetz, *Behind Closed Doors.*

40. Steinmetz, "The Battered Husband Syndrome," pp. 499-509.

41. Ibid.

42. K. Yllo and M. A. Straus, "Interpersonal Violence Among Married and Co-habitating Couples" (Paper presented at the annual meeting of the National Council on Family Relations, Philadelphia, 1978).

43. See J. Gayford, "Wife-Battering: A Preliminary Survey of 100 Cases," *British Medical Journal* 1 (1975): 194-97; Bonnie E. Carlson, "Battered Women and Their Assailants," *Social Work* 22 (1977): 456.

44. Straus, Gelles, and Steinmetz, *Behind Closed Doors.*

45. G. Levinger, "Sources of Marital Dissatisfaction Among Applicants for Divorce," *American Journal of Orthopsychiatry* 36, no. 5 (1966): 803-7.

46. Bulcroft and Straus, "Validity of Husband, Wife, and Child Reports."

47. Lenore E. Walker, *The Battered Woman* (New York: Harper & Row, 1979); Terry Davidson, *Conjugal Crime: Understanding and Changing the Wife-Beating Pattern* (New York: Hawthorne, 1979).

48. Straus, Gelles, and Steinmetz, *Behind Closed Doors.*

49. Gelles, *The Violent Home.*

50. J. E. O'Brien, "Violence in Divorce-Prone Families," *Journal of Marriage and the Family* 33 (1971): 692-98.

51. Straus, Gelles, and Steinmetz, *Behind Closed Doors.*

52. Gelles, *The Violent Home.*

53. Straus, Gelles, and Steinmetz, *Behind Closed Doors.*

54. S. Prescott and C. Letko, "Battered: A Social Psychological Perspective," in Maria Roy, ed., *Battered Women: A Psychosociological Study of Domestic Violence* (New York: Van Nostrand Reinhold, 1977), pp. 72-96.

55. Gelles, *The Violent Home.*

56. Straus, Gelles, and Steinmetz, *Behind Closed Doors.*

57. Gelles, *The Violent Home;* Carlson, "Battered Women and Their Assailants."

58. Gayford, "Wife-Battering."

59. Maria Roy, "A Current Survey of 150 Cases," in Maria Roy, ed., *Battered Women: A Psychosociological Study of Domestic Violence* (New York: Van Nostrand Reinhold, 1977).

60. Ibid.; Prescott and Letko, "Battered: A Social Psychological Perspective;" J. A. Bayles, "Violence, Alcohol Problems and Other Problems in Disintegrating Families," *Journal of Studies on Alcohol* 39 (1978): 551-63.

61. Karen S. Peterson, "The Nightmare of a Battered Parent," *USA Today* (March 18, 1983): A6.

62. Straus, Gelles, and Steinmetz, *Behind Closed Doors.*

63. See, for example, J. A. Bergman, H. O'Malley, and H. Segars, "Legal Research and Services for the Elderly. Elder Abuse in Massachusetts: A Survey of Professional and Paraprofessionals," in *Elder Abuse: The Hidden Problem* (Washington, D.C.: Government Printing Office, 1980).

64. Suzanne K. Steinmetz, "Violence-Prone Families," *Annals of New York Academy of Sciences* 347 (1980): 251-65.

65. Suzanne K. Steinmetz, "The Use of Force for Resolving Family Conflict: The Training Ground for Abuse," *Family Coordinator* 26 (1977): 19.

66. Straus, Gelles, and Steinmetz, *Behind Closed Doors.*

67. Ibid.

68. Steinmetz, "The Use of Force for Resolving Family Conflict."

69. Richard J. Gelles and Murray A. Straus, "Determinants of Violence in the Family: Toward a Theoretical Integration," in W. R. Burr, R. Hill, F. I. Nye, and I. L. Reiss, eds., *Contemporary Theories About the Family* (New York: Free Press, 1979).

70. Ibid.

71. Ibid.

72. See, for example, B. F. Feingold, *Why Your Child Is Hyperactive* (New York: Random House, 1975).

12

Prisoners

The demographic makeup of the prisoner population in the United States is largely a reflection of the characteristics of criminals and arrestees in general. In this chapter, we will examine the demographic trends among prisoners. Much of the discussion will center on male prisoners, since they comprise the vast majority of the inmates in this country.

PRISON INMATES

On December 31, 1986, there was a record-high 546,659 prisoners in state and federal institutions—a rise of 8 percent from 1985 and an increase of nearly 66 percent since 1980.[1] Ninety-two percent of the inmates were in state custody; however, the number of sentenced prisoners increased from 1985 to 1986 at a greater rate in the federal system (11.7 percent) than in state prisons (8.6 percent). "Sentenced prisoners"—prisoners with sentences of more than a year—comprised 96 percent of the aggregate prison population. The rate of prisoners per 100,000 at the end of 1986 was 216, also setting an all-time high and representing a 55 percent increase since 1980.

Regionally

There are more than twice as many prisoners in the South as there are in the next highest region, the Midwest, followed by the West and the Northeast (Table 12.1). In 1986, the South also had the highest per capita incarceration rate in the nation (249); the Northeast had the lowest rate (158). The rate for the West was second highest at 198, followed by the Midwest at 173.

Between 1980 and 1986, the per capita incarceration rates have risen most rapidly in the West, climbing by almost 89 percent, compared to 82 percent in the Northeast, 59 percent in the Midwest, and 32 percent in the South.

Table 12.1
Prisoners under the Jurisdiction of State and Federal Correctional Authorities,
by Region, Year-end 1985 and 1986

Region	1985	1986	Percent Change 1985–86	Incarceration Rate 1986[a]
U.S. Total	503,271	546,659	8.6%	216
Northeast	75,706	82,388	8.8%	158
Midwest	95,704	103,101	7.7%	173
South	202,926	215,713	6.3%	249
West	88,712	101,049	13.9%	198

[a]The rate is for the number of prisoners sentenced to more than a year per 100,000 resident population. Population estimates are for July 1, 1986.

Source: U.S. Department of Justice, Bureau of Justice Statistics Bulletin, *Prisoners in 1986* (Washington, D.C.: Government Printing Office, 1987), p. 2.

The West also showed the greatest percentage increase of prisoners from 1985 to 1986, at nearly 14 percent, while the South had the lowest percentage change among the regions (6.3 percent).[2]

Among states, aggregate prison populations increased most rapidly in 1986 as compared to 1985 in Nevada (19.5 percent), California (18.7 percent), New Mexico and Michigan (16.8 percent), and Oklahoma (15.2 percent). The greatest percentage increases in the number of sentenced inmates occurred in New Mexico and Maine, each rising by more than 20 percent during the year.[3]

Gender

At year-end 1986, male prisoners constituted 95.1 percent of the total of U.S. prisoners, compared to female prisoners at 4.9 percent. The federal prisoner male to female breakdown stood at 93.6 percent to 6.4 percent, while male prisoners accounted for 95.3 percent of the state prisoners and female prisoners, 4.7 percent. The rate of incarceration for sentenced male prisoners per 100,000 male residents in the population was 432, about 21 times greater than the rate for sentenced female prisoners. However, female inmates have increased at a faster rate than male inmates in recent years. From 1985 to 1986, women prisoners rose 15.1 percent, compared to 8.3 percent for males.[4]

Offenses

The crimes for which most prisoners are serving sentences in state and federal penitentiaries are Crime Index offenses. More than half of those incarcerated are convicted for violent crimes such as murder, robbery, and assault; over 40 percent of the nation's prisoners are serving time for property-related offenses (such as larceny-theft). The remainder are in prison for drug-related and public-order offenses.[5]

Age

The vast majority of U.S. prisoners (not including those housed in juvenile facilities) fall between the ages of 20 and 29, with the median age being around 25.[6] The percentage of prisoners under 20 was about 9 percent, compared to approximately 15 percent aged 40 and over.[7] Adult prisoners in this country tend to be much younger than the national average age.

Race and Ethnicity

More than half of the aggregate prisoners in the United States are white (Table 12.2). However, blacks and other minorities are overrepresented in prison facilities. At the end of 1985, blacks accounted for 45 percent of the total prison population, while comprising only 12 percent of the general population. Their totals are slightly higher in state institutions. In fact, blacks are disproportionately represented as prisoners in every state except for those in which the black population is extremely low. Hispanics accounted for 25 percent of the federal prisoners in 1985, more than three times their proportion of the national population, and 11 percent of the total prisoner population. One out of every 16 prisoners in this country is Hispanic. Although Native Americans constitute a very low percentage of the prison population, they are disproportionately represented nevertheless, while Asian-Americans are underrepresented. Native American prisoners are especially likely to be overrepresented in states where there are a large number of Native Americans, such as Oklahoma.[8]

Table 12.2
Percentage Distribution of Prisoners in State and Federal Institutions, by Race and Ethnicity, 1985

	Total[a]	White	Black	Native American	Asian	Hispanic[b]
United States Total	100.0	51.9	45.2	1.0	0.4	10.9
State Institutions	100.0	50.8	46.3	0.9	0.3	9.7
Federal Institutions	100.0	84.9	32.5	1.8	0.8	25.0

[a]Includes prisoners of unknown race or ethnicity.

[b]Hispanic prisoners are counted in the total prisoners by either race or unknown.

Source: Computed from U.S. Department of Justice, *Correctional Populations in the United States 1985* (Washington, D.C.: Government Printing Office, 1987), p. 57.

Social Class

Most research suggests that prisoners are likely to be from the lower social classes and to be under- or unemployed.[9] Using the Hollingshead scale to rate the social class of prisoners in Louisiana, one study found that the inmates were predominantly drawn from the lower two of Hollingshead's total of five classes.[10] Another study found a strong relationship between imprisonment and poverty, unemployment, and unsteady employment among inmates prior to incarceration.[11] The highest rate of incarceration among males aged 16 to 64 was found to be with those who were unemployed at the time of arrest.

Occupation

Occupational and income data on prisoners reflect the social class findings. The most extensive demographic profile of prisoners may be a 1974 survey conducted by the Law Enforcement Assistance Administration (LEAA).[12] This survey of prisoners in state penitentiaries found that 69 percent of the prisoners had been employed in blue-collar occupations prior to arrest, compared to 10 percent who were in service fields, 3 percent in farm labor, and only 15 percent in white-collar jobs. Fifty-four percent of the prisoners had prearrest incomes below $5,000, and 30 percent made between $5,000 and $9,999. Only 16 percent of the prisoners, before arrest, had incomes of $10,000 or more. Although these data exclude any income obtained illegally by the prisoners, they clearly indicate that most were from the lower classes of the social and economic ladder. Seventy-two percent of the prisoners were actually employed full-time one month prior to arrest, while half of the remaining inmates were seeking employment during the month before their arrests, and the balance were not looking for work at all.

Education

Prisoners in American institutions are less educated than society in general. Research has shown that about half of the men incarcerated have failed to complete high school. The median grade completed is the 10th. Less than 1 in every 100 prisoners has obtained a college degree.[13] The evidence suggests that the educational level of prisoners is actually lower than they claim. A study of Florida prisoners who had maintained that they possessed a 10th grade education tested at an average educational achievement of just over grade seven.[14] Intelligence quotient tests have shown that prisoners score below average, a further indication that the prisoner population has less education and a lower level of intelligence than does the general population.[15]

Marital Status

The majority of prisoners are unmarried. A study of state prisoners found that, although more than half of the prisoners were married upon entering the correctional facilities, by the time of the survey this percentage had shrunk to under one-quarter.[16] On average, the prisoners had served a year and a half between entry to prison and the time of the survey. During this same period, the number of inmates who were divorced climbed 66 percent, while those who were separated rose 19 percent. Prisoners were more likely to be divorced if they were to serve or were in the midst of serving long prison sentences.

Family Dynamics

Most prisoners tend to come from broken homes. A recent Justice Department report on crime and criminals in America shows that 53 percent of the state prisoners grew up in a household with only one parent or were raised by relatives.[17] The study also found that 40 percent of the prisoners had a member of their immediate family who had served time in a correctional facility.

The LEAA survey reported that 60 percent of those inmates who had been self-supporting prior to arrest had dependents.[18] It can be presumed that the majority of these dependents were children. This is supported by the Justice Department study, which found that over half of the prisoners had children, the majority of which were under 18.[19]

Attesting to the economic strain of imprisonment on the families of prisoners is the fact that 38 percent of the dependents in the LEAA study were on welfare when the survey was conducted. The survey, however, does not reveal how many were on welfare prior to the arrest of the prisoners. Based on other social and economic characteristics already discussed, the assumption is that many of the dependents were receiving financial assistance, a situation whose difficulty became compounded upon the imprisonment of the supporter.

Substance Abuse

There is much evidence to show a strong correlation between imprisonment and a history of alcohol and drug abuse. Sixty-five percent of Wisconsin state prisoners acknowledged recent use of illicit drugs, and 42 percent admitted abusing alcohol. More than one out of every three inmates confessed to drug addiction at some point in their past.[20] Studies of prisoners in Virginia[21] and Florida[22] found that 70 percent and 51 percent of the inmates respectively either heavily abused alcohol, used illicit drugs, or both. A study of New York state inmates showed that, while more than 50 percent of the inmates used illegal drugs prior to arrest, only 11 percent of the males and 22 percent of the females were incarcerated for drug law violations.[23] A 1979 survey of prison inmates found that more than three-quarters of all state prisoners had used one or more illegal drugs during their lifetime—roughly double the rate for the U.S. population.[24]

Although these studies are obviously not necessarily indicative of the offense for which inmates are incarcerated, they do serve to give us an important demographic correlate of prisoners that can be used to study further the relationship between criminality and substance abuse. Some research, however, has found a direct link between the commission of crime that led to imprisonment and substance abuse.[25]

The Prevalence of Imprisonment

According to a recent report by the Bureau of Justice Statistics, the prevalence of imprisonment in state institutions is as follows:[26]

Imprisonment on Any Given Day:
- Males have a 26 times greater likelihood of imprisonment than females
- Blacks are 8 times as likely to be incarcerated than other races
- Black males are 8 times more likely to be imprisoned than white or other males, 204 times more likely than white females, and 25 times more likely than black females
- White females are least likely to be imprisoned
- Black males in their 20s have the highest prevalence of imprisonment

Lifetime Prevalence of Imprisonment:
- Males have a 1 in 40 chance of being imprisoned
- Females have a 1 in 370 likelihood of serving a prison term
- Black males are 6 to 7 times more likely than white males to go to prison
- Black females are 6 to 8 times as likely as white females to be imprisoned
- A white female has a 1 in 714 chance of serving a prison sentence

Probation and Parole

In 1986, the number of persons on probation or parole rose for the eighth straight year. The probation population grew by 6.4 percent to 2,094,405, while those on parole increased 8.9 percent to 326,752. The ratio of probationers and parolees per 100,000 adult residents was highest in the South, followed by the Northeast, West, and Midwest.[27]

Table 12.3 compares selected characteristics of probationers and parolees at the end of 1985. Males were put on probation 5 times as often as females,

Table 12.3
Characteristics of Adults on Probation and Parole, 1985

	Probation		Parole	
	Number of Probationers from State or Federal Courts	Percent of Those with A Known Status	Number of Parolees from State or Federal Prisons	Percent of Those With A Known Status
Sex	1,657,516	100	262,854	100
Male	1,384,878	84	245,707	93
Female	272,638	16	17,147	7
Race	1,243,311	100	254,061	100
White	872,905	70	137,990	54
Black	355,408	29	110,906	44
Other	14,998	1	5,165	2
Hispanic Origin	768,596	100	187,231	100
Hispanic	109,532	14	31,315	17
Non-Hispanic	659,064	86	155,916	83
Type of Offense[a] of Probationers	1,346,924	100		
Felony	677,074	50		
Misdemeanor	657,114	49		
Infractions	12,706	1		

[a]Similar information is not provided for parolees.

Source: U.S. Department of Justice, *Correctional Populations in the United States 1985* (Washington, D.C.: Government Printing Office, 1987), pp. 24, 90.

and were paroled more than 14 times as often. Blacks had a higher percentage of being paroled than put on probation without being incarcerated. The opposite was true of whites. Seven out of every ten probationers and over half the parolees were white. The Hispanic and non-Hispanic percentages of probation and parole were comparable to each other: non-Hispanics received probation or parole at a ratio of better than four to one over Hispanics. Fifty percent of the probationers were convicted of felonies, 49 percent of misdemeanors, and 1 percent of infractions.

Recidivism

Recidivism—or previous incarceration as an adult, juvenile, or both—was explored most comprehensively in a 1979 Bureau of Justice Statistics–sponsored nationwide survey of inmates in state institutions.[28] The survey found that:

- 61 percent of those entering prison were recidivists
- 42 percent of the recidivists were on probation or parole for previous offenses at the time of their prison admittance
- "Avertable recidivists" committed 20 percent of the violent crimes reported by prison admissions, 28 percent of the burglaries and auto thefts, 31 percent of the stolen property crimes, and 30 percent of the fraud, forgery, and embezzlement offenses[29]
- Almost half of those who leave prison will return within 20 years
- Most recidivism occurs within the first three years after release
- Half of the recidivists had four or more prior sentences of probation, jail, or imprisonment

Capital Punishment

There were 18 executions in the United States in 1986, bringing the aggregate number of persons put to death since the death penalty was reinstated in 1976 to 68. In all, 1,781 prisoners were under sentence of death at the end of 1986 (Table 12.4). The majority were male, white, and non-Hispanic. Blacks and Native Americans were disproportionately likely to be sentenced to death. The median age of death row inmates was 31.9, the median educational level, 10.6 years. Nearly half of the inmates were never married, and 21 percent of the others were divorced or separated. All but one of the prisoners under sentence of death in 1986 were convicted of murder. More than 60 percent of those on death row were incarcerated in the South, with the majority of the others in western or midwestern states. Florida had the greatest number of death row inmates, followed by Texas, California, Georgia, and Illinois.[30]

Table 12.4
Demographic Profile of Prisoners under Sentence of Death, 1986

	Yearend 1986	1986 Admissions	1986 Removals
Total Number Under Sentence of Death	1,781	297	91
Sex			
Male	99.0%	98.7%	96.7%
Female	1.0%	1.3%	3.3%
Race			
White	56.5%	55.2%	59.3%
Black	42.1%	41.4%	40.7%
Other[a]	1.4%	3.4%	0%
Ethnicity			
Hispanic	6.0%	5.4%	6.6%
Non-Hispanic	94.0%	94.6%	93.4%
Age[b]			
Less than 20 years	1.1%	617%	0%
20-24	12.2%	22.2%	9.9%
25-29	26.2%	30.3%	27.5%
30-34	22.8%	16.5%	19.8%
35-39	17.8%	14.5%	19.8%
40-54	18.1%	9.1%	16.5%
55+	1.9%	0.7%	6.6%
Median age	31.9 years	27.4 years	32.6 years
Education			
7th grade or less	10.4%	6.9%	7.9%
8th	11.1%	7.3%	6.6%
9th-11th	36.7%	41.3%	36.8%
12th	32.7%	35.1%	42.1%
Any college	9.1%	9.3%	6.6%
Median education	10.6 years	10.7 years	10.2 years
Marital Status			
Married	31.0%	26.1%	37.1%
Divorced/separated	21.3%	18.7%	18.0%
Widowed	2.2%	3.4%	4.5%
Never married	45.5%	51.9%	40.4%

[a]Consists of 16 American Indians and 9 Asians present at the end of 1986 and 6 American Indians and 4 Asians admitted during the year.

[b]The youngest person under sentence of death was a black inmate in Arkansas born in October 1969. The oldest was a white inmate in Kentucky born in October 1911.

Source: U.S. Department of Justice, *Bureau of Justice Statistics Bulletin: Capital Punishment, 1986* (Washington, D.C.: Government Printing Office, 1987), p. 6.

JAIL INMATES

The Annual Survey of Jails estimate that on June 30, 1986, there were 274,444 persons held in local jails nationwide, a 7 percent increase over the previous year. Jail inmates generally mirror the demographic characteristics of prison inmates.[31] Males comprised 92 percent of all jail prisoners in 1986. The racial distribution shows that white inmates accounted for 58 percent of the total, while blacks comprised a disproportionate share at 41 percent, and other races totaled 1 percent. Hispanics, 18 percent of which were also listed as white and 5 percent as black, were overrepresented as well, constituting 14 percent of all jail inmates. The vast majority of jail prisoners are adults. Less than 1 percent of those housed in adult jails across the country in 1986 were juveniles.[32]

The most recent detailed description of the sociodemographic features of jail inmates can be seen in the 1978 Survey of Jail Inmates (Table 12.5). The median age of jail inmates was 25, with 70 percent under 30. Over half of the inmates had never been married, while the majority of the others were either separated, divorced, or widowed. At the time of admission, more than 40 percent of the inmates had dependents. The median grade of schooling completed for male and female inmates was the 10th grade. More than 40 percent were unemployed at the time of arrest. The median income of those receiving income was $3,714; for females it was only $2,416. Nearly 70 percent of the inmates reported using drugs at some point; 40 percent of them were daily users. The jail survey indicated further that most inmates were incarcerated for property crimes, followed by violent offenses, public order offenses, and drug violations.

INCARCERATED WOMEN

Women make up a very small percentage of those in correctional facilities. The latest figures show that females comprise 8 percent of all jail inmates and 4.9 percent of the prison detainees. Between 1983 and 1986, the number of women in local jails increased 37 percent.[33] A similar increase has been found for women in prisons.

The demographic makeup of incarcerated women parallels that of incarcerated men. A study by Laura Bresler and Donald Leonard of jailed women in San Francisco found that they were disproportionately minority, unemployed, under age 30, and unmarried.[34] The authors also learned that over one-third of the inmates had children; most of the women who worked recently were employed in unskilled, semiskilled, sales, or personal service occupations; and two-thirds attributed the use of alcohol or drugs to their arrest.

A 1978 survey of jail inmates found that relatively more female than male inmates had, prior to incarceration, depended on welfare, social security, and unemployment benefits; financial assistance through family and friends; and income from illegal activities.[35] Nearly twice as many black as white women had income other than from wages or salaries—primarily from unemployment and welfare benefits.

A 10-year study of the backgrounds of women in Michigan penitentiaries produced much the same results.[36] Nearly three-quarters of the prisoners were minority members, 70 percent had not completed high school, 90 percent were from lower-class families, and half had been unemployed or

Table 12.5
Demographic and Prearrest Characteristics of Jail Inmates, 1978

Characteristic	Total[a]	Percent Distribution Male	Female
Sex			
Male	94	*	*
Female	6	*	*
Race			
White	56	57	49
Black	41	41	48
Other	2	2	3
Age			
Under 30	70	69	73
30 and over	30	31	27
55 and over	2	2	1
Median age	25	25	25
Marital Status			
Married	21	21	19
Separated/divorced	23	23	30
Widowed	2	2	4
Never married	54	54	47
Dependents at Time of Admission			
With dependents	44	43	48
Without dependents	56	57	52
Education			
0-8 years	19	19	13
9-11 years	42	42	46
12 years	30	30	30
13 or more	10	9	12
Median grade	10	10	10
Employment Status			
Employed	57	58	33
Full-time	45	46	26
Part-time	12	12	7
Unemployed	43	42	67
Annual Income			
With income	93	93	90
Without income	7	7	10
Median income	$3,714	$3,821	$2,416
Drug Experience			
Never used	31	31	34
Used drugs	69	69	66

[a]Percentages derived from reported numbers.

Source: U.S. Department of Justice, *Profile of Jail Inmates: Sociodemographic Findings from the 1978 Survey of Inmates of Local Jails* (Washington, D.C.: Government Printing Office, 1980).

employed in unskilled work at the time of their arrest. Another study mirrored these findings and confirmed the similarities in the distribution of the offenses for which female and male prisoners were imprisoned, with the majority being for violent offenses, followed by property crimes.[37]

JUVENILES IN CUSTODY

Juvenile delinquents and nondelinquents are predominantly detained in juvenile custody facilities. With little variation, their demographic characteristics are much the same as those of adult prisoners (Table 12.6). The most recent Children in Custody census shows that males make up 80 percent of all juveniles in custody. However, there are proportionately more females in juvenile facilities than in jails and prisons. The average age of a juvenile detainee is 15 years old.

Whites comprise 64 percent of the juveniles in custody; 33 percent are blacks, and 3 percent are of other races. Hispanics make up 10 percent of the total. The percentage of blacks in public institutions (38 percent) is higher than it is in private facilities (25 percent); the same can be said for

Table 12.6
Demographic Characteristics and Adjudication Status of Juveniles Held in Public and Private Juvenile Facilities, 1983[a]

	Public & Private Facilities	Public Facilities	Private Facilities
TOTAL	80,091	48,701	31,390
Sex			
Male	64,424	42,182	22,242
Female	15,667	6,519	9,148
Race			
White	50,182	27,805	22,377
Black	25,842	18,020	7,822
Other[b]	2,020	1,104	916
Not reported	2,047	1,772	275
Ethnicity			
Hispanic	7,844	5,727	2,117
Non-Hispanic	72,247	42,974	29,273
Age			
9 years and under	661	42	619
10-13 years	8,523	3,104	5,419
14-17 years	63,808	39,571	24,237
18-20 years	5,890	4,804	1,086
21 years and over	115	86	29
Not reported	1,094	1,094	0
Average age	15.2 years	15.4 years	14.9 years
Adjudication Status			
Committed	59,590	35,178	24,412
Detained	14,376	13,156	1,220
Voluntarily admitted	6,125	367	5,758

[a]February 1, 1983.

[b]American Indians, Aleuts, Asians, and Pacific Islanders.

Source: U.S. Department of Justice, Children in Custody: 1982/83 Census of Juvenile Detention and Correctional Facilities (Washington, D.C.: Government Printing Office, 1986), p. 5.

Table 12.7
Juveniles Held in Public and Private Facilities, by Reason Held, 1983

Number and Percent of Juveniles in:

Reason Held	Public and Private Facilities Number	Percent	Public Facilities Number	Percent	Private Facilities Number	Percent
Total	80,091	100.0	48,701	100.0	31,390	100.0
Delinquents[a]	56,063	70.0	45,351	93.1	10,712	34.1
Violent offenders	13,687	17.1	12,164	25.0	1,523	4.9
More serious[b]	9,617	12.0	8,901	18.3	716	2.3
Less serious	4,070	5.1	3,263	6.7	807	2.6
Property offenders	27,720	34.6	22,624	46.5	5,096	16.2
More serious[c]	19,516	24.4	16,644	34.2	2,872	9.1
Less serious	8,204	10.2	5,980	12.3	2,224	7.1
Alcohol/drug offenders	2,850	3.6	2,239	4.6	611	1.9
Public order offenders	2,981	3.7	2,582	5.3	399	1.3
Other offenders	8,825	11.0	5,742	11.8	3,083	9.8
Nondelinquents[d]	17,903	22.4	2,983	6.1	14,920	47.5
Status offenders	9,042	11.3	2,390	4.9	6,652	21.2
Nonoffenders	8,861	11.1	593	1.2	8,268	26.3
Voluntary admissions[e]	6,125	7.6	367	0.8	5,758	18.3

[a]Delinquents are those whose offense would be a criminal offense for adults.

[b]Includes those held for murder, forcible rape, robbery, and aggravated assault.

[c]Includes those held for burglary, arson, larceny-theft, and motor vehicle theft.

[d]Status offenders are those whose offense would not be a criminal offense for adults (runaways, truants, incorrigibles, etc.). Nonoffenders are those held for dependency, neglect, abuse, emotional disturbance, and mental retardation.

[e]Voluntary admissions are those who are admitted without adjudication.

Source: U.S. Department of Justice, Children in Custody: 1982/83 Census of Juvenile Detention and Correctional Facilities (Washington, D.C.: Government Printing Office, 1986), p. 7.

Hispanics (12 percent to 7 percent). Minorities account for a smaller proportion of juvenile inmates than adult institution prisoners; however, the proportion still considerably exceeds their representation in the general population.

In 1983, committed (postadjudication) juveniles constituted 74 percent of the juveniles in custody, compared to 18 percent who were detained (preadjudication) juveniles, and 8 percent who were voluntarily admitted (without adjudication). Delinquents accounted for nearly three out of every four juveniles in custody (Table 12.7). Eighty-one percent of the delinquents were housed in public facilities, whereas 83 percent of the nondelinquents were detained in private facilities. Nearly half of the delinquents in custody are property offenders, and one-fourth are violent offenders, with the balance detained for drug, alcohol, and public order offenses. Nondelinquents are more likely to be nonoffenders than status offenders, and females are more likely than males to be detained for noncriminal offenses. Delinquent detainees are typically from broken or distressed homes and low-income families, and are undereducated compared to juveniles in general.[38]

The general characteristics of the correctional population in this country tend to form a profile similar to that of arrestees. They are inclined to be

- Male, young, and unmarried
- Disproportionately members of minority groups and the lower classes
- Without a high school education
- Unemployed or underemployed at the time of detention
- With dependents at the time of arrest
- With a history of alcohol or drug use
- Repeat offenders

Nevertheless, while this tells us who is in prison, it may not be indicative of all criminals, since such factors as a differential system of justice and imprisonment have kept many criminals out of the correctional system.

NOTES

1. U.S. Department of Justice, *Bureau of Justice Statistics Bulletin: Prisoners in 1986* (Washington, D.C.: Government Printing Office, 1987), pp. 1-2.
   2. Ibid.
   3. Ibid.
   4. Ibid., pp. 2-3.
   5. U.S. Department of Justice, *Bureau of Justice Statistics Bulletin: Prisons and Prisoners* (Washington, D.C.: Government Printing Office, 1982); Ann Goetting and Roy Michael Howsen, "Women in Prison: A Profile," *Prison Journal* 63 (1983): 29.

6. Margaret Werner Calahan, *Historical Corrections Statistics in the United States, 1850-1984* (Rockville, Md.: Westat, Inc., 1986), p. 66.

7. Ibid.; Law Enforcement Assistance Administration, *Profile of State Prison Inmates: Sociodemographic Findings from the 1974 Survey of Inmates of State Correctional Facilities* (Washington, D.C.: Government Printing Office, 1979).

8. Ronald B. Flowers, *Minorities and Criminality* (Westport, Conn.: Greenwood Press, 1988).

9. See, for example, U.S. Department of Justice, *Prisoners and Drugs* (Washington, D.C.: Government Printing Office, 1983); U.S. Department of Justice, *Prisoners and Alcohol* (Washington, D.C.: Government Printing Office, 1983).

10. Patricia B. Sutker and Charles E. Moan, "A Psychosocial Description of Penitentiary Inmates," *Archives of General Psychiatry* 29 (1973): 663-67.

11. *Prisons and Prisoners.*

12. *Profile of State Prison Inmates.*

13. U.S. Department of Justice, *Bureau of Justice Statistics Special Report: Examining Recidivism* (Washington, D.C.: Government Printing Office, 1985), p. 6; *Profile of State Prison Inmates.*

14. Florida Department of Corrections, *Annual Report, 1977-1978* (Tallahassee, 1978).

15. Ibid.; Sutker and Moan, "A Psychosocial Description of Penitentiary Inmates."

16. *Profile of State Prison Inmates.*

17. U.S. Department of Justice, Bureau of Justice Statistics, *Report to the Nation on Crime and Justice: The Data* (Washington, D.C.: Government Printing Office, 1983), pp. 30-40.

18. *Profile of State Prison Inmates.*

19. *Report to the Nation.*

20. Wisconsin Division of Corrections, *Drug Abuse Survey* (Madison, 1976).

21. Virginia Department of Corrections, *Annual Statistical Report of Felons and Misdemeanants Committed to the Virginia State Penal System During the Year Ended June 30, 1976 and Felons Confined in the Penal System on June 30, 1976 Including Felony Recidivists Committed and Confined* (Richmond, 1976).

22. Florida Department of Corrections, *Annual Report, 1977-1978.*

23. New York, Department of Correctional Services, *Characteristics of New Commitments—1978* (Albany, 1979).

24. As cited in *Report to the Nation.*

25. Ibid.; S. Gettinger, "Addicts and Crime," *Police Magazine* 2 (1979): 35; Peter Kerr, "Drugs Play Key Crime Role," *Sacramento Bee* (January 22, 1988): A19.

26. U.S. Department of Justice, *Bureau of Justice Statistics Special Report: The Prevalence of Imprisonment* (Washington, D.C.: Government Printing Office, 1985).

27. U.S. Department of Justice, *Bureau of Justice Statistics Bulletin: Probation and Parole 1986* (Washington, D.C.: Government Printing Office, 1987).

28. *Examining Recidivism.*

29. *Avertable recidivists* are recidivists who would still have been incarcerated from a previous conviction at the time of their readmission had they served the maximum term of their prior sentence.

30. U.S. Department of Justice, *Bureau of Justice Statistics Bulletin: Capital Punishment, 1986* (Washington, D.C.: Government Printing Office, 1987).

31. U.S. Department of Justice, *Bureau of Justice Statistics Bulletin: Jail Inmates 1986* (Washington, D.C.: Government Printing Office, 1987).

32. Ibid.

33. Ibid.

34. Laura Bresler and Donald Leonard, *Women's Jail: Pretrial and Post-Conviction Alternatives* (San Francisco: Unitarian Universalist Service Committee, 1978).

35. U.S. Department of Justice, *Profile of Jail Inmates: Sociodemographic Findings from the 1978 Survey of Inmates of Local Jails* (Washington, D.C.: Government Printing Office, 1980).

36. Josefina Figueira-McDonough, Alfred Iglehart, Rosemary Sarri, and Terry Williams, *Females in Prison in Michigan, 1968-1978* (Ann Arbor: University of Michigan Institute for Social Research, 1981), p. 15.

37. Goetting and Howsen, "Women in Prison."

38. *Report to the Nation;* Ronald B. Flowers, *Children and Criminality: The Child as Victim and Perpetrator* (Westport, Conn.: Greenwood Press, 1986).

IV

DEMOGRAPHICS, CRIME, AND THE FUTURE

13

Responding to the Demographic Makeup of Criminality

Now that we have explored the demographic characteristics of criminality in America, the most important question is how do we best utilize this data in terms of theory and crime control? Let us address each area separately.

CRIMINOLOGICAL THEORY AND DEMOGRAPHIC PATTERNS

In general, theories of criminality have been guilty of only selectively taking into account significant demographic variations in crime, and in some instances have ignored such data altogether. As a result, many criminological propositions have inadequately explained crime trends. Demographic knowledge of criminal behavior and victimization is critical to our understanding of why crime exists and how best to mitigate its impact on society. In order for theory to make a more substantive contribution in the areas of crime causation and prevention, greater attention must be given to the following characteristics of criminality and the questions they pose.

Ecological Dimensions

Important ecological trends in the spatial variation of crime need to be incorporated into theory. Specifically, answers are needed for the following questions:

- What is the relationship between criminal ecology and culture?
- Why does crime occur more often in densely populated and urban areas?
- How can temporal variations in crime be explained?
- How does crime relate ecologically, in absolute terms, to relative amounts of crime?
- What are the significance of ecological variations in crime and other characteristics of criminality?

Age

Age is believed to be one of the most important determinants of criminality and victimization. From a theoretical standpoint, we need to know more about:

- The relationship between age and hidden crime
- The relationship between the age of victims and the age of criminals
- Why the peak age for crime tends to vary according to the type of crime (for example, violent versus nonviolent crime)
- Why criminal activity declines as people grow older
- How age relates to other correlates of crime and victimization

Gender

Gender variations in crime have been shown strongly to favor males. Yet theory has failed properly to address:

- Why males are more criminally active than females
- The relationship between gender, age, and crime
- The roles of hidden crime and differential treatment in the known distribution of crime between the sexes
- Why females are making relative gains in criminal participation
- The significance of various measurements of crime and gender
- The correlation between gender and other correlates of crime and victimization

Race and Ethnicity

Minorities are disproportionately represented in most data as offenders and victims of crime. Criminological theory on racial disparities in crime must better address the following questions:

- Why do some minority groups (such as blacks) have much higher crime rates than other minority groups (for example, Asians)?
- What are the cross-racial explanations for crime, and how do they relate to race-specific explanations?
- How significant is race to social class theories of crime and vice versa?
- What effect does official data have on explanations of race- and ethnic-related criminal behavior?
- How do biological differences effectively explain crime?
- How can criminological theory account for differential racial/ethnic treatment within the criminal justice system?

Sociodemographic Correlates of Crime

Studies have indicated that criminal participants are disproportionately single, under- or unemployed, of low income, and likely not to have a high school diploma. To become more useful, crime theories must explain:

- The relationship between various sociodemographic variables and crime
- The causes of factors related to criminality
- Why crime exists among individuals who are married, gainfully employed, of high income, and highly educated
- How race, class, and age relate to sociodemographic variations in crime

Substance Abuse

As substance abuse has been shown to be a direct or indirect factor in crime, theory must adequately expound:

- The effect of substance use/abuse as a determinant in crime
- The relative role of substance use in crime
- How substance abuse relates to other crime factors
- The relationship between age and substance abuse
- How alcohol abuse differs from drug abuse with respect to criminal behavior
- Who is most susceptible to the use and influence of alcohol and drugs

Chronic Offenders

Habitual offenders are involved in a disproportionate amount of crime and have thus attracted the attention of law enforcement and legislators. Criminological theorists must use demographic data on chronic offenders to help:

- Assess the relative strengths and weaknesses of criminological theories
- Distinguish between the various types of chronic offenders
- Interpret the relationship between career criminals and background factors
- Explain how age relates to repeat criminality
- Establish why chronic offenders exist
- Assess the role of the criminal justice system and its policies in the labeling of habitual criminals
- Theorize the relationship between chronic and nonchronic criminality

Family Violence

Violence in the family has become an increasingly serious problem in our society. Yet theories of domestic violence have inadequately explained the dynamics of this branch of violent behavior. What is needed, therefore, are theories that:

- Account for the many variables of family violence
- Effectively relate domestic violence to the overall picture of criminal violence
- Address the social and economic implications of family violence
- More comprehensively explore intergenerational aspects of family violence
- Explain the characteristics of violence in the family
- Focus more closely on the relationship between victim provocation or participation and domestic violence

Prisoners

Prison offenders are generally a reflection of the criminals we are most familiar with (arrestees) in terms of background, types of crimes committed, and social, economic, and demographic correlates. Yet because they are imprisoned they are also unique as criminals and thus present further questions, which the criminologist must address more profoundly when formulating theory, such as:

- What are the differences between imprisoned and nonimprisoned offenders?
- Are jailed criminals more a reflection of their criminality or of discriminant criminal justice treatment?
- What is the role of the correctional system in creating more chronic, hardened criminals?
- How can race relations be improved within the prison system?
- How can inmates be better prepared to lead productive lives upon return to society?
- Does incarceration effectively deter crime?

CRIME CONTROL AND DEMOGRAPHIC TRENDS

Demographic data is perhaps most useful in controlling and preventing crime, for once it is known what particular groups and individuals are most likely to be involved in crime, appropriate measures can be taken to target resources, personnel, legislation, and policies accordingly. Recent years have seen improvements in crime control measures, such as tougher laws, longer jail terms, new jails and prisons, beefed up street patrols, and greater media attention on serious crimes. However, it is likely that there will be more sophisticated, diverse, and serious crime as we head into the 1990s, and therefore a greater reliance on the demographic characteristics of crime will be needed to control more effectively the criminal element of society and to protect victims. Specifically, more demographic attention must be accorded to crime in general, to offenders, and to victims.

Crime

In the future, more effective crime control will require greater demographic knowledge of:

- The spatial distribution of crime
- The relationship between urbanity and crime
- Suburban and rural crime
- The relative and absolute rates of crime geographically and temporally
- The ecological concentration of violent crime
- Class-related crime
- Crime and age
- Crime and substance abuse
- Crime and spatial conduciveness
- Comparative demographic correlates of crime
- Criminal justice employees, their backgrounds, substance abuse, and attitudes

Offenders

The relationship between crime control and the demographic characteristics of offenders will take on increased importance in the future and, therefore, will require law enforcement and legislators to focus greater attention on

- The relationship of age, gender, race, ethnicity, and offenders
- The relationship between offenders and victims
- The sociodemographic characteristics of violent criminals
- The spatial distribution of criminals
- Substance abuse among offenders
- The background characteristics of chronic offenders
- The socioeconomic distribution of offenders
- Family dynamics and criminality
- Hidden crime and criminals
- Prisoner characteristics
- Discriminatory treatment within the system of criminal justice

Victims

Since most crimes have victims, it is in this area where we need to acquire perhaps the clearest demographic perspective in order to help control crime. What is particularly needed in future demographic data is:

- Knowledge of the characteristics of victims under the age of 12
- More detailed victimization data
- Statistics on hidden victimization
- Greater knowledge of the victims' role in victimization
- The spatial dimensions of victimization
- The relative risks of victimization by geographical location, gender, age, and socioeconomic class
- The study of repeat and violent victimizations
- Greater knowledge of the characteristics of nonvictims of crime

Despite the preference in criminological study for sociological and cultural explanations and solutions for crime, the demographic characteristics of criminality are a vital component of our basic knowledge of the variables and distribution of crime, criminals, and victims. It is my hope that this volume illustrates effectively the significance of the demography of crime in America and that it may therefore contribute gainfully to the study and understanding of criminality.

Bibliography

Beasley, Ronald W., and George Antunes. "The Etiology of Urban Crime: An Ecological Analysis." *Criminology* 11 (1974): 439-61.

Blumstein, Alfred, and Jacqueline Cohen. "Characterizing Criminal Careers." *Science* 237 (1987): 985-91.

Braithwaite, John. "The Myth of Social Class and Criminality Reconsidered." *American Sociological Review* 46 (1981): 36-57.

Calahan, Margaret Werner. *Historical Corrections Statistics in the United States, 1850-1984*. Rockville, Md.: Westat, Inc., 1986.

Carpenter, Cheryl, Barry Glassner, Bruce D. Johnson, and Julia Loughlin. *Kids, Drugs, and Crime*. Lexington, Mass.: Lexington Books, 1988.

Cernkovich, Steve A., and Peggy C. Giordano. "A Comparative Analysis of Male and Female Delinquency." *Sociological Quarterly* 20 (1979): 131-45.

"Climate and Crime." *New York Times* (September 3, 1985): C5(L).

Collins, James J., Jr., ed. *Drinking and Crime*. New York: Guilford Press, 1981.

Conrad, John P. *The Dangerous and the Endangered*. Lexington, Mass.: Lexington Books, 1985.

Elliot, Delbert S., and Suzanne S. Ageton. "Reconciling Race and Class Differences in Self-Reported and Official Estimates of Delinquency." *American Sociological Review* 45 (1980): 90-110.

Farrington, David P. "Age and Crime." In Michael Tonry and Norval Morris, eds. *Crime and Justice: An Annual Review of Literature*. Vol. 71. Chicago: University of Chicago Press, 1986.

Figlio, Robert M., Simon Hakim, and George F. Rengert, eds. *Metropolitan Crime Patterns*. Monsey, N.Y.: Willow Tree Press, 1986.

Figueira-McDonough, Josefina, Alfred Iglehart, Rosemary Sarri, and Terry Williams. *Females in Prison in Michigan, 1968-1978*. Ann Arbor: University of Michigan Institute for Social Research, 1981.

Flowers, Ronald B. *Children and Criminality: The Child as Victim and Perpetrator*. Westport, Conn.: Greenwood Press, 1986.

_____. *Minorities and Criminality*. Westport, Conn.: Greenwood Press, 1988.

_____. *Women and Criminality: The Woman as Victim, Offender, and Practitioner.* Westport, Conn.: Greenwood Press, 1987.

Freedman, Jonathan L. *Crowding and Behavior.* New York: Viking, 1975.

Gelles, Richard J. *The Violent Home.* Beverly Hills: Sage Publications, 1987.

Greenberg, David F. "Age and Crime." In Sanford H. Kadish, ed. *Encyclopedia of Crime and Justice.* New York: Free Press, 1983.

Haberman, Paul W., and Michael M. Baden. *Alcohol, Other Drugs and Violent Death.* New York: Oxford University Press, 1978.

Hancock, D. N. "Alcohol and Crime." In G. Edwards and M. Grant, eds. *Alcoholism: New Knowledge and New Responses.* London: Croom Helm, 1977.

Hindelang, Michael J. "Class and Crime." In Sanford H. Kadish, ed. *Encyclopedia of Crime and Justice.* Vol. 1. New York: Free Press, 1983.

Kerr, Peter. "Study: Drugs Play Key Crime Role." *Sacramento Bee* (January 22, 1988): A19.

Law Enforcement Assistance Administration. *Profile of State Prison Inmates: Sociodemographic Findings from the 1974 Survey of Inmates of State Correctional Facilities.* Washington, D.C.: Government Printing Office, 1979.

Lystad, Mary, ed. *Violence in the Home: Interdisciplinary Perspectives.* New York: Brunner/Mazel, 1986.

Nagel, Ilene H., and John Hagan. "Gender and Crime: Offense Patterns and Criminal Court Sanctions." In Michael Tonry and Norval Morris, eds. *Crime and Justice: An Annual Review of Research.* Vol. 4. Chicago: University of Chicago Press, 1983.

Okun, Lewis. *Woman Abuse: Facts Replacing Myths.* New York: State University of New York Press, 1986.

Petersilia, Joan, Peter Greenwood, and Marvin Lavin. *Criminal Careers of Habitual Felons.* Washington, D.C.: National Institute of Justice, 1978.

Roy, Maria, ed. *The Abusive Partner: An Analysis of Domestic Battering.* New York: Van Nostrand Reinhold, 1982.

Shelley, Louise I. *Crime and Modernization: The Impact of Industrialization and Urbanization on Crime.* Carbondale: Southern Illinois University Press, 1981.

Shover, Neal. *Aging Criminals.* Beverly Hills: Sage Publications, 1985.

Sltomer, Curtis J. "Drugs, Drink, and Youth Crime." *Christian Science Monitor* (November 18, 1985): 3.

Snyder, Howard N., and Terrence A. Finnegan. *Delinquency in the United States 1983.* Pittsburgh: National Center for Juvenile Justice, 1987.

Steffensmeier, Darrell. "Sex Differences in Patterns of Adult Crimes, 1965-77: A Review and Assessment." *Social Forces* 58 (1980): 1080-1108.

Straus, Murray A., Richard J. Gelles, and Suzanne K. Steinmetz. *Behind Closed Doors: Violence in the American Family.* New York: Doubleday, 1980.

"Study Tells of Role of Chronic Juvenile Criminals." *New York Times* (December 8, 1985): 61(L).

Trebilcock, Bob. "Crime Comes to the Country." *Country Journal* 13 (1986): 62-71.

U.S. Department of Justice. *BJS Data Report, 1986.* Washington, D.C.: Government Printing Office, 1987.

U.S. Department of Justice. *Bureau of Justice Statistics Bulletin: Capital Punishment, 1986.* Washington, D.C.: Government Printing Office, 1987.

U.S. Department of Justice. *Bureau of Justice Statistics Bulletin: Jail Inmates 1986.* Washington, D.C.: Government Printing Office, 1987.

U.S. Department of Justice. *Bureau of Justice Statistics Bulletin: Prisoners in 1986.* Washington, D.C.: Government Printing Office, 1987.

U.S. Department of Justice. *Bureau of Justice Statistics Bulletin: Probation and Parole 1986.* Washington, D.C.: Government Printing Office, 1987.

U.S. Department of Justice. *Bureau of Justice Statistics Special Report: Career Patterns in Crime.* Washington, D.C.: Government Printing Office, 1983.

U.S. Department of Justice. *Bureau of Justice Statistics Special Report: The Economic Cost of Crime to Victims.* Washington, D.C.: Government Printing Office, 1984.

U.S. Department of Justice. *Bureau of Justice Statistics Special Report: Examining Recidivism.* Washington, D.C.: Government Printing Office, 1985.

U.S. Department of Justice. *Bureau of Justice Statistics Special Report: Family Violence.* Washington, D.C.: Government Printing Office, 1984.

U.S. Department of Justice. *Bureau of Justice Statistics Special Report: Locating City, Suburban, and Rural Crime.* Washington, D.C.: Government Printing Office, 1985.

U.S. Department of Justice. *Children in Custody: 1982/83 Census of Juvenile Detention and Correctional Facilities.* Washington, D.C.: Government Printing Office, 1986.

U.S. Department of Justice. *Correctional Populations in the United States 1985.* Washington, D.C.: Government Printing Office, 1987.

U.S. Department of Justice. *Criminal Victimization in the United States, 1985: A National Crime Survey Report.* Washington, D.C.: Government Printing Office, 1987.

U.S. Department of Justice. *Criminal Victimization in the United States, 1986: A National Crime Survey Report.* Washington, D.C.: Government Printing Office, 1987.

U.S. Department of Justice. *Profile of Jail Inmates: Sociodemographic Findings from the 1978 Survey of Inmates of Local Jails.* Washington, D.C.: Government Printing Office, 1980.

U.S. Department of Justice, Bureau of Justice Statistics. *Report to the Nation on Crime and Justice: The Data.* Washington, D.C.: Government Printing Office, 1983.

U.S. Federal Bureau of Investigation. *Crime in the United States: Uniform Crime Reports 1987.* Washington, D.C.: Government Printing Office, 1988.

"Wide Drug Use Found in People Held in Crimes." *New York Times* (June 4, 1986): A14.

Wolfgang, Marvin E., Robert M. Figlio, and Thorsten Sellin. *Delinquency in a Birth Cohort.* Chicago: University of Chicago Press, 1972.

Index